Empty Suffering

Interdisciplinary in approach, tl [illegible] y, sociology, history and psychology in the analy [illegible] ms of suffering. With attention to depression, anxiety, cl [illegible] addiction, it examines both particular forms of suffering and tak [illegible] ad view of their common features, so as to offer a comprehensive and parallel view both of the various forms of suffering and the treatments commonly applied to them. Highlighting the challenges and distortions of the available treatments and identifying these as contributory factors to the overall problem of contemporary suffering, *Empty Suffering* promises to widen the horizon of critical theories of modernization, therapeutic interventions and social policies. As such, it will appeal to scholars across the social sciences and humanities with interests in mental health and disorder, social theory and social pathologies.

Domonkos Sik is an associate professor of Sociology at the Eötvös Loránd University, Budapest, and alumni of CEU-IAS, Budapest-Vienna. He is the author of several monographs in critical theory, including *Radicalism and Indifference*.

The Social Pathologies of Contemporary Civilization

Breaking decisively with the often ideological and moralistic approach of treating problems of health and well-being as discrete and individual problems to be addressed in isolation both from one another and their broader social contexts, this series pursues the investigation of the ways in which contemporary malaises, diseases, illnesses and psychosomatic syndromes are related to cultural pathologies of the social body and disorders of the collective ésprit de corps of contemporary society.

It avoids reductive psychological and biomedical understandings of pathologies – including depression, stress-related illnesses, eating disorders, suicide and deliberate self-harm – to focus instead on the socio-cultural contexts in which they occur, examining the radical changes to social structures and institutions, and the deep crises in our civilization as a whole to which such conditions are connected.

The Social Pathologies of Contemporary Civilization thus welcomes manuscripts from a broad range of disciplinary perspectives across the humanities and social sciences – sociology, philosophy, psychology, anthropology, politics, economics and cultural studies, as well as from the fields of medicine social care, therapeutic practice and the healing arts – that explore the fruitfulness locating health and well-being not simply in the individual body or soul but within a trans-disciplinary imagination that takes into account the integral human person's situatedness within collective social bodies, particular communities, entire societies, or even whole civilizations.

Series editors
Anders Petersen, Kieran Keohane and Bert van den Bergh

Titles in the series

For more information about this series, please visit:
https://www.routledge.com/The-Social-Pathologies-of-Contemporary-Civilization/book-series/ASHSER1434

Empty Suffering

A Social Phenomenology of Depression, Anxiety and Addiction

Domonkos Sik

Routledge
Taylor & Francis Group
LONDON AND NEW YORK

First published 2022
by Routledge
2 Park Square, Milton Park, Abingdon, Oxon OX14 4RN

and by Routledge
605 Third Avenue, New York, NY 10158

Routledge is an imprint of the Taylor & Francis Group, an informa business

British Library Cataloguing-in-Publication Data
A catalogue record for this book is available from the British Library

Library of Congress Cataloging-in-Publication Data
Names: Sik, Domonkos, 1982- author.
Title: Empty suffering : a social phenomenology of depression, anxiety and addiction / Domonkos Sik.
Description: Abingdon, Oxon ; New York, NY : Routledge, 2022. | Series: The social pathologies of contemporary civilization | Includes bibliographical references and index.
Identifiers: LCCN 2021023982 (print) | LCCN 2021023983 (ebook) | ISBN 9781032045573 (hbk) | ISBN 9781032053899 (pbk) | ISBN 9781003197355 (ebk)
Subjects: LCSH: Suffering. | Anxiety. | Social sciences--Philosophy.
Classification: LCC BF789.S8 S56 2022 (print) | LCC BF789.S8 (ebook) | DDC 152.4--dc23
LC record available at https://lccn.loc.gov/2021023982
LC ebook record available at https://lccn.loc.gov/2021023983

ISBN: 978-1-032-04557-3 (hbk)
ISBN: 978-1-032-05389-9 (pbk)
ISBN: 978-1-003-19735-5 (ebk)

DOI: 10.4324/9781003197355

Typeset in Bembo
by KnowledgeWorks Global Ltd.

Contents

Acknowledgements

I started to work on the sociology of mental disorders and social suffering during a Bolyai Fellowship (2016–2018) provided by the Hungarian Academy of Science. A related project about solidarity in late modernity (2018–2021) was financed by NKFI (FK-129138). Since 2019, the Higher Education Excellence Program of the Ministry of Human Capacities at Eötvös Loránd University (ELTE-FIKP) provided support for analysing online depression forums. My workplace, Eötvös Loránd University also provided generous support while I was finalizing the manuscript.

I would like to express my gratitude to the members of the Social Pathologies of Contemporary Civilisation research network (http://socialpath.simplesite.com/), their conferences provided an invaluable platform for discussing the challenges of late modernity in a critical and interdisciplinary manner. I would like to thank Sabine Flick, Anders Petersen, Bert van den Bergh and especially Kieran Keohane, who supported and encouraged me in the publication process. Finally, I would like to thank Ildikó Zakariás, who was the first reader of most chapters – her comments and support mean a lot to me.

The first version of Chapters 1–5 and 7 appeared previously in the following journals:

Chapter 1: From naturalized suffering to futile ownership – A genealogy of depressed lifeworld. *Journal of Historical Sociology*, 33(4): 546–566. https://doi.org/10.1111/johs.12305.

Chapter 2: Towards a social theory of fear: A phenomenology of negative integration. *European Journal of Social Theory*, 23(4): 512–531. https://doi.org/10.1177/1368431019850074.

Chapter 3: Power from indirect pain – A historical phenomenology of medical pain management. *Continental Philosophy Review*, 54(1): 41–59. https://doi.org/10.1007/s11007-020-09518-5.

Chapter 4: From mental disorders to social suffering: Making sense of depression for critical theories. *European Journal of Social Theory*, 22(4): 477–496. https://doi.org/10.1177/1368431018760947.

Chapter 5: Networks of anxiety – From the distortions of late modern societies to the social components of anxiety. *Phenomenology & Mind* (18). https://doi.org/10.17454/pam-1817.

Chapter 7: From dealing with the contingencies of biomedicine to secular ritual healing – An online ethnography of depression forums. In: *Culture, Medicine, and Psychiatry.* https://doi.org/10.1007/s11013-020-09702-5.

Introduction

Phenomenology emphasizes that things and events (reality) have no meaning in themselves. Meaning must be shared in order for people to live together.

Exposedness to suffering is one of the fundamental aspects of human existence. As the attributed causes constitute the horizon of the 'problematic', suffering does not merely affect a passive actor but also contributes to the emergence of agency. The process of constructing a meaningful horizon is inseparable from the past memories, the present experiences and the future projections of suffering. These phenomenological components shape the individual lifeworld (which is partly built around them) while also affecting the institutionalization of cultural praxes shared by an intersubjective community (which are developed to commemorate, treat or prevent suffering). Vice versa, by providing an interpretative framework, the collective discourses also frame the experience of suffering. Due to these narrative representations, suffering does not exist as a raw impression, but a potentially meaningful experience embedded in a historical and social context. Every society elaborates various ways of relating to suffering, including the attributes of its paradigmatic forms; the explanatory or justifying narratives; and the technologies of treatment. Accordingly, the experience of suffering is a two-fold phenomenon: it happens to the subject, while being intersubjectively constructed at the same time.

Similar to any other eras, contemporary, 'late modern' societies are also characterized by a specific paradigm of suffering. The notion of late modernity refers to a dividing line: while 'classic modernity' is characterized by an unreflected identification with rationalist utopic prospects (i.e. social, technological or scientific development), unquestioned epistemic authorities (i.e. expertise based on formal rationality) and triumphant institutions and structures (i.e. bureaucratic organizations, capitalist market); late modernity is characterized by the doubting and dissolving of these constituents. That does not mean, however, the complete giving up on the project of modernity (as theories of post-modernity claim it), rather its reconfiguration as a contingent and ambiguous horizon. This book focuses on this era: by analyzing the idealtypical contemporary forms of suffering, the related interpretative narratives and interventions, an attempt is made to describe some of the key constituents of late modern existence. In order to reveal its specific characteristics, suffering is reconstructed as a historical phenomenon, in a genealogical

DOI: 10.4324/9781003197355-1

fashion. This creates opportunity for understanding the broader social, economic, cultural and political context of contemporary suffering.

The various forms of suffering fall within the competence of several disciplines, such as philosophy, psychology, social sciences and history. Consequently, an enterprise aiming at the genealogy of late modern suffering is inevitably an interdisciplinary one. This raises the methodological question concerning the possibility of mediating between divergent disciplinary semantics. In this book, phenomenology plays the role of a common denominator. Its rich tradition incorporates analyses explaining the process of experiencing and the construction of meanings from various perspectives. Phenomenologically oriented philosophy, psychology, social sciences and history elaborate complementary models, which focus on either subjective or intersubjective; mental or corporeal; universal or particular; and structural or intentional processes of constructing a meaningful world. The synthesis of these models holds the key to understand suffering in a non-reductionist way: the experience of suffering may be born as a consequence of various distorted phenomenological processes. As none of the mono-disciplinary models provide a comprehensive explanation to suffering, the various disciplinary approaches are combined on a phenomenological level throughout the book. In this sense, late modern suffering is analyzed in a phenomenologically grounded, interdisciplinary fashion. The various distortions of constructing a meaningful world – revealed by phenomenological philosophy, psychology, social sciences and history – are viewed as complementary mechanisms, which explain together the emergence and the shaping of contemporary suffering.

The book is constituted of three parts. Firstly, those long-term transformations are overviewed, which result in a structural environment threatening with the emergence of new phenomenological patterns of suffering, such as depression, anxiety or addiction (Part I). These genealogical overviews ground the analysis of the distortions of contemporary societies: those specific integration mechanisms and networks are described, which create an overall depressive, anxious and addictive lifeworld on individual level (Part II). These social phenomenological analyses not only enable the expansion of the horizon of critical theories, but also prepare the ground for sociologically informed interventions. In the last part, the possibilities and the actual efforts of countering modern suffering are explored including the spontaneous practices, the horizon of solidarity and the targeted interventions (Part III).

In the first part of the book, three phenomenologically grounded social historical analyses take place. While these analyses vary according to their substantive and historical focus, they are driven by the same intention: mapping those transformations, which shaped the way suffering is framed in contemporary societies. Chapter 1 deals with the transition between the late medieval era and early modernity, from the perspective of the phenomenology of depression. A depressed lifeworld is characterized by burdensome embodiment, disorganization of linear time, hopelessness and guilt, loss of agency and distorted intersubjectivity. The idealtypical late medieval and early modern lifeworld is analyzed along these dimensions. The lifeworlds are initially reconstructed according to the social history literature of mentalities and everyday life. This step is followed by a comparative analysis of the two eras revealing the structural transformations responsible for the increasing prevalence of depression. Even if the medieval era is characterized by the naturalization of suffering, limited agency and lacking worldly hope, these experiences are counterbalanced by an eschatological horizon of time providing transcendental framework for resolving guilt; furthermore, a continuous presence of the others, who prevented complete isolation and consequent despair. During early modernity, such formula has changed: the gradual expansion of agency promising control over suffering and enjoyment lead to the emergence of a parallel horizon of worldly time and ambiguities of intersubjectivity at the same time. In order to handle these ambiguities and improve worldly control, the modern notion of property as 'absolute dominion' was born. By linking the potential of control to the detachment from the others a dangerous compound emerged. Being deprived of property or being failed by it renders the subject hopeless, isolated and ultimately helpless – which are the constituents of depression.

Modernization fundamentally changes the horizon of suffering: it is not naturalized anymore, but challenged. By transforming suffering into an eliminable phenomenon, on the one hand, its previously existing, primary forms (such as starving, illness or limited agency) are not treated anymore as inevitable trials or punishments of transcendental origin, but rather as obstacles to be overcome through owning the required means. However, such promise of control – and the trajectory of a life based on pursuing it – did not only reduce the primary forms of suffering; it also created a new, secondary source of suffering. As the birth of absolute dominion implies the expectation of handling suffering, in case of the failure of such promise, the burdensome experience is complemented with the sense of finality. While in the early modern era, suffering still could have been narrated and resolved according to various religious and intersubjective ways, the attempt of increasing control through the concept of absolute dominion gradually eliminated these alternative framings. Thus, suffering became not only a personal burden but also the final proof of the personal inadequacy. This element of finality transforms the otherwise episodic suffering into depression.

Chapter 2 complements this line of thought by analyzing the transforming horizon of suffering from a different angle. While in Chapter 1, the resigned premodern relation to suffering is contrasted to the proactive modern one, in Chapter 2, the inner dynamics of modernization is analyzed by comparing the social constituents of fear and trust in early and late modernity. This time, the sources of the phenomenological analysis are not the traces of everyday mentalities, but the classical social contract theories reflecting upon the possibility of a secular political order. Hobbes' and Rousseau's theories are reinterpreted from a phenomenological perspective: negative (based on fear) and positive (based on hope) motivational bases of self-limiting one's freedom are reconstructed, which are capable of motivating the subjects to subordinate their will to collective regulations, without referring to religious or metaphysical dogmas. These 'motivations for cooperation' are the prerequisite of any modern, secular society, as their absence results in disintegration. From the perspective of these two phenomenological types of motivation, two modalities of integration are identified. Based on analyses targeting classical (Weber, Durkheim, Habermas) and late modernity (Beck, Castells), it is argued that contemporary societies are characterized by the upset of the balance of the two modalities leading to the predominance of 'negative integration', relying exclusively on fear instead of hope.

Accordingly, a second type of modern suffering is identified: the unmanageable fear originating from negative integration. Such experience is labelled by philosophers and psychologists as existential or generalized anxiety, which is considered to be either the consequence of the universal incertitude of human existence, or the individual traumas and maladaptation. However, as the genealogical analysis reveals it, these experiences are neither universal nor individually situated; instead, they are closely related to the way integration mechanisms phenomenologically ground late modern societies. As contemporary societies lack positive integration mechanisms capable of providing a horizon of worthy collective goals (that is a social constellation, where one can be at home in the world), fear remains the main motivational source of forming social units. In this constellation, a secondary form of suffering emerges, which is based on the lost horizon of security implying a perpetual sense of being on the run.

Chapter 3 complements these analyses by focusing on the *par excellence* bodily form of suffering, physical pain. Pain is a two-sided phenomenon: on the one hand, it occurs as a consequence of injuries or illnesses; on the other hand, it originates from intentional harming, which aims at engraving power. Thus, the phenomenology of pain has to take into consideration both aspects: the emergent technologies of treating pain and the transforming technologies of harming have to be reconstructed in parallel. In this spirit, Husserl's and Merleau-Ponty's ideas are used for clarifying the experience of pain itself and Scarry's analyses are overviewed in order to reconstruct how pain contributes to the establishing of power. This two-sided approach is applied initially on early modern context: the parallel processes of the decline of a transcendental and the emergence of a medical interpretation of pain are introduced, along with the marginalization of violence. These social historical analyses ground the reconstruction of the contemporary constellation, an era characterized by the triumph of medical pain management. Based on medical anthropological sources, it is argued that the constitutive role of pain in establishing power does not fade away with the emergence of technologies of discursive governance and the decline of violence. Instead, those institutional actors, which are responsible for controlling pain, become the managers of power as well, not by directly causing pain, but by indirectly withholding the technologies capable of eliminating it.

Similarly to the violence in premodernity, the indirect pain also plays a constitutive role in grounding power, even if the authority born as its consequence does not belong to a recognizable entity, but a faceless, obscure will. The representatives of the biopolitical complex do not act out of cruelty, rather out of ignorance justified by professionalism. However, as their interventions are based on a hegemonic discursive position – claiming to access not only the adequate treatment of pain but also the capability of describing every form of pain in a positivist language – they leave no alternatives to the sufferers, but the adaptation to their reifying perspective. As power creates not only social hierarchies but also shapes subjectivities (Foucault), the objectifying biomedical pain management also establishes a specific relation to the self. These experiences constitute the third dimension of late modern suffering: the self is transformed into an object-body (*Körper*), which can be managed as an automaton through switching the buttons of pain (and also pleasure). In this constellation, even if the physical suffering is neutralized, it costs self-objectification: the subjects become dependent upon the technologies managing their medicalized suffering. In these power relations, a hybrid subjectivity is born, which is particularly susceptible to addictive behaviour patterns.

The transformations introduced in the first part express the key dimensions of emptying suffering. They include the early modern reframing of suffering as a meaningless obstacle, which can be exceeded by owning and controlling the world; the late modern restructuring of social integration according to exclusively negative motivations (fear without the element of hope); and the emergence of a power structure implying self-objectification. In contemporary societies, not only those transcendental meanings disappear, which used to make sense of suffering; but also those utopic horizons are eliminated, which used to balance out suffering with promising collective prospects while the suffering subject is reduced to a dysfunctional body-object (*Körper*) treatable by medical pain management. As a consequence of the emptying of suffering, the failure of control through ownership threatens with the collapse of the totality of the lifeworld (that is the experience of depression); the lack of promising collective expectations leads to the obsession with fear (that is the experience of anxiety); and the subordination to a reifying power structure leads to the dependence on technologies of pleasure and pain (that is the precondition of addiction). All in all, from a genealogical perspective, the most common pathologies of the modern subject are explained as consequences of complex structural transformations emptying suffering on transcendental, social and subjective levels.

In late modernity depressive, anxious and addictive patterns of suffering do not replace, rather complement those types, which dominated the premodern lifeworld. However, their possibility does not automatically imply their generalization. Even in late modernity, those specific social constellations need to be identified, where the new types of suffering occur with high probability. In the second part of the book, this goal is pursued. Chapter 4 attempts to reconstruct those integration mechanisms, which are responsible for the emergence of depression as a late modern form of social suffering. For this purpose, clinical explanations of depression are reinterpreted from the perspective of their latent references to the social. Post-Freudian psychoanalytic theories of insecurity; behaviourist explanations emphasizing conditioning through feedbacks; cognitive models of maladaptive automatic thoughts and learned helplessness equally include latent references to social distortions. These hidden dimensions are explored with the help of contemporary social theories dealing with the distortions of competition (Bourdieu) and cooperation (Habermas). By combining psychological models of depression with the critical theoretical models of distorted integration, those structural constellations may be described, which trap the actors in a constraining environment depriving them from agency.

Social constellations organized according to the logic capitals or linguistic and mediatized communication may contribute to a depressive pattern of suffering in a different way. The cruel, biased, arbitrary, segregating competitions are just a few examples of how the otherwise inevitable social confrontations may constitute an environment threatening with insecurity, deprivation from positive feedback and learned helplessness. Also, the overly complex, discredited system, or the incompetent, moralizing, unsuccessful communicative action are examples of how the attempts of cooperation may contribute to the emergence of negative automatic thoughts and self-blaming collective representations. Overall, the relation between certain distortions of integration and a depressive pattern of suffering highlights those social mechanisms, which systematically reproduce a constellation, where not only the attempts of controlling suffering fail but also this experience is complemented with the sense of finality.

Chapter 5 continues this line of thought by analyzing social constellations responsible for the emergence of anxiety. Based on psychoanalytic, cognitive psychological and existentialist descriptions, anxiety is defined as a non-reactive, non-targeted fear, resulting in the generalization of worry. In order to reconstruct the hidden social component of this phenomenological pattern, those forms of sociability need to be taken into consideration, which manage fear by differentiating between its reasonable and unrealistic forms. Instead of focusing on interactions, the continuously changing network environment is taken into consideration (White). On the one hand, the traditional and reflexive networks of ontological security play a key role: while the former are responsible for orienting the actors' evaluation of danger by referring to collective memory, the latter enables the navigation in a post-traditional world by evaluating risks (Giddens). On the other hand, those social mechanisms are taken into consideration, which reproduce a secure social environment characterized by trust instead of suspicion: various forms of recognition play a constitutive role by reinforcing confidence, self-esteem and dignity (Honneth). Combining psychological models of anxiety, with descriptions of distorted social environments (preventing the actors in finding security) reveals those networks of negative integration, which enclose the actors in a disquieting world.

Chapter 6 focuses on the network constituents of addiction as an element of empty suffering. Addiction is not only a major public concern in late modernity but also a phenomenon challenging basic epistemic distinctions. In order to adequately address it, the sociological model of networks constituted solely of subjects needs to be complemented with a model incorporating objects as well. That is why, addiction is reinterpreted from the perspective of actor-network theory (Latour). Firstly, the phenomenological constituents of addiction as a consequence of reification are reconstructed. Secondly, various social theoretical frameworks are overviewed: various theories of reification (e.g. Honneth) and information society (Lash) are used as substantive supplements to actor-network theory. Addiction is reinterpreted as a consequence of reifying actor-networks limiting the human 'actant' in becoming 'mediator': it emerges, if complementary actor-networks are established in order to overcome the exclusivity of 'intermediator' roles. If the generally reifying social relations are incorporated by the actors themselves, addiction emerges as self-reification, expressing an existential compromise. In order to extend their agency, actors instrumentally use technologies of joy and pain, despite the danger of further transforming them into semi-automatons. While such hybrid subjectivities express adaptation to the constraints of late modernity, they also lead to the further emptying of existence.

While in the first part of the book, those historical transformations are introduced, which resulted in structures characterized by various forms of meaninglessness (i.e. futile ownership, negative integration, power from indirect pain management), in the second part, those constellations are analyzed, where these effects become dominant (i.e. depressing competitive and communicative forms of integration, networks of anxiety, actor-networks of addiction). If one is incorporating such a distorted social environment, the phenomenological patterns of depression, anxiety and addiction emerge. Accordingly, the second part can be read as a criticism of reducing these patterns of suffering to mere 'mental illnesses' originating from either physical or psychic causes. It is argued that they should also be understood as various expressions of empty suffering originating from the structural constraints of late modernity. From this perspective, besides the biomedical or psychopathological attempts of treating suffering, the need for new forms of intervention arises. The third part of the book seeks such countermeasures having the potential of addressing the specific challenges of empty suffering – both on phenomenological and structural levels, in a genealogically reflective manner.

As one of the main difficulties of empty suffering is related to alienated self-narratives, firstly the lay attempts of making sense of the experience are mapped. Chapter 7 analyzes online depression forums as platforms of lay discussions of expert biomedical discourses and also peer support. Online forums are reinterpreted as public spheres capable of hosting debates between the two positions. Based on such premises, the results of an online ethnography are introduced: the main topics appearing in online discussions are summarized (explaining how the abstract tensions between lay and expert discourses appear in the actual discussions); and the various supportive communicative acts are identified (pragmatic advises, attempts of reframing self-narratives and expressions of unconditional recognition). Based on these analyses, an attempt is made to explore the latent functionality of online peer support by referring to a secular 'ritual healing' (Csordas) existing as an unreflected, contingent potential.

Chapter 8 expands the analyses to a more abstract direction by elaborating the space of possibility of late modern solidarity. Most theories of solidarity are embedded either in sociological or moral philosophical framework while not paying much attention to the empirical forms. This chapter aims at overcoming both types of one-sidedness by elaborating a model, which is sociologically grounded, normatively clarified and empirically refined. The following questions are analyzed: what are those mechanisms, which could complement or replace the weakening institutions of the welfare state (previously responsible for a system of 'organic solidarity' in Durkheimian sense)?; how can an appropriate normative basis of such hybrid solidarity be grounded?; how do local and global power struggles affect these processes? While attempting to answer these questions, a model of 'post-organic solidarity' is elaborated. It is constituted of networks temporarily managing global risks, without the prospect of long-term institutional solutions; justified by a set of negative moral principles, which balance the dialectical dynamics of countermeasures and their distortive unintentional consequences; undermined by the paradox of emergency, which is a constitutive element and a distortive factor at the same time. Late modern solidarity continuously balances between emancipatory and reifying tendencies: it does not aim to overcome the structural constituents of empty suffering in a revolutionary way, rather to facilitate change by taming these constraints and reflectively widening the space of agency.

Chapter 9 concludes the line of thought of the book by elaborating the basis of a therapeutic praxis fitting empty suffering. A more detailed phenomenological analysis of suffering reveals that the only way out from the meaninglessness of suffering is through replacing its solitary model with an intersubjective one (Levinas). Not only does suffering emerge in an intersubjective space, the treatment also depends on it: finding narratives, which are capable of giving sense to otherwise meaningless hardships, becomes possible only by turning to the suffering other (from the suffering self); thus, ethical meanings (such as responsibility and care) may be born. The details of such process are refined by reflecting on the possibilities and limitations of various psychotherapies and social work praxes. The technics elaborated by psychoanalysis (targeting the identification and correction of inner tensions), cognitive therapy (targeting the maladaptive automatic thoughts) and person-centred therapy (targeting the boundary issues of the self, related to insecure relationships) are reintroduced on social level. Networks enabling reflection on latent and manifest interpersonal conflicts or the dysfunctionality of social relations; along with the ones providing supplementary experiences of interpersonal approval are reintroduced as quasi-therapeutic intersubjectivities. Being connected to the distorted networks of late modernity, they might counter empty suffering originating from them.

While these nine chapters constitute a coherent argumentation, each of them (except Chapter 9) can be read as a distinct line of thought as well. The main argument tells the story of the emergence, the social context and the countermeasures of various forms of suffering related to the late modern condition. However, it may occur that someone is interested solely on the phenomenological, historical or sociological aspects of depression, anxiety or addiction. In their case, either a single chapter or the combination of chapters may prove to be useful: Chapters 1, 4 and 7 are focusing on depression; Chapters 2 and 5 focus on anxiety; Chapters 3 and 6 are related to the broad field of addiction. Therefore, despite the optimal order of chapters is expressed in the structure of the book, the readers are invited to discover them according to their own interest.

Part I

Genealogies of late modern suffering

Contemporary societies relate to suffering in a peculiar fashion: it is exclusively viewed as an obstacle in the way of a liveable or authentic existence. Consequently, suffering is emptied: it becomes a redundant experience, which is only meant to be overcome. However, such one-dimensional relation to suffering is not a cultural or historical universality – rather it is inseparable from modernization. Part I explores some of those historical processes in Occidental societies, which are responsible for the transformation of the experience of suffering. Chapter 1 explores the transition from late medieval times to early modernity: while suffering loses its transcendental meaning, the means of elimination also become widely available and acceptable. As a consequence of these transformations, an existence free from suffering becomes more desirable than unworldly values. Social interactions are reorganized along these lines: a struggle for a suffering-free existence begins, leading to the birth of individualized property as a key to secure it. However, the emergence of 'absolute dominion' indirectly also enables a new type of suffering: the parallel collapse of time consciousness, agency and intersubjectivity, which is described first as melancholia, later as depression. This is considered to be the first variant of empty suffering. Chapters 2 and 3 complement these conclusions by analyzing the transition from classic to late modernity. As the mechanisms of action coordination are reconfigured in a purely negative fashion (motivated by fear, instead of a combination of fear and hopes), anxiety becomes the phenomenological texture of social structures. With the emergence of modern biomedicine as a hegemonic discourse, the relation to physical pain is also reconfigured: while being exclusively interpreted as a bodily matter (to be handled by biomedical intervention), its latent relation to power structures shaping subjectivities is ignored. In case of medically untreatable, or unhandled pain, the experience of a senseless power is born. The only way to relate this structure is self-objectification: the subordination to a substance-based management of pleasure and pain, that is the birth of addictive subjectivities. These structural transformations outline the genealogy of empty suffering: the dissolving of transcendental meaning, the disappearance of positive integration and the rise of objectifying power structures explain the phenomenological patterns identified as depression, anxiety or addiction.

DOI: 10.4324/9781003197355-2

1 From naturalized suffering to futile ownership

A genealogy of depressed lifeworld

Depression is deeply connected to modernity. Even though similar forms of suffering have been registered since the ancient Greek era, depression has emerged as a central problem only since the consequences of modernization became widely experienced.[1] It has appeared not only in the medical discourses (Jackson, 1986) but also in various artworks indicating a general mood of times (Flately, 2008). In our days, depression is considered to be one of the greatest medical threats: a 'leading cause of disability worldwide', continuously on the rise (WHO, 2018). Unsurprisingly social scientific diagnoses of times have tried to explain the relationship between the distortions of modern societies and various mood disorders since their birth. Classic social theories referred to notions like 'alienation' (Marx), 'anomie' (Durkheim), 'loss of meaning' (Weber), which are not the equivalents of clinical depression, but express similar distortions. Contemporary critical theories refer to causes like the liquidity of social structures (Bauman, 2000), or the information society dissolving the space of narrative identity formation (Lash, 2002). While these analyses successfully establish some links between structural dysfunctions and depressive mood, they lack depth in both historical and phenomenological sense. They do neither make an effort to elaborate a sociologically grounded concept of depression nor do they raise the question concerning its prevalence in premodern times. Thus, they lack the potential of systematically explaining specific modernization trends responsible for the emergence of depression. Of course, these critical theories are not to be blamed for such imperfection, as depression is far from being at the centre of their interest – instead, it usually plays only an illustrative role, exemplifying a concrete consequence of social distortions. Various other theories attempt to understand depression as a *par excellence* late modern experience, implied by the cultural over-stressing of performance and autonomy (Ehrenberg, 2009), or by the acceleration of everyday life and social change (Rosa, 2010). While these analyses connect historical transformations with pathological phenomenological patterns, they limit their scope to classic and late modernity, and therefore miss the chance of grasping important *long durée* trends.

This chapter aims at identifying the long-term structural transformations that are related to the emergence of depression as a distorted phenomenological

DOI: 10.4324/9781003197355-3

pattern. In order to do this, a 'genealogical' analysis is conducted. From a methodological point of view, genealogy is an approach combining structural and phenomenological levels. It explains the emergence of moral (Nietzsche, 2013) or everyday discursive interpretations of the world (Foucault, 1977) considered to be evident by the contemporaries. While processes of *naturalizing* arbitrary interpretations are never independent from power relations, they are neither deterministic. The task of a genealogical analysis, therefore, is to map specific contingent mechanisms that play a decisive role in the reproduction of a certain interpretative framework, as also interrelated with forces structuring social existence. In this spirit, this chapter aims at tracking complex social historical transformations that resulted in a structural constellation implying a depressed lifeworld. As a result of this analysis, not only the social historical preconditions of depression may be identified, but also those alternative patterns of social suffering, which were free from the threat of depression.

In order to ground such genealogical study, firstly a framework is needed bridging psy- and social sciences. A common conceptual denominator is required, which could mediate between ahistorical models of mental disorders and historically situated models of social suffering. Phenomenology does have such potentials, as it provides access points for both psychological and sociological explanation. As it is explained in the first section, depression can be understood from a phenomenological approach as a distortion of one's relation to the world, including disembodiment, disrupted relation to the future and the past, lost agency and distorted interaffectivity (Fuchs, 2013; Ratcliffe, 2015). On such phenomenological grounds, an ideal-type of a depressive being in the world may be elaborated as an inherently social phenomenon, inseparable from the disturbed patterns of intersubjectivity, social suffering and the collective construction of time. This conceptualization enables a historical analysis: by reconstructing the premodern and early modern structural components of the intersubjective lifeworld; those distortive dimensions of modernization that are responsible for the emergence of its depressed version can be highlighted.

While such phenomenology of depression provides invaluable conceptual tools for analyzing historical transformations, it also has its methodological limitations. Undoubtedly, no matter how detailed it is, a single idealtype inevitably reduces the wide spectrum of depressive experiences (Rodríguez et al., 2012). Therefore, first person accounts have to be considered too in order to grasp the different aspects of depression, including descending, inhabiting or overcoming phases (Cvetkovich, 2012). Furthermore, for a historical phenomenology, the level of discursive framings also needs to be reflected upon: depressive being in the world includes not only a certain pattern of experiences but also their narrative interpretation and related attempts of treatment. Accordingly, a historical phenomenological study must cover the widest possible spectrum of related experiences, while reflecting on the transformation of their structural constituents and interpretative frames as well. Even though an overview such as this one is inevitably limited in its scope, an attempt is made to provide a comprehensive analysis taking most of these aspects into consideration.

Based on the phenomenological grounding, the second section attempts to reconstruct late medieval lifeworlds, with a special focus on embodiment, time consciousness, agency, intersubjectivity and also the discursive framing of melancholia. Such reconstruction relies on social historical studies, which – inspired by the school of *Annales* – aim at understanding the mentalities of late medieval actors based on their structural circumstances. We use these analyses as empirical sources for the purposes of elaborating the basic phenomenological dynamics of premodern societies.[2] After overviewing the known structural constraints of late medieval societies, the potential of depression is evaluated, which allows us to formulate our fundamental claim. While medieval existence was characterized by extreme levels of material deprivation and physical suffering, the intense focus on providence and the afterlife was capable of neutralizing these experiences, which made depression an overall improbable phenomenon. However, despite its hegemonic status, the power complex built upon such religious discourses was far from omnipotent: in various social positions, religious dogmas became doubted, often given up for heretic views or personal drives. Revealing such a latent conflict potential of medieval societies, our reconstruction, while analyzing the preconditions of depression in medieval societies, also allows for a dynamic understanding of the transition into the early modern era.

The idealtypical forms of social suffering have a mobilizing force in a sense that they designate the directions of the probable changes (Renault, 2010). Accordingly, early modern structural transformations may be explained as reactions to the medieval legitimacy crises that emerged around the paradoxes and inadequacies of the feudal power techniques (e.g. religious discourses) naturalizing and justifying suffering. The reconfiguration of internal social structures (the rise of the bourgeoisie) and of global economic structures (commercialization and colonization) severely challenged the medieval social order: everyday experience of these processes resulted in questioning the evidence of physical suffering and undermined religious dogmas legitimizing it. In the third section, this complex transformation is analyzed from the perspective of embodiment, time consciousness, agency and intersubjectivity. As the feudal system of labour, market and solidarity, with religious orientations at their core, was gradually complemented by one based on worldly orientations, the intersubjective lifeworld was fundamentally transformed. As an alternative to the ontological security provided by religion, which made bearable the material hardship and helplessness, the desire of taking control over the world became first a possibility, then a claim. The key to realize such goals was no longer held by a transcendental force – it assigned agency more and more to the actors themselves. In early modernity, these claims appeared first as complementary to the religious interpretation of the world resulting in an ambivalent constellation. Later on, in order to overcome these ambivalences, the relation to the world was reorganized according to the logic of control. The idea of controlling by owning – the objects, the others and the self – meant the expansion of property as absolute dominion, that is, a horizon deconstructing both the unworldly and the other.

A phenomenology of depression

Despite its widespread prevalence, depression is yet to become an uncontroversial notion – not only within the wider scientific community but also in the narrower circle of psy-experts. While the Diagnostic and Statistical Manual of Mental Disorders (DSM) seems to provide clear diagnostic criteria for identifying various forms of depression (APA, 2013), doubts have been raised both from outside and from inside the psy-discourse regarding the adequacy of such diagnostic criteria (Horwitz and Wakefield, 2007). Although differing in their content, these controversies all originate from the unclarified ontological status of depression: as it is situated in the middle of an inextricable conceptual web of biological, social and psychological causes, the exclusive choice of either of these perspectives inevitably results in oversimplification. Despite the evident need for a multidisciplinary approach, the multitude of ontological and epistemological disciplinary differences creates a seemingly unbridgeable distance. In order to overcome this difficulty, a common conceptual framework is needed, which is capable of linking diverging – and in many aspects incommensurable – disciplinary approaches. Since its birth, phenomenology has been dedicated to the task of grounding disciplines by revealing and elaborating their pre-scientific, evidently given presuppositions (Husserl, 1970). In this vein, phenomenology carries the potential of playing a similar role in the process of reconstructing depression in a pre-disciplinary way: elaborating the constitution of the depressive experience results in a pre-disciplinary description, which could then be related to medical, psy- and socio-discourses. In the following section, the most important phenomenological analyses of depression are overviewed in this spirit.

While most phenomenological analyses of depression agree on conceptualizing it as a distortion of one's 'relation to the world', the exact nature of such distortion is still debated. Some argue that depression should be understood as a mood, that is, an attunement based on a narrowed horizon of possibilities (Aho, 2013). Others argue that instead of understanding it simply as a mood, it should be defined as an 'existential feeling'. While the former provides a particular framework for relating to the world, the latter refers to the totality of being in the world. Depression as an existential feeling is characterized by the experience of losing the horizon of satisfaction or enjoyment paralleled by the experience of their impossibility as well (Ratcliffe, 2015: 67). Following this line of thought, others aim at embedding depression on a more fundamental level of experiencing. They argue that instead of interpreting it as a transformation of the modality of human existence, it should be described as the distortion of the very structure of existence. Depressed subjects lack certain abilities, such as relating to others (interaffectivity), or navigating in time (inter-temporality). In this sense, they are not simply characterized by a specific attunement or an existential feeling (which can be changed), but incapable of accessing the dynamic sphere of attunements (that is being trapped out of time and sociability). Accordingly, depression is a degradation of the existential structure itself (Fernandez, 2014).

While these accounts highlight various phenomenological approaches to depression, they are not necessarily incompatible with each other.[3] As depression itself includes a wide variety of experiential patterns, these analyses may be interpreted as idealtypical descriptions of different elements of the phenomenological continuum addressed as depression. Moods, existential feelings and structural degradation respectively represent gradually more and more severe distortions of one's horizon of possibilities. Such a unitary approach may not only enable a more comprehensive understanding of the heterogeneous experience of depression but also reveals the limitations of conceptualizations that attempt to link it exclusively either to the body or to the mind. Depression is not simply a bodily illness, or the pathological state of the affective or cognitive structures; instead, it involves the irreducible totality of being in the world. From a phenomenological point of view, the material world, the others and the self together constitute an intertwining continuum (Merleau-Ponty, 1968). This means that any modification of our relation to the world appears on all of these levels. As it is most obvious in case of illness: not only our body but also the whole world around us is transformed from a comfortable environment into a burdensome totality (van der Berg, 1972: 45). Accordingly, being depressed involves experience that indistinguishably relates to the external world, to the others, to our body and to our feelings: the loss of agency means at the same time the impassable barriers of the physical environment, the limitations set by the others, the unbearable fatigue of the body and the helplessness of the mind. This paralysing reconfiguration of being in the world constitutes the first component of the phenomenological description of depression.

There is a common element in the experience of depression and illness, as in both cases, the structure of existence is transformed: the world loses its plasticity, the others become inaccessible and the self loses its potency (Ratcliffe, 2015: 97). However, while in the case of illness, the transformation is considered to be temporal, in the case of depression it is perceived as permanent. Such sense of unchangeability originates from a distortion specific to depression, that is, the modification of the temporal structures of the lifeworld. The depressed person loses the access to the horizon of both the future (expressed by hopelessness) and the past (expressed by guilt). The temporal structures of the lifeworld play a fundamental role in inhabiting the world: inability to place events on a timeline renders it impossible to think in terms of causes and consequences, that is, to give sense to the world by constructing coherent narratives. First-person narratives of depression reveal several different types of turmoil, including the slowing or freezing of time, the parallel flowing of time or its annihilation by the proximity of death (Ratcliffe, 2015: 176). While these disturbances vary on a substantive level, they share a mutual experience of losing control over time, more specifically tipping the balance of linear and circular dimensions of time that enable teleological action and familiarity, respectively (Stanghellini et al., 2017). The experience of depression is characterized by the predominance of circular time: if linear time becomes inaccessible, the world does not seem changeable anymore (Ratcliffe, 2015: 185). As no phenomenon could be perceived as exceptional, time flows in an undifferentiated manner and the experience of permanency is born. This incapability of differentiating between relevant and irrelevant elements of the lifeworld and the consequent lack of structured time constitutes the second layer of the phenomenological description of depression.

Many depression symptoms may be understood as implied by such temporality distortions: without the horizon of linear time, operations relying on projections to the future, such as desiring or hoping, become impossible. Related first-person narratives emphasize not only the lack of trust in the world as a place of potential improvement but also demoralization including the loss of personal future, aspirations for particular goals and the general experience of incapability of hoping (Ratcliffe, 2015: 125). In order to understand such a sense of hopelessness, however, we cannot solely focus on the lack of differentiation, as a timeless horizon is not necessarily depressing. In case of hopelessness, besides the actual incapability of projecting into the future, there is also an element of being aware of this state as a deprivation. The birth of hopelessness includes an element of loss, that is, a reference of a quality that is used to characterize the world, but does not do so any longer.[4] A traumatic experience is born as the world itself becomes damaged, and the future – imagined as the future of the whole continuum – ceases to make sense.[5] Losing a significant object, symbolic or material, may result in the experience of an 'incomplete death': the world as it used to be known is partly destroyed by the loss, making the life linked to the lost object experienced as fundamentally non-continuable. That also explains the emergence of suicidal thoughts (i.e. attempts of completing the incomplete death): a non-continuable future is characterized by not only the lack of hopeful events but also the firm belief of the impossibility of hope as such (Ratcliffe, 2015: 116). This negative experience of loss constitutes the third dimension of depression.

The destruction of the horizon of future also affects the relation to the past. The lack of perspectives to proceed forwards makes the consequences of past deeds definitive. If previous mistakes are unredeemable, freedom becomes a trap: personal mistakes stick to the actor, which results in existential guilt. Unlike remorse originating from a particular event, existential guilt reframes one's relation to the self and to others (Ratcliffe, 2015: 133). If mistakes are considered unredeemable, then the regrettable events prevent identification with one's own past, which undermines the organizing of one's life story into a coherent narrative. Besides being alienated from their own identity, those who suffer from existential guilt are isolated from the others as well: they are perceived as judges for the unresolvable crimes, generating exclusively shame. Therefore, existential guilt gradually invades the depressed person's thoughts, and without a chance for escape through the future, it becomes the sole source of one's preoccupations (Ratcliffe, 2015: 194). As it fills one's circular time with repetitive intrusive content, existential guilt further contributes to the reproducing of a depressive lifeworld (especially when depression itself becomes the reason for guilt). In this sense, existential guilt complements the burdensome, undifferentiated, hopeless world, by highlighting those substantive elements, which, despite all the hiatuses, keep the depressed persons busy. This experience of unresolvable sins constitutes the fourth dimension of the phenomenology of depression.

As a consequence of guilt and hopelessness, one's agency is also gradually dissolved. Freedom is never experienced as a distinctive feeling, but as a state of world, which enables one to realize their potentials. In case of depression, this horizon is replaced by an alternative one, where activities are considered to be inevitably futile. Various forms of lost agency may include the loss of goals, lack of motivation, general sense of meaninglessness or complete passivity and ignorance (Ratcliffe, 2015: 170). Giving up on action further strengthens the other aspects of depressive being in the world, as it provides proof for the vanity of resistance. In passivity and acts of procrastination, the actor resolves from interacting with the world, thus missing any chance for finding elements that do not prove to be burdensome. Also, they miss the chance of finding any basis for differentiating between relevant and irrelevant phenomena, which prevents them from reopening the horizon of the future and the past (thus decreasing hopelessness and guilt). Accordingly, it is passivity itself that transforms the particular experiences of limited freedom into an experience of general deprivation from freedom. As the depressed person gradually becomes isolated because of the transformation of their bodily and temporal horizons, they gather experiences about the impossibility of agency. This impression of complete helplessness constitutes the fifth layer of depression.

Various dimensions of depression are equally related to the question of isolation, that is, the withdrawal of bodily involvement, initiation and claim for shaping the future and reframing the past. Amongst the intertwining material, embodied and social components of the world, one segment plays a distinctive role when it comes to the question of isolation. Withdrawal from the world means most importantly the suspension of social interactions, that is disconnecting from the intersubjectively constructed material world (inter-corporality), time (inter-temporality) and attunements (inter-affectivity). Even if empirical solitude is a well-known symptom of depression, it still requires a phenomenological grounding, as depressed persons do not simply avoid the company of others, but actually lose their ability of relating to them. On the one hand, this transformation includes the incapability of attributing mental states to elements of the world; therefore, the other is degraded into a thing. On the other hand, it includes the incapability of stimulation, that is, the mutual impacting of each other's relation to the world (Ratcliffe, 2015: 208). As the others, who enable sharing and receiving are not part of the horizon anymore, the experience of their hiatus reinforces the experience of the impossibility of relating.

While intersubjectivity requires both the ability of attributing mental states to others and the ability of stimulation, solely these two factors do not explain it completely. On a dynamic level, intersubjectivity is maintained through the resonance of embodied selves. The affective and cognitive motivational basis of action is accessible for the actors due to their bodily expression (e.g. one becomes aware of being afraid because their body is shaking). The fact that living through and expressing an impression are inseparable from each other implies that experiences mediated by the body are not accessible only for the subject – instead, they belong to the sphere of intersubjectivity (Fuchs, 2013: 222). Even those emotions or thoughts, which are considered to belong exclusively to the individual, are potentially open to influences originating from the others. On a pre-intentional level, actors are continuously synchronizing their attunement in the same bodily mediated process that enables self-consciousness as well. Therefore, depression as isolation is explained by the incapability of participating in such processes of resonance. The distortion of interaffectivity is principally a disorder of inter-corporeality, that is a transformation of the living body capable of mediating for the self and the other (*Leib*) into a dead body existing as a mere object (*Körper*). As a consequence, the whole intertwining world loses its living character and becomes unrelatable, dead matter.[6] The individual remains alone with the task of inhabiting the fundamentally intersubjective world. This paradoxical situation could be expressed on the one hand by deprived, negative emotions, and on the other hand by the pathological reconfiguration of the whole lifeworld including depersonalization, derealization or delusions (Fuchs, 2013: 229). This incapability of inter-corporeal synchronization with the others constitutes the sixth dimension of depression.

While each of the above analyzed dimensions plays a crucial role in the emergence of depression, none of them can be picked as the single most important one. This means that even if they are interrelated, none of them is reducible to any other. These dimensions may be understood as entry points of the phenomenological transformation potentially culminating in clinical depression as a pathological being in the world. The transformation of the (embodied) world into an environment full of obstacles; the disturbance of temporality caused by the incapability of differentiating between relevant and irrelevant elements of the lifeworld; the experience of hopelessness as partial death; the sense of unresolvable guilt caused by an uncontinuable past; the experience of deprivation from freedom reassured by passivity or loneliness caused by the inability of relating to the other could all equally initiate a depressive transformation of the lifeworld. However, the full process requires not only the existence of one or several dimensions but also their gradual interconnection. Depression emerges if the experience of a burdensome world is complemented with getting stuck in circular time, the elimination of future, the preoccupation with the past, passivity or isolation. If more and more of these elements are linked up, then a coherent lifeworld is constituted, wherein all the different layers strengthen and reinforce a depressive being in the world. In this sense, from a phenomenological perspective, depression is not as much a state, but rather a dynamic process.

Such a phenomenological description of depression allows for the social and historical analysis of its prevalence. Experiences belonging to the above dimensions are rendered likely by various social constellations that outline the horizon of possibilities – in what follows, these will be defined as the structural components of depression. Unsurprisingly, quantitative data on the historical prevalence of depression are entirely unavailable; luckily at this point, these are rendered unnecessary for our purposes. The idealtypical reconstruction of the social structures in pre-modern and modern social constellations that make each phenomenological dimension – and especially their interconnections – likely, shall enable us to analyze the relation of modernity and depression. In the following sections, this objective is pursued.

Late medieval lifeworlds: The dominance of the unworldly

In order to understand the specific phenomenological dynamics of modernity, the structural transformations of late medieval and early modern Europe need to be explored. Even if there are significant local specificities in each region and period, there are also common factors determining the space of possibilities of the medieval era. In what follows, these material and symbolic living conditions are reconstructed as idealtypical structures of the medieval lifeworld.[7] As it would be an over-ambitious goal to provide a comprehensive overview of the medieval lifeworld, we restrict our focus on those aspects that are relevant for the phenomenology of depression. These include bodily and temporal experiences, agency and intersubjectivity. As the distortion of these dimensions determines the likelihood of the emergence of a pathological form of depression, they are evaluated first separately and then according to their interferences. Besides highlighting the medieval structural constituents of depression, an attempt is also made to reflect upon the contemporary interpretations of depressive experiences, based on the medieval accounts of melancholia.

The quality of embodied existence depends on the capability of fulfilling desires (expressing the enjoyment of the world) and the level of unhandled suffering (implying a burdensome relation to the world). Material culture sets a framework for the process of embodiment, as it provides tools for cultivating the body, that is, not only for securing its needs but also for learning how to maintain balance with the environment. If such tools are missing, then the environment unfolds in a harsh and hostile form, resulting in physical suffering. From this perspective, medieval societies are characterized by poorly developed material culture. The basis of such poor development was a general suspicion towards any technical novelties, considered to be sinful (Le Goff, 1992: 200). The most drastic consequences of this technophobia concerned the agricultural sector: as the technology required for effective cultivation of lands was missing, extensive farming was barely capable of securing the nourishment of the population. Accordingly, the medieval life-world was fundamentally characterized by the naturalization of hunger (Le Goff, 1992: 228). This bodily experience was complemented on the one hand by the constant threat of various illnesses and diseases, which were frequent due to the lack of countermeasures, malnutrition and exhaustive physical labour. On the other hand, physical violence was a profound experience: in the public and private feudal relations, it was applied as a means of punishment or as an expression of social hierarchies (Le Roy Ladurie, 1984: 194). The suffering of the body, however, was not only endured – in some cases, it also became idealized based on religious reasons. As the always lustful body was considered to be the source of devilish influence, the suppression of desires, or self-induced pain was considered to be a virtue and a key to salvation and providence (Le Goff, 1992: 161). Due to these various reasons, physical suffering was not perceived as exceptional and avertible, instead, as an inevitable experience, often cultivated by mostly religious narratives and practices.[8] Overall, while suffering was a decisive experience, it did include not only negative meanings of hiatus or deprivations but also transcendental ones.

The structure of medieval time was based on the concept of eschatology. Within this framework, everyday life was lacking teleological structure: it did not include worldly goals to achieve, only the principle of following the divine regulations (Le Goff, 1992: 187). The life course was not divided into qualitatively distinct phases, such as the childhood as a preparation for the adult life. Instead, the whole life was conceived to be of a homogeneous duration, without the horizon of change (Ariés, 1962: 128). The succession of generations was also lacking any historical significance: the order of events was registered only contingently, without the motivation of reconstructing tendencies or providing a credible chronology. In this sense, linear time consciousness was not only missing on the individual level, but on the collective level as well (Le Roy Ladurie, 1984: 281). As a consequence of lacking any perspective of structuring worldly life in a teleological fashion, the repetitive, circular framework remained the basis of time consciousness. Such circular perception of time, however, did not imply idleness: as it was considered to be a major sin, work consumed the majority of time (Le Goff, 1992: 174). Despite its consistency, the traditional forms of work did not create a rigid order for everyday actions; they also provided space for flexibility and relaxing (Le Roy Ladurie, 1984: 278). Overall, the medieval temporality was characterized by the lack of worldly teleological structure and by an interrelated system of religious and natural orders of circular time. In other words, linear time existed beyond the empirically testable reality while circular time was applied as a non-deterministic framework.

Based on such structure of time, the horizon of hope became also limited. Development on individual or collective level was considered not only to be impossible but also to be a sinful attempt. This resulted in a paradoxical concept of labour: on the one hand, goal-oriented work was forbidden; on the other hand, continuous activity was expected (Le Goff, 1992: 223). As the accumulation of worldly goods could not provide any ground for securing the future, the attention was oriented towards other worldly hopes. The relation to the world was based on a quasi-magical attunement, where the visible and the invisible constituted an inextricable texture; thus, any phenomenon could be perceived as a sign of the divine (Le Goff, 1992: 165). This interrelatedness of the mundane and the transcendental enabled the anchoring of religious beliefs to the tangible world. However, despite the coherent framework provided by the church dogmas, the detachment of hope from empirical experiences often proved to be limited. Primordial sensations such as hunger, desire or parental affections could often overwrite the horizon of unworldly hope while demanding actual solutions to worldly problems (Le Roy Ladurie, 1984: 153). Such situations could either result in the emergence of alternative paths within the system of beliefs, which implied the blame of heresy, or in some sort of naïve materialism imply the retreat to non-religious practices. The most common acts of revolt were mainly motivated by unbearable living conditions such as starvation. While aiming at solving a concrete problem, they also expressed the anger caused by the general lack of recognition of human needs (Le Goff, 1992: 301). Overall, the structure of medieval hope was characterized by the ambivalence of lacking a worldly horizon and the transcendental promise of providence and salvation, complemented with sparks of revolt.

Such perspective of the future was affecting the relation to the past as well. As action had mostly unworldly relevance, the possibility of correcting previous mistakes was also embedded into the transcendental horizon. Humans were considered to be natural sinners; thus, the sin itself was a regularity requiring proper mechanisms capable of handling it. Such mechanisms included the practice of confession providing chance for forgiveness and negotiating divine support (Le Roy Ladurie, 1984: 312). In order to provide further assurances of salvation and providence, the concept of purgatory was born as a liminal place between hell and heaven, a last chance for redeeming sins and gaining entrance to paradise. While originally not being part of Christian theology, the concept became more and more important during the middle ages: as the time between death and resurrection had to be filled with content, the horizon of a last opportunity for working off the debts of worldly sins emerged (Le Roy Ladurie, 1984: 292). The purgatory allowed for the birth of a limited sense of control, as it was imagined analogously to a court of justice, where the decision could be influenced by the living: if they prayed, fasted and devoted masses for the dead, salvation was possible despite previous sins (Le Goff, 1984: 305). As in death everyone became dependent on those who survived them, a horizon of worldly activities oriented to secure the afterlife by establishing networks of support (based on either solidarity or money) emerged (Le Goff, 1984: 332). Overall, faith provided several ways of handling guilt: by keeping the past open for change both in life and after death, no sins remained unredeemable.

Religious practices that were supposed to handle the persistent forms of suffering in a transcendental way were affecting not only temporal structures but also the horizon of agency. A concept of freedom referring to the ability of acting according to the individual's will was completely lacking, as everyone was dependent on the other. In such a chain of dependencies, to be free meant to have strong protectors, who could secure one's position in the hierarchical order (Le Goff, 1992: 280). The capability of acting on one's own was also partly prevented by the lack of technological knowledge enabling the manipulation of nature. Even more importantly, it was blocked by the lack of secure property: in case of common people, the lords had access to any household goods while the lands of the lords were given and potentially taken away by the superior liege lords (Duby, 1988: 22). The lack of technical competence and the insecurity of social positions resulted in attempts of realizing agency through less consistent ways. The first hiatus was often resolved with prayers or pilgrims aiming at gaining divine favour based on an elaborated order of personal sacrifices and expectable miracles (Finucane, 1977). Alternatively, superstitious or magical praxes aiming at manipulating reality in non-Christian ways were also applied (Le Roy Ladurie, 1984: 342). The second hiatus, that is the lack of secure social positions, was treated by various forms of small-scale revolts against the *status quo*, including the denial of the feudal-religious authority complex (Le Roy Ladurie, 1984: 260), or the forming of social spaces inaccessible to the others' gaze (Duby, 1988: 511). A less trivial example of the struggle for agency is the phenomenon of the carnival: by depicting worldly and religious authorities as ridiculous, these festivities provided opportunity not only to suspend the existing hierarchies but also to acquire agency, even if only for a limited time (Bakhtin, 1984: 30). The grotesque realism of the carnival represented a relief from the strict regulations of the church and the lords, that is, an alternative way of relating to the world: a chance for liberating laughter, instead of the anxious focus on sins and on fears from retribution. Overall, even if medieval agency was limited by both lack of competence and recognition of freedom, that did not imply passivity, not only because of the prohibition of idleness but also because of those subtle strategies, which enabled actions outside the official lifeworld governed by worldly authorities and the church.

The limitations of personal agency affected the framework of intersubjectivity as well. The basic division of the world differentiated between the wilderness, occupying the majority of the known world, being full of actual and mystical threats, and the relatively small islands of inhabited territories, representing security provided by the presence of the others (Le Goff, 1992: 133). In this constellation, the interdependence of mankind constituted the basic level of intersubjectivity: the proximity of the other was not a choice, but a necessity for survival. Within these frames, the very horizon of the individual was missing: people were identified, by themselves and by their environment, primarily with the family they belonged to (Le Goff, 1992: 281). Besides interaction patterns, religious beliefs also thwarted the construction of personhood: being alone was considered to be not only a dangerous practice but also a sinful one. As the individual was thought to be vulnerable to devilish influence, every possible moment of life was spent in the company of others (Duby, 1988: 515). This included not only activities like eating or working but also most bodily activities such as sleeping, cleaning or even urinating or defecating. This naturalization of permanent intersubjectivity was mirrored by the spatial structure of buildings lacking private spaces (Le Roy Ladurie, 1984: 142). As the chance for privacy was missing from the horizon of medieval actors, the lifeworld was almost exclusively constructed in interactions. Such immediacy of giving sense to the world together resulted not only in a strong collective consciousness but also in the relative unity of beliefs and affections. Even if these interactions were not at all free from hierarchies, they still maintained a strong sense of solidarity: the family and the local community were literally the sole chance of survival (Le Goff, 1992: 290). Overall, the constant, collectivist and immediate medieval intersubjectivity existed primarily as a necessity while being legitimized by religious dogmas as well. As a consequence, despite its authoritarian tendencies, such a strong social network provided a permanent chance for relating to the other and sharing an interaffective attunement.

In sum, the idealtypical medieval lifeworld is characterized by permanent physical suffering naturalized by religious principles; the lack of the horizon of an empirically inhabitable linear timeframe; the prospect of salvation as the main source of hope; religious techniques of resolving mistakes and sins; limited instrumental capabilities complemented by the practices rooted in popular culture and oppressive, but omnipresent intersubjectivity. Within such framework, even if several factors rendered the emergence of certain depressive experiences probable, there was only a small overall chance of them to build up a consistent pattern exclusively dominating one's horizon. Even if the physical suffering, the limitations of linear time and hope, the agency lacking competences and technology, or the oppressive intersubjectivity equally had the potential of threatening with depressive experiences, religious interpretations and strategies of the popular culture were capable of counterweighting them. More importantly, the permanent presence of the others could prevent overwhelming hopelessness by exposing the subject to the synchronizing effects of the others. In this sense, a pathological pattern of depression was improbable: while the medieval lifeworld exposed the subjects to various other forms of suffering, it systematically prevented the emergence of unresolvable despair.

Despite the improbability of a consistent pattern of depressive condition, moods resembling depression were not completely unknown in the medieval era. The terms 'melancholia' and 'acedia' refer to distinct approaches of unresolvable despair, which can be related to the modern experience of depression. The former originates from the ancient Greek medical tradition, which relates depressive symptoms to a generally disturbed behaviour pattern: 'causeless fear, sadness, anguish, preference of solitude, loss of appetite, suspiciousness and absurd talk' were explained with the turmoil of the balance of the 'black bile' (Jackson, 1986: 62). According to the Hippocratic-Galenic tradition, the treatments were also centred around re-establishing the balance by appropriate diet and activities (Lindeman, 1999: 17). Unlike the medical approach of melancholia, explaining depressive behaviour mainly as a bodily illness, acedia is anchored in the religious tradition. Originally elaborated to explain the crisis of devotion among monks, acedia is defined by the symptoms of 'carelessness, weariness, exhaustion, apathy, anguish, sadness, low spirits, and sloth or negligence from excessive attention to worldly matters' (Jackson, 1986: 66). Later on, these signs of failing faith were applied to the lay population, with the intention of interpreting the loss of agency as a consequence of evil influences. In this framework, the depressed condition becomes inseparable from the domain of sins; therefore, the treatments are also religious (e.g. confession – Jackson, 1986: 70). All in all, while more severe depressive symptoms were partly explained by physiological causes originating from the ancient Greek tradition, less severe depressive symptoms were explained according to the transcendental dialectics of sin and penance.[9] In this sense, the medieval actor had no alternative but to interpret their own depressed mood according to the same religious frames that naturalized any other suffering as well.

Transition to early modernity: The emergence of the worldly

Despite the common perception of the medieval world as a stable, unchanging era, social historical research highlighted several latent tensions straining it. One of the most important tensions was between the moral teachings of the church legitimizing a worldly order and the actual experience of the corrupted and oppressive worldly and religious elite (Le Roy Ladurie, 1984: 317). Another tension emerged around the status of wealth: its accumulation was not only forbidden but also turned into a taboo, while it gained more and more significance in the power struggles between and within the three orders (Duby, 1980: 327). In this sense, the medieval era was characterized by a prolonged, underlying legitimation crisis, which was partly pacified by faith and the ridiculing strategies of popular culture, but regularly emerged to the surface through outbursts of local revolts often paired with heresy. As these acts were both motivated by unbearable physical suffering or starvation and the outrage caused by the contrast between the teachings and the acting of the worldly and church elite, they targeted the whole power complex. The answer of the elites to these attempts was the gradual centralization of power and the increase of oppression (Duby, 1980: 336). However, these tendencies were capable of maintaining the *status quo* only temporarily – beneath the surface, the structural tensions slowly reshaped the phenomenological horizon. During the early modern era, besides the surviving medieval lifeworld, slowly new tendencies emerged that aimed to reconfigure the controversial relation to the worldly matters neglected by the transcendental focus of Christianity. This liminal state makes early modernity a distinct era: while the medieval other-worldly mentality still prevailed, it was increasingly complemented with worldly orientations (Ariés, 1989: 2).[10] In order to understand how depression became a fundamental experience in modernity, first the transformations of being in the world need to be analyzed among the liminal conditions of early modernity, which should be complemented by analyzing the reconfiguring discourses of melancholia.

While embodiment among medieval conditions was principally characterized by naturalized suffering and a consequent neglecting of the cultivation of the body, the early modern era was characterized by a shift in corporeality. The body becomes the terrain of expressing social status and experiencing pleasure. It was not anymore treated exclusively as the platform of sin, but rather as the primary indicator of social position (Cohen and Cohen, 2001: 217). As healthiness and beauty started to provide prestige, the cultivation of the body became a legitimate goal. This included on the one hand a greater focus on training the body, ornamenting it and also disciplining it according to the etiquette (Elias, 2000). Furthermore, the dissolution of the taboos around the body enabled not only its instrumentalization in public interactions but also its rediscovery as a source of enjoyment. Pleasing the body through various sensations, such as pleasant smells, good tastes or the soft touch of clothes, became not only a status symbol but also a legitimate luxury goal (Cohen and Cohen, 2001: 276). However, despite every attention given to the body, the most basic elements of suffering caused by illness and heavy physical labour remained untreatable. As the density of the population significantly increased, new types of health risks appeared due to the lack of hygiene and medical expertise. Infections and epidemics became a major problem, which were still handled with magical and religious practices (Chamberlin, 1965: 134). Despite these similarities, suffering was not seen any more as an inevitable 'punishment of God', but instead as something which can be fought (Ginzburg, 1992: 68). Furthermore, illness raised not only individual but also public awareness as authorities developed the techniques of quarantine as an effective way of stopping epidemics (Cohen and Cohen, 2001: 241).[11] Overall, the framework of embodiment changed significantly compared to the medieval era: although still a constitutive element mainly fought with superstitious methods, suffering was not treated anymore as a necessity, but instead, as a hardship to be resisted. Furthermore, the body emerged as a terrain of pleasure and prestige.

Due to commercialization and the explorations of foreign lands, the social order and the geography of the world were slowly transforming, and along with them the structure of time. Cities functioning as centres for enterprise opened the perspectives of mobility: although inequalities were still considered inevitable characteristics of the world, the horizon of social mobility also emerged. Having the right skills and a little luck, moving across the social hierarchy became possible: merchants could accumulate wealth measurable to that owned by nobility; craftsmen could advance in the hierarchy of the guild system and peasants could become tenants (Cohen and Cohen, 2001: 15). This general experience of mobility enabled access to a linear worldly time complementing the transcendental one. Besides such individual experiences, the development of administration of business and governance created a new sense of historical time. Events were documented in a new, more detailed manner, which resulted in the birth of a narrative reflectivity structuring the past, present and future events (Cohen and Cohen, 2001: 164). Obviously, the birth of a rival temporal order was in conflict with the religious one: a claim for transforming the social order perceived to be unjust emerged (Burke, 1978: 175). While similar claims were not completely unknown in medieval times either, they became a general impression, independent from acute crises of suffering or starvation, only during early modernity. As a consequence of such criticism, the very horizon of eschatology was weakened (Ginzburg, 1992: 64). Overall, as linear time became accessible on individual and collective levels, the 'time lived through' gradually replaced the 'time promised'; thus, one's temporal horizon became more and more anchored in the empirical world.

The emergence of a worldly horizon of linear time transformed the relation to the future and the past as well. The experience of personal mobility and historical transformation contributed to the formation of a plastic future, which gradually complemented the horizon of salvation. Instead of the medieval concept of providence as an unchangeable fate, the future became populated by various risks, which were considered to have probability, and thus predictability and controllability (Nacol, 2016). While both natural and social risks were constitutive of the horizon of a controllable future, in the early modern era – without adequate scientific knowledge – the latter played a decisive role (Cohen and Cohen, 2001: 43). In order to control the future, those skills had to be perfected that gained others' approval, such as moral (i.e. 'honour' in opposition to Christian morality), aesthetic (i.e. attractiveness or charisma), intellectual (i.e. capability of autonomous reflection) or manual (i.e. dexterous craftsman) skills (Cohen and Cohen, 2001: 80). As a consequence of commercialization, not only personal perfection but also adaptation to the increasing pressure of specialization and the demands of the market took part in structuring the relation to the future (Cameron, 2001: 49). They exposed the actors to a novel experience: failure as a consequence of personal inadequacy. Unlike in the medieval lifeworld, where success or failure was beyond human reach, after the horizon of mobility was opened in early modernity, competition also became sharp and cruel (Cohen and Cohen, 2001: 72). Overall, the early modern framing of hope became a mixture of enduring unworldly securities and the new perspective of personal development. Religious motivations for perfection and the preserved hope for salvation became sided by the chance of taking responsibility for one's life, and the danger of failing.

A similar controversy also prevailed in the relation to the past. One of the most important technological innovations of early modernity is printing and the consequent expansion of literacy. By making classical and contemporary texts available for a wider readership and presenting new genres (e.g. journals), printing provided a vivid relation to the past. Worldly events were not automatically fading away, but a written domain for remembrance emerged (Cohen and Cohen, 2001: 129). This worldly collective memory gradually complemented the eschatological: by providing an alternative, empirically accessible past, it enabled a different relation to sins and mistakes. Based on such framing, sinful acts were not only considered to be redeemable in the afterlife (or indirectly by affecting the afterlife) but also through intervening in worldly events in a restorative way. In order to elaborate adequate mechanisms, narrative interpretations capable of arranging the series of events in a causally coherent framework were needed. On an institutional level, the registration of official events (Cohen and Cohen, 2001: 143) and on an individual level diaries (Ariés, 1989: 5) and confessions (Stegner, 2016) provided opportunity for constructing such narratives and trajectories. However, even though the importance of the worldly past gradually increased, it still remained complemented by the horizon of the religious medieval relation to the past. The concept of purgatory remained in use throughout the early modern era, providing a less and less convincing, though always available sanctuary. Death was still treated as a transition (Ariés, 1976); it was still the living's duty to secure the fate of the departed and the afterlife was still a period requiring attention, even if these aspects ceased to dominate the horizon of everyday life (Cohen and Cohen, 2001: 210). Overall, the transcendental framing of guilt in the early modern era was complemented with a worldly one, which on the one hand provided opportunity for the resolution of past mistakes, and on the other hand increased uncertainty by weakening the hegemony of religious faith (Ginzburg, 1992: 76).

These characteristics of the early modern lifeworld provided a new framework for agency and freedom as well. Even if the birth of the modern subject is shaped by several parallel historical tendencies, one of them stands out, that is the expanding space of accumulating property. Property was acquired for several reasons: on the one hand, the unreliability of banks and the financial system did not leave other alternatives than the investment in durable, easily sellable goods instead of cash or deposit (Cameron, 2001: 257). In other cases, property played a religious function: according to protestant ethics, worldly success was considered to be the expression of being chosen for salvation (Weber, 1992). Furthermore, property played a purely symbolic function as well: as the boundary between status groups became more and more blurred, hierarchy had to be expressed by visible indicators, such as owned objects (Cohen and Cohen, 2001: 82). In this sense, acquiring property became the main terrain of everyday agency: the merchant, the craftsman, the mercenary, the proprietor and the tenant-farmer were involved in different activities, but all shared the same experience of autonomy.[12] They invested in acquiring skills, took risks, made alliances and competed with others in order to step forwards in the social hierarchy by accumulating material property and showing it off (Chamberlin, 1965: 76).

Besides the acquisition of wealth, other opportunities also became available for the early modern actor. The spreading of printed texts not only relativized the official religious interpretation of the world but also provided opportunity for forming personal opinions and claiming the right to do so (Ginzburg, 1992: 112). Power struggles also drastically changed. While in the medieval era, the claim for power had to rely on some form of traditional legitimacy (inheritance) or transcendental legitimacy, in early modernity, such factors became less relevant, as best exemplified by Machiavelli's classic novel *The Prince*. Honour gained emphasis compared to Christian duties, and in the name of the former, many deeds forbidden by the latter became justifiable (e.g. blood revenge, scheming) (Cohen and Cohen, 2001: 90). As the normative field became multidimensional, a space of manoeuvre was born, and a strategic relation to norms emerged. Overall, early modernity is characterized by increased freedom in both material and cognitive senses. However, these novel fields of agency were not only unequally distributed, but completely lacking any sense of solidarity, which implied the naturalization of cruel and competitive social relations (Cohen and Cohen, 2001: 110).

It is important to emphasize at this point that the phenomenon of early modern autonomy should not be confused with modern individualism, for the reason that the former was completely lacking the element of independence from the others. Similar to medieval patterns of intersubjectivity, agency in the early modern era still relied upon the others as constitutive elements of one's existence. Not only were they the main providers of various resources (the 'social capital' of the family or clan) but others also constituted the main public whose recognition was desired (Cohen and Cohen, 2001: 53). Social ties were cultivated by defending honour and more importantly by continuously giving and asking for favours. Unlike market exchange, favour is less concrete concerning both its content and its timeframe. Such uncertainty had its own functionality: instead of being a clearly defined, atomic transaction between individuals, favours interlaced the whole existence, and were thus capable of maintaining trust and a sense of belonging (Cohen and Cohen, 2001: 64). Patron-client relations built upon unequal relations of favour replaced earlier feudal chains and provided a more flexible social structure, which was, however, still based on personal dependencies and familiarity.

As norms and roles became increasingly negotiable, uncertainty was rising as well. A basic social contract providing the basis for potential further agreements was missing: while the medieval religious-feudal order was gradually weakened, an adequate substitute, that is, some sort of 'rule of law', was yet to be developed. Without a binding force, agreements could not ground expectations for the future, and instead they became games of honour, of favours and patronizing (Cohen and Cohen, 2001: 112). Uncertainty prevailed, and social interactions became increasingly chaotic and uncontrollable. Such intensive, yet chaotic intersubjectivity on the one hand lead to the emergence of new phenomena, such as the birth of friendship as a relationship free from rivalries and mutual suspicion, autonomously shaped by the participants (Cohen and Cohen, 2001: 65), or the emergence of micro public spheres of debating religious or political issues (Ginzburg, 1992: 31). On the other hand, it resulted in the dire need for breaking away from often suffocating interpersonal social networks, which was expressed by the transformation of spatial structures and the birth of isolated, private spaces (Ariés, 1989: 7). Overall, early modern intersubjectivity was similar to medieval intersubjectivity in its density; however, it was much more contingent and competitive. Consequently, it provoked the need not only for new mechanisms of social control but also for means of disconnecting.

In sum, the idealtypical early modern lifeworld was characterized by the gradual expansion of possibilities. The experiences of embodiment still included the element of untreatable suffering, although not anymore in a naturalized way, as physical pleasure and the cultivation of the body appeared on the horizon. The eschatological framework of time still prevailed, but it was complemented with linear historical time on an individual and collective level. The differentiation of time enabled a new relation to the future and the past as potentially controllable by actors. The space of freedom increased on both material and reflective levels, while it remained dependent on the social environment. Intersubjectivity remained dense, yet it also became more contingent and intrusive. In many ways, the early modern lifeworld provided new solutions to previous forms of suffering while creating challenges of its own. The primary terrain of the newly acquired agency was the social sphere, where the opening paths of mobility provided opportunity for personal and collective progress through accumulating wealth. However, the price of this transformation was the profound reconfiguration of intersubjectivity. Without new regulations capable of handling insecurity and rivalry, it became a controversial terrain, full of dangers.

In this sense, while trying to handle the specific sufferings of the medieval era, social innovations of the early modern era unintendedly dismantled social structures that previously prevented depression. From a genealogical perspective, it may be argued that the horizon of depression was opened as a consequence of these early modern transformations. This is also reflected in the slowly changing discourse of melancholia. While the medieval era was mostly preoccupied with a religious-moral framing of the depressive mood, during the renaissance, a new interpretative horizon emerged. Melancholia was gradually detached from the religious context and became a natural condition to be treated or endured. Also the concept of 'melancholic temperament' emerged, as an indicator of an intellectual, creative, insightful character, who sacrificed a balanced mood for greater personal achievements (Jackson, 1986: 99).[13] This figure originated from Italy, but became popular in the Elizabethan era, greatly influencing the emerging drama literature in the 16th–17th centuries (Lindeman, 1999: 33). The gradual reinterpretation of melancholia (as an illness) or acedia (as a sin) into melancholic temperament (as an inevitable cost of self-fulfilment) indicates the transformation of its status: it increasingly becomes the experience of the individual aiming at establishing themself as an autonomous agent.[14]

These transformations, however, did not result automatically in the widespread experience of melancholia. Those who successfully navigated the labyrinth of social mobility preoccupied themselves with shaping their personal future while maintaining a balance of social embeddedness and independence in relation to others. The experience of defeating suffering could then be born and the world could be inhabited in an autonomous way. Such 'promise of early modernity' provided a solution for the paradoxes of the medieval era, without threatening with depression. Melancholia emerged only in those cases where suffering proved to be unmanageable (as a result of failed attempts of social mobility) or intersubjective relationships were suffocating (as a result of overly sharp competition) while at the same time, faith also lost its comforting potential. As these dimensions were independent from each other, overall the early modern subject was still relatively protected from depression, while also holding the potential of overcoming the idealtypical medieval forms of suffering. This constellation changed only after further structural transformations, which – while trying to handle the ambivalences of early modernity – made depression not only a possible, but a rather probable phenomenon.

Absolute dominion and depression

After overviewing the late medieval and early modern structural components of depression, the conclusions may be summarized. It may be argued that due to the complex transformations affecting the economic, social and political levels of medieval society, the constellation that had prevented the generalization of depression for centuries gradually dissolved in the early modern era. However, that did not instantly result in a constellation resembling the contemporary one: in early modernity, the paradoxes of the medieval era were handled in a mixed way, by relying on previous technologies of the self and experimenting with new forms of social existence (Table 1.1).

As the transition from the late medieval to early modern era is explained by the social suffering related to medieval structures (e.g. the lack of material well-being, the contrast between the religious principles and the worldly elite), the transformations leading to classical modernity can also be understood as reactions to the discrepancies of the early modern *status quo*. Among

Table 1.1 The structural components of depression in late medieval and early modern era

Phenomenological dimensions of depression/era	*Late medieval era*	*Early modernity*
Embodied existence	Permanent physical suffering naturalized by religious principles	The element of untreatable suffering is still present, but not anymore in a naturalized way (horizon of pleasure and unjustified suffering)
Time consciousness	Lacking horizon of an empirically inhabitable linear timeframe; the prospect of salvation as the main source of hope; religious techniques of resolving mistakes and sins	Eschatological time prevails, but complemented with linear historical time on individual and collective levels; new relation to the future and the past as potentially controllable
Agency	Limited instrumental capabilities complemented by practices rooted in popular culture	Freedom increased on both material and reflective levels, still dependent on social status, making social mobility a priority
Intersubjectivity	Oppressive, but omnipresent intersubjectivity	Intersubjectivity still dense, but also more contingent and competitive
Narrative framing	Melancholia (black bile), acedia (sins)	Melancholic temperament (as a cost of individual greatness)

these discrepancies, the dependence on uncertain social relationships seems to stand out in importance: as the others became the key to replace suffering with enjoyment, the securing of social positions also became a priority. Consequently, the unpredictability of interactions was treated more and more as an eliminable problem. It is not surprising that the very first theoretical reflections on the possibility of a modern social order were aimed at reconstructing a fundamental 'social contract' as a precondition of overcoming the unsustainable coexistence of individuals not constrained anymore by a common religious tradition (Hobbes, 1997). The trajectory of modernization was greatly affected by various economic, political and legal attempts of answering the interrelated questions of finding a way to secure property (as a safeguard against suffering) and to regulate intersubjectivity (as a terrain of the competition for property).

To explore these transformations in detail is beyond the grasp of this chapter. In this concluding section, only two interrelating tendencies are highlighted: the birth of a modern concept of ownership and its impact on the emergence of depression. According to the approach originating from Locke's ideal of workmanship, as God gave the world to man, everything cultivated by someone becomes their property (Shapiro, 1995: 23).[15] Even if the secularization and generalization of this concept provided the theoretical basis for institutionalizing property, its translation to actual legal texts and social practices remained a challenge for centuries. In the medieval and early modern eras, property was generally collective and under-defined: it was shared by a family, whose members had various rights of accessing and using it; it could also be alienated, under the right circumstances (Gordon, 1995: 96). This constellation functioned properly until market exchange became a priority, and the insecure, non-individualized property became an obstacle in the way of trading. Such difficulty had to be eliminated. Gradually, legal clarifications were elaborated concerning the owner, the boundaries of property and the meaning of owning as well, resulting in the birth of 'absolute dominion'. This concept granted total freedom over the property for the owning individual while excluding everyone else from accessing that property (Gordon, 1995: 104).[16] In many ways, this legal practice connected the element of total control with the right of owning. Controlling through owning became the paradigm of modern agency: the world became reconstructed as a horizon of possible acquisitions, including nature, the other and the self as well, which also meant a potentially exclusive and total control over the material and symbolic sphere.

Such transformation of property did not leave unaffected the horizon of faith and the space of intersubjectivity either. On the one hand, as suffering and enjoyment could be controlled within the sphere of the absolute dominion of property, there was less need for pursuing transcendental goals (Weber, 1992). Therefore, as ownership became legally secured, actors could focus exclusively on instrumental action. On the other hand, the privatization of property resulted in the reconfiguration of social ties as well: as owning became endowed with the meaning of exclusive authority over the world, the control over various dimensions of existence became dependent on the separation from the others, instead of navigating within social networks. The informal framework of interactions based on personal acquaintances was gradually shifting to a formal one based on contracts (Tönnies, 1957).[17]

As a result of these transformations originating from the emergence of absolute property, the early modern structural background of depression drastically changed. In this historical moment, a new form of suffering emerged characterized by complete meaninglessness. All dimensions that used to be independent from the logic of accumulation became dependent on property: the horizon of suffering, time, the other and the self all started to be perceived within the framework of ownership, and thus became subordinated to the logic of acquisition. This new type of interrelatedness of the previously independent dimensions of the lifeworld created a dangerous compound. Unlike in the early modern period, when depression emerged in cases of worldly failure, the discrediting of dogmas, and social exclusion occurring simultaneously, after the transformation of property into absolute individual dominion, only a single factor remained decisive.[18]

With the decreasing number of independent structural dimensions affecting depression, modern subjects became exposed to it to a greater extent, turning depression from an improbable possibility into a highly probable hazard. Even if absolute dominion potentially provides previously unseen chances for taking control over one's life, it endangers the subject, for its failure results in the collapse of the entire lifeworld. Being deprived from property or not being able to control suffering through owning equally leave the subject without alternative escapes. As modernization is committed to an existence which is based on actively eliminating suffering at the cost of deconstructing the transcendental and isolating from others, the failure of this attempt undermines being in the world as such. If absolute property fails, then the whole horizon collapses at once: suffering becomes imminent, the future hopeless, the past haunting, freedom lacking and others non-existent.[19] In these moments, the dreadful emptiness of existence is experienced. From the perspective of the historical phenomenology of depression, modernization proves to be a risky enterprise, in so far as by exclusively aiming at more personal control over the world through absolute dominion, the potential of failed ownership risks losing it all.[20]

It is important to note that 'commodification' itself does not necessarily imply the emergence of mood disorders, as is suggested by most classic and contemporary critical theories relying on related notions like alienation (Marx), anomie (Durkheim), loss of meaning (Weber), colonization (Habermas) or desynchronization (Rosa).[21] One can still inhabit a world built around property (that is by owning things, experiences or others) without suffering, losing hope, feeling helpless or isolated: all that is required are satisfying properties. Instead, what explains the contemporary increase of depression is the interrelatedness of the previously independent phenomenological factors contributing to the emergence of depression, along with their common dependence on satisfaction provided by absolute dominion. In this sense, modern ownership becomes futile: even if it promises to provide control over particular problems, by becoming absolute, it causes suffering unresolvable within the phenomenological framework related to it.

Contemporary analyses of depression as social suffering provide a detailed account of the long term consequences of these transformations. It may be argued that the relative economic prosperity of the second half of the 20th century resulted not only in the shift from the moral of obligations to the moral of self-fulfilment but also in a 'worship of performance'. This is exemplified in the figure of the sports champion, the popular hero of late modernity (Ehrenberg, 1991). Transforming the self into an autonomous agent became a normative expectation in the private, economic and political spheres at the same time. Such an expectation became a particularly burdensome pressure, considering that self-realization takes place in an increasingly competitive and atomized structural framework. Self-fulfilment hindered by structural constraints; its failure being interpreted as personal responsibility; the related insecurity of self-esteem – these factors are all contributing to a 'depressive breakdown' (Ehrenberg, 2009). These diagnoses can be complemented by describing depression as a late modern 'pathology of time': undesired time pressure and the hectic rhythm of change, along with stagnation and futurelessness, result not only in the increased stress of self-realization but also in its emptying (Rosa, 2010: 248). These analyses highlight some of the contemporary structural constraints related to depression – however, without a phenomenological and genealogical background, they remain inevitably one-sided.

From such a comprehensive perspective, a parallel history of emptying suffering and controlling it through owning reveals itself. Late medieval times are characterized by both naturalized suffering and the lacking horizon of individual agency. As a reaction to these long-lasting challenges, in early modernity, the passive relation to suffering was partly replaced by an active one, which resulted in the expansion of worldly agency. Property became a key component within this constellation: as the access to material means (promising to treat agony) and social status (becoming a central aspect of the worldly oriented self) were both dependent on it, the possibility of overcoming suffering became fundamentally related to its acquisition. The transformation of the originally contingent early modern property into the modern absolute dominion indicates a new phase in this process. While its birth was originally validated by the need for overcoming the long-lasting uncertainties related to property, absolute dominion implied unintended consequences as well. It created a new experience of total control over owned things, and previously unseen freedom was guaranteed by the contractual approval of others. Such experience not only contributed to the marginalization of a less attractive religious relation to suffering, but also created a horizon of exclusive personal responsibility of suffering. The individuals entitled to control the world by owning are completely dependent on the success of their efforts. If these fail, not only does suffering prevail but also time (structured by accumulation), intersubjectivity (based on competition) and agency (related to instrumental rationality) collapse, as they are equally subordinated to the logic of absolute dominion. Depression emerges in these empty moments. Diagnoses either focusing on the 'worship of performance' or the 'acceleration' miss the chance of accessing the common root of these tendencies – the naturalized horizon of property as absolute dominion. Only by revealing its genealogy may those deep structures be identified, which explain the late modern interrelatedness of the previously independent phenomenological components of depression. Chapters 4 and 7 further explore these issues.

Notes

1 Such a claim cannot be made on a direct statistical basis, as health statistics measuring depressive disorder exist only in modern times. While there is an ongoing debate about the prevalence in last 50 years, where arguments supporting the increase (e.g. Murphy et al., 2000) and stagnation (e.g. Bretschneider et al., 2018) are equally present, this chapter does not contribute to these discussions. Instead, an indirect approach is applied: the changing probability of depression is explained by analyzing the transformation of the related structures. Based on a similar approach, there are convincing arguments concerning the transformation

of physical conditions related to depression (e.g. overfeeding, malnourishing, sedentary, sunlight-deficient, sleep-deprived and socially-isolated lifestyle – Hidaka, 2012). This chapter complements these analyses by exploring the social factors.

2 The greatest methodological difficulty that follows from such an approach is the proper handling of the inevitably fragmented empirical material. In order to avoid the trap of overemphasizing certain tendencies, while neglecting others, my analysis follows the logic of constructing ideal-types (Weber, 1949).

3 Although, the various phenomenological accounts of depression have various strengths and blindspots, two of them stands out: Fuchs pioneered the incorporation of the influences originating from Merleau-Ponty's theorizing on the 'invisible' and the 'intersubjectivity' (2013); Ratcliffe elaborated the most systematic phenomenological theory of depression (2015). This explains why the overview focuses mostly on their contributions.

4 In his classic essay about depression, Freud puts grief at the centre of explaining melancholia (1917), which could orient phenomenological analysis as well. As the world is constituted as an intertwining continuum of objects, the others, and the embodied self, the loss of any particular significant elements affects the whole.

5 Hopelessness is closely related to the experience of trauma, which also irreversibly disrupts the relation to time (Stolorow, 2007). The wide literature connecting trauma and depression can be understood from this perspective: traumatic events are impossible to be transformed into a meaningful experience, and thus become incorporated by the subject, while resurging uncontrollably (Bernet, 2000). Accordingly, trauma is a rupture in the time consciousness: it represents a randomly reappearing past, which can never be integrated in the present, and thus cannot ground any possible future.

6 In this sense, the metaphorical description of being depressed as feeling partly dead may be phenomenologically related to the lack of actual experience of being alive (Fuchs, 2012).

7 The historical sources referred below focus on the 11th–13th century feudal, Christian Europe, including most territories of the former Roman Empire (Le Goff, 1992: 56).

8 From a sociological perspective, religion involves not only a specific interpretation of the visible and transcendental world but also those social rites, which indirectly reproduce the distinctions between the sacred and the profane, while also classifying the world according to the performed social distinctions (Durkheim, 1995). Of course, in the case of late medieval Christianity, both the rites and the consequent worldviews varied greatly, as it is exemplified by frequency of heterodoxy (Le Roy Ladurie, 1984). However, the various interpretations and technologies equally provided performative and phenomenological tools for dealing with suffering in a religious way.

9 This emphasis on the divine can be exemplified by one of the few personal accounts of medieval suffering appearing in Abelard's letters: 'Do not torment yourself that you have been the cause of this great good, or doubt that God created you for this. And do not grieve over what I may have suffered, except when the blessings that flow from the suffering of the martyrs and the death of our Lord himself will also make you sad (...) Nonetheless, it may relieve the bitterness of your grief if I demonstrate to you that what happened to us was both in accord with justice and to our advantage as well, (...) You know how shamelessly we acted in that holy place, consecrated to the Blessed Virgin. Now even if there were no other sins, that one alone deserves a heavy retribution. But do I need to remind you of those shameful and polluting acts that came before our marriage?' (Levitan, 2007: 94). The reference to suffering is inseparable from the divine semantics of sins and retributions: as suffering expresses the will of God, it should not be resisted, instead understood and penanced.

10 The historical sources referred to below identify early modernity as a period roughly between the 14th and 17th centuries characterized by various phenomena such as the Renaissance, humanism, the reformation, counter-reformation, the colonization, the invention of printing and an intensive commercialization (Chamberlin, 1965: 14; Cameron, 2001). While all of them cannot be analyzed in detail here, an idealtype of early modernity is elaborated: those structural transformations are emphasized, which express the gradual reconfiguration of the perception of suffering, time consciousness, agency and intersubjectivity.

11 Such an excluding mechanism proved to be the forerunner of the institutions governing the body by proactive technologies of discipline, instead of reactive sanctions (Foucault, 1995).

12 Of course, such early modern property differs from its later versions. It was closer to those substantively embedded forms of owning and giving, which are called 'gifts' (Mauss, 1966). Unlike an abstract concept of property being exchanged in competitive market transactions and secured by legal warranties, gift-like goods express social recognition between individual actors, while being secured by the traditions of a community. In early modernity, the small and large scale properties – such as the alms given for the beggars or the bounties of the monarch – were equally embedded in the complex of family, economic, politic and religious relations implying a meaningful content for the owners beside the mere exchange value (Davis, 2000).

13 This emphasis on the worldly can be exemplified by one of the personal accounts of early modern melancholy, an excerpt from the diary of Samuel Pepys (9 September 1665): 'The fleete come home with shame to require a great deale of money, which is not to be had, to discharge many men that must get the plague then or continue at greater charge on shipboard, nothing done by them to encourage the Parliament to give money, nor the Kingdom able to spare any money, if they would, at this time of the plague, so that, as things look at present, the whole state must come to ruine. Full of these melancholy thoughts, to bed; where, though I lay the softest I ever did in my life, with a downe bed, after the Danish manner, upon me, yet I slept very ill' (Pepys, 2009). Unlike in the case of the medieval excerpt, the early modern sufferer is no longer worrying about sins or retributions; instead their mind is on everyday hardships to be overcome (such as the plague or lacking money) and their own involvement in the process – including the emotional cost of melancholy.

14 Such normalization of even the more unusual forms of melancholy is explained by the generally more accepting attitude towards strange, atypical behaviour patterns, which lasted until the 16th century (Midelfort, 1994: 20). Starting from the 17th century, this tolerance was gradually replaced by the stigmatizing and isolating praxes targeting the abnormal and deviant (Foucault, 2006). The illness paradigm of depression was born in this later era, as a consequence of the further transformation of early modern subjectivity discussed in the last section.

15 Later on the religious basis of the legitimacy of ownership was weakened due to the secularization. As a reaction to this constellation, the modern myth of the 'entrepreneur' was born in the public sphere, who not only conquers the world but also proves their morality through refined manners (Klein, 1995).

16 In order to place such alienated idealtype in the right context, the commodification of households provides a tangible example: what used to be the platform of care and affections has been deprived from any substantive moral content and reduced to mere exchange value. Accordingly, the crisis of the market of households does not simply affect a specific commodity, but the totality of intersubjectivity (Keohane, 2013).

17 The endpoint of this tendency is experienced in contemporary societies, where 'ultra-liberalism' results in the birth of Sadean 'isolist' subjects (van den Bergh, 2013).

18 That does not mean absolute dominion becomes the single (social) *cause* of depression in modernity. Instead, its emergence expresses the transformation of the *space of possibility* of depression: the elimination of the previously independent dimensions of success and failure (by subordinating them to the logic of ownership) results in vulnerability. However, whether this potential is transformed into actual depression still depends on various social factors (e.g. see Chapter 4) besides psychological and biological ones.

19 In contemporary sociology of depression, this possibility is explained as the transformation of the normative expectation of 'authentic self-realization' into a stress factor (Petersen, 2011). This potential is closely related to economic failure, as authenticity is more and more anchored in consumption (Petersen, 2009).

20 The interrelatedness of socio-economic status and depression is a well-known phenomenon (e.g. Lorant et al., 2003). However, beside detecting the correlation, this research seldom analyzes the phenomenological mechanisms linking structural deprivation with depression. The exceptions argue that the lacking of resources results in the loss of agency, which is one of the key factors of depression if being internalized as 'learned helplessness' (Seligman, 1975). The present historical analysis further enriches these argumentations: it is more likely that the reduced agency due to lacking resources leads to a depressive collapse in a world which is built around the promise of agency acquirable by owning the world. In other words, depression is not simply the consequence of poverty, but a poverty being embedded in the modern sphere of possibilities, where meaningful life is inseparable from absolute dominion; thus poverty is imbued with existential failure.

21 Similar diagnoses of capitalism have a long tradition claiming that structural transformations of modernization are responsible for depriving human existence from its essential aspects. While this book continues this tradition, it also applies a more specific focus by linking social distortions to mental disorders. In this sense, it aims at enriching the recently lively discourse on 'occidental madness' (Dufour, 2014), or the 'social pathologies of contemporary civilization' (Keohane et al., 2017).

References

Aho, K. A. (2013) Depression and Embodiment: Phenomenological Reflections on Motility, Affectivity, and Transcendence. *Medicine, Health Care and Philosophy*, 16(4): 751–759.

American Psychiatric Association (2013) *Diagnostic and Statistical Manual of Mental Disorders* (5th edition). Washington, DC: American Psychiatric Publishing.

Ariés, P. (1962) *Centuries of Childhood. A Social History of Family Life*. New York, NY: Alfread A. Knopf.

Ariés, P. (1976) *Attitudes Toward Death from the Middle Ages to the Present*. Baltimore, MD: Johns Hopkins University Press.

Ariés, P. (1989) Introduction. In Chartier, R. (Ed.), *A History of Private Life, Volume III: Passions of the Renaissance*. Cambridge, MA: Harvard University Press.

Bakhtin, M. M. (1984) *Rabelais and His World*. Bloomington, IN: Indiana University Press.

Bauman, Z. (2000) *Liquid Modernity*. Cambridge: Polity.

Berg, J. H. (1972) *A Different Existence: Principles of Phenomenological Psychopathology*. Pittsburgh, PA: Duquesne University Press.

Bergh, B. (2013) Depression: Resisting Ultra-Liberalism? In Keohane, K. and Petersen, A. (Eds.), *The Social Pathologies of Contemporary Civilization*. London: Routledge, 41–68.

Bernet, R. (2000) The Traumatized Subject. *Research in Phenomenology*, 30(1): 160–179.

Bretschneider, J., Janitza, S., Jacobi, F. et al. (2018) Time Trends in Depression Prevalence and Health-Related Correlates: Results from Population-Based Surveys in Germany 1997–1999 vs. 2009–2012. *BMC Psychiatry*, 18(1): 394.

Burke, P. (1978) *Popular Culture in Early Modern Europe*. London: Harper and Row.

Cameron, E. (Ed.) (2001) *Early Modern Europe: An Oxford History*. Oxford: Oxford University Press.

Chamberlin, E. R. (1965) *Everyday Life in Renaissance*. New York, NY: Capricorn Books.

Cohen, E. S. and Cohen, T. V. (2001) *Daily Life in Renaissance Italy*. Westport, CT and London: The Greenwood Press.

Cvetkovich, A. (2012) *Depression: A Public Feeling*. Durham: Duke University Press.

Davis, N. Z. (2000) *The Gift in Sixteenth-Century France*. Madison, WI/Oxford: University of Wisconsin Press/Oxford University Press.

Duby, G. (1980) *The Three Orders: Feudal Society Imagined*. Chicago, IL: University of Chicago Press.

Duby, G. (Ed.) (1988) *A History of Private Life, Volume II: Revelations of the Medieval World*. Cambridge, MA: Harvard University Press.

Dufour, D.-R. (2014) *Le délire occidental: et ses effets actuels dans la vie quotidienne: Travail, loisir, amourr*. Paris: Les liens qui libèrent.

Durkheim, Émile (1995) *The Elementary Forms of Religious Life*. New York, NY: The Free Press.

Ehrenberg, A. (1991) *Le Culte De La Performance*. Paris: Calmann-Lévy.

Ehrenberg, A. (2009) *The Weariness of the Self: Diagnosing the History of Depression in the Contemporary Age*. Montreal: McGill-Queen's University Press.

Elias, N. (2000) *The Civilizing Process*. Oxford: Blackwell.

Fernandez, A. V. (2014) Depression as Existential Feeling or De-Situatedness? Distinguishing Structure from Mode in Psychopathology. *Phenomenology and the Cognitive Sciences*, 13(4): 595–612.

Finucane, R. C. (1977) *Miracles and Pilgrims: Popular Beliefs in Medieval England*. London: Dent.

Flately, J. (2008) *Affective Mapping: Melancholia and the Politics of Modernism*. Harvard, MA: Harvard University Press.

Foucault, M. (1995) *Discipline and Punish*. New York, NY: Vintage Books.

Foucault, M. (1977) Nietzsche, Genealogy, History. In Bouchard D. F. (Ed.), *Language, Counter-Memory, Practice: Selected Essays and Interviews*. Ithaca, NY: Cornell UP.

Foucault, M. (2006) *History of Madness*. New York, NY: Routledge.

Freud, S. (1917) Mourning and Melancholia. In *Collected Papers* (Vol. 4). London: Hogarth Press and the Institute of Psychoanalysis, 243–258.

Fuchs, T. (2012) The Feeling of Being Alive. Organic Foundations of Self-Awareness. In Fingerhut, J. and Marienberg, S. (Eds.), *Feelings of Being Alive*. Berlin and New York, NY: De Gruyter, 149–165.

Fuchs, T. (2013) Depression, Intercorporeality and Interaffectivity. *Journal of Consciousness Studies*, 20(7–8): 219–238.

Gordon, R. W. (1995) Paradoxical Property. In Brewer, J. and Staves, S. (Eds.) *Early Modern Conceptions of Property*. London: Routledge. 95–111.

Ginzburg, C. (1992) *The Cheese and the Worms: The Cosmos of a Sixteenth-Century Miller*. Baltimore, MD: John Hopkins University Press.

Hidaka, B. H. (2012) Depression as a Disease of Modernity: Explanations for Increasing Prevalence. *Journal of Affect Disorder*, 140(3): 205–214.

Hobbes, T. (1997) *Leviathan*. New York, NY: Simon and Schuster.

Horwitz, A. V. and Wakefield, J. C. (2007) *The Loss of Sadness: How Psychiatry Transformed Normal Sorrow into Depressive Disorder.* New York, NY: Oxford University Press.

Husserl, E. (1970) *The Crisis of European Sciences and Transcendental Philosophy.* Evanston, IL: Northwestern University Press.

Jackson, S. W. (1986) *Melancholia and Depression. From Hippocratic Times to Modern Times.* New Haven, CT: Yale University Press.

Keohane, K. (2013) The Value of Houses in the Libidinal Economy: Financialization as Social Pathogenesis. In Keohane, K. and Petersen, A. (Eds.), *The Social Pathologies of Contemporary Civilization.* London: Routledge, 63–80.

Keohane, K., Petersen, A. and van den Bergh, B. (2017) *Late Modern Subjectivity and Its Discontents Anxiety, Depression and Alzheimer's Disease.* London: Routledge.

Klein, L. E. (1995) Property and Politeness in the Early Eighteenth-Century Which Moralists. The Case of the Spectator. In Brewer, J. and Staves, S. (Eds.), *Early Modern Conceptions of Property.* London: Routledge, 221–233.

Lash, S. (2002) *The Critique of Information.* London: Sage.

Le Goff, J. (1992) *Medieval Civilization: 400–1500.* Oxford: Blackwell Publishers Ltd.

Le Roy Ladurie, E. (1984) *Montaillou: Cathars and Catholics in a French Village 1294–1324.* London: Penguin.

Levitan, W. (2007) *Abelard and Heloise: The Letters and Other Writings.* Cambridge, MA: Hackett Publishing.

Lindeman, M. (1999) *Medicine and Society in Early Modern Europe.* Cambridge: Cambridge University Press.

Lorant, V., Deliège, D., Eaton, W., Robert, A., Philippot, P. and Ansseau, M. (2003) Socioeconomic Inequalities in Depression: A Meta-Analysis. *American Journal of Epidemiology,* 157(2): 98–112.

Mauss, M. (1966) *The Gift.* London: Cohen and West.

Merleau-Ponty, M. (1968) *The Visible and the Invisible.* Evanston, IL: Northwestern University Press.

Midelfort, H. C. E. (1994) *Mad Princes of Renaissance Germany.* Charlottesville and London: University of Virginia Press.

Murphy, J. M., Laird, N. M., Monson, R. R., Sobol, A. M. and Leighton, A. H. (2000) A 40-Year Perspective on the Prevalence of Depression: The Stirling County Study. *Archives of General Psychiatry,* 57(3): 209–215.

Nacol, E. C. (2016) *An Age of Risk Politics and Economy in Early Modern Britain.* Princeton, NJ: Princeton University Press.

Nietzsche, F. (2013) *On the Genealogy of Morals.* London: Penguin Classics.

Pepys, S. (2009) *Diary of Samuel Pepys.* The Project Gutenberg EBook of Diary of Samuel Pepys https://www.gutenberg.org/files/4162/4162-h/4162-h.htm.

Petersen, A. (2009) Depression – A Social Pathology of Action. *Irish Journal of Sociology,* 17(2): 56–71.

Petersen, A. (2011) Authentic Self-Realization and Depression. *International Sociology,* 26(1): 5–24.

Ratcliffe, M. (2015) *Experiences of Depression.* Oxford: Oxford University Press.

Renault, E. (2010) A Critical Theory of Social Suffering. *Critical Horizons,* 11(2): 221–241.

Rodríguez, M. R., Nuevo, R., Chatterji, S. and Ayuso-Mateos, J. L. (2012) Definitions and Factors Associated With Subthreshold Depressive Conditions: A Systematic Review. *BMC Psychiatry,* 12(1): 181–188.

Rosa, H. (2010) *Social Acceleration. A New Theory of Modernity.* New York, NY: Columbia University Press.

Seligman, M. E. P. (1975) *Helplessness*. San Francisco, CA: Freeman.

Shapiro, I. (1995) Resources, Capacities, and Ownership. The Workmanship Ideal and Distributive Justice. In Brewer, J. and Staves, S. (Eds.), *Early Modern Conceptions of Property*. London: Routledge. 21–43.

Stanghellini, G., Ballerini, M., Presenza, S., Mancini, M., Northoff, G. and Cutting, J. (2017) Abnormal Time Experiences in Major Depression: An Empirical Qualitative Study. *Psychopathology*, 50(2): 125–140.

Stegner, P. (2016) *Confession and Memory in Early Modern English Literature*. New York, NY: Palgrave Macmillan.

Stolorow, R. D. (2007) *Trauma and Human Existence: Autobiographical, Psychoanalytic, and Philosophical Reflections*. New York, NY: Routledge.

Tönnies, F. (1957) *Community and Society*. Oxford, England: Michigan State University Press.

Weber, M. (1949) *The Methodology of the Social Sciences*. Glencoe, IL: Free Press.

Weber, M. (1992) *The Protestant Ethic and the Spirit of Capitalism*. London: Routledge.

WHO (2018) *Depression*. https://www.who.int/news-room/fact-sheets/detail/depression.

2 The social constituents of fear

A phenomenology of negative integration

Although fear is considered to be a universal emotion, it is affected by many historical factors. According to various critical theories, late modernity is an era of extreme uncertainty and worry due to the dissolving of integration mechanisms capable of reliably handling social contingencies (e.g. Bauman, 2000; Giddens, 1994). Such theoretical diagnoses are supported by surveys reporting an increasing level of perceived threats (e.g. Collins, 2018), analyses detecting the increased media coverage of fearsome events (e.g. Glassner, 1999) and the naturalizing of fear (e.g. Brower, 2011). Even if these researches conclude that fear plays a fundamental role in our societies, none of them succeeds in explaining which particular mechanisms are responsible for its emergence. While most theories tend to rely on over-generalizing structural changes without paying attention to the phenomenological details (Wilkinson, 1999, 2001), empirical analyses either neglect or fail to elaborate a comprehensive social theoretical framework (Tudor, 2003). This hiatus is the starting point of the following chapter: an attempt is made to reintroduce fear at a fundamental level of social integration in order to analyze its late modern specificities.

While fear is an essential, constitutive factor of the human condition, social theories relate to it in a controversial way.[1] As a 'primary emotion', fear is considered to be cross-culturally universal, making it primarily belong to the territory of psy-sciences (Kemper, 1987).[2] On the other hand, fear plays a constitutive role in sociability: basic concepts such as norms, power or solidarity can hardly be described without referring to the fear from sanctions, subordination or external danger (Moon, 2013; Vannelli, 2015). Most social theories react to such ambiguity by neglecting fear while latently building on it. Therefore, fear is seldom in the focus of theoretical analysis; instead, it is considered to be a self-evident component of social phenomena. However, such attitude prevents sociology from explaining convincingly the increase of fear in contemporary societies. In order to falsify or reinforce such hypothesis, the general and historical aspects of fear need to be differentiated so that the increase can be explained through the latter. Such analysis requires a social phenomenological approach capable of operating both on the level of structural components and the experiences of the actors. Fear is not considered

DOI: 10.4324/9781003197355-4

to be a substantive element of the lifeworld, but an underlying dimension, which is constructed intersubjectively.[3] This approach enables the linking of the probability of fear to certain types of integration mechanisms – that is the key of answering the question: in what extent and how did late modernity become an epoch of extreme fear?

For this purpose, a theoretical framework is required, which is broader than the horizon of classic sociology. Social contract theories are reinterpreted from this perspective: they deal with fundamental questions of sociability, without limiting their scope to the functional questions of action coordination. They focus on the tension between autonomy and sociability while exploring the reasons for limiting one's originally unlimited freedom for the sake of the social. In this sense, social contract theories start their investigation at the fundamental level of the motivational basis of cooperation, whereas social theories consider such commitment to be self-evident. Relying on the ideas of Hobbes and Rousseau, the ideal types of negative and positive *motivation for cooperation* are described, grounding two different modalities of social integration: one based on the fear from something, the other based on the hope for something. Social contract theories enable the reintroduction of fear on the fundamental level of theorizing: it becomes a definitive dimension of the lifeworld in those constellations, where integration is based mostly on negative motivation for cooperation.

These conceptual tools revived from early modern social philosophy are applied in the second and third sections for the purpose of exploring the specificities of classic and late modern social integration. On the one hand, the positive and negative modalities of the classical modern 'integration mechanisms' introduced by Weber (legal-bureaucratic legitimacy), Durkheim (division of labour) and Habermas (communicative lifeworld and systems) are elaborated. On the other hand, the modalities of late modern 'technics of adaptation' appearing in the theory of Castells (networks) and Beck (reflexivity) are reinterpreted.[4] Such overview provides the opportunity for describing the balance of negative and positive modalities of social integration in each epoch. According to the diagnosis of times of classical modernity, positive and negative motivations played an equally important role in organizing social interactions. However, based on the descriptions of late modernity, it can be argued that sociability is emptied: as negative modalities became predominant, promising collective horizons are not available anymore. This change affects not only the newest mechanisms of integration but also the ones inherited from previous times.

After reintroducing fear on a fundamental level of social integration and explaining late modernity as an upset of the balance of negative and positive motivation for cooperation, an attempt is made to link empirical patterns of fear with negative integration. In the last section, those mechanisms are introduced, which are responsible for translating the abstract negative motivation for cooperation into actual patterns of fear. By reintroducing fear as a phenomenological texture of late modern social structures and revealing its specific expressions related to various forms of integration, its overall emergence can be explained in a comprehensive way. Fear does not expand in general; instead, its divers patterns appear in constellations coordinated by various mechanisms of negative integration.

Social contract and the motivation for cooperation

Social contract theories born at the dawn of modernity express a liminal condition, characterized by turbulent transformations and uncertainties. As the religious worldview and the related feudal structures lost their unchallenged validity, the question of freedom became once again central in epistemology, ethics and social philosophy. Without naturalized hierarchies based on religious dogma, it required clarification why actors should limit their – originally unlimited – freedom of pursuing individual goals. Social contract theories start their investigation with the intention of answering this question: what are those universally accessible reasons, which are capable of motivating actors not sharing any sort of mutual belief system to cooperate? This question is prior to the one about the potential forms of society, as only the clarification of the motivational basis of cooperation enables the elaboration of a typology of society. As the theologically grounded, quasi-natural, external reasons of limiting one's freedom lost their relevance, normative regulation could only be based on the autonomous, voluntary decision of the actors. In this sense, classic contract theories are inevitably operated on a phenomenological level: they argued that the constitution of society cannot depend on natural or transcendent forces, only on the actors' self-limitation.[5]

While each social contract theory provides alternative answers to these questions, it was Hobbes and Rousseau, who elaborated two fundamentally different motivational bases of self-limitation. Their contrasting ideas originate from the differences of their anthropological and historical assumptions. Hobbes relies on a concept of human existence purified from any metaphysical preconceptions: humans are considered to be sensing and processing automatons, not determined by any inherent, essential goal or value. In such constellation, actors are motivated primarily by their desires and fears. Among these, the fear from death is particularly important, as it is fundamental for any reasonable actors. If avoiding death is the single most elementary interest, then everyone is motivated to increase their power, which is the only way to relative security. These basic premises outline a dynamic, yet chaotic, hypothetical 'state of nature' (the war of all against all), where everyone has unlimited freedom, but nobody is secure. As the elementary interest of avoiding death is in contradiction with the state of nature (the risk of becoming a victim is high), reasonable actors are motivated to overcome such constellation. In order to do it, they have to give up their unconditional freedom and transfer it to a single authority (the Leviathan) responsible for protecting everyone by monopolizing power. In this sense, the social contract is a collective agreement about self-limiting freedom and centralizing power, motivated by the elementary fear from the unconditionally free other. The state being born in such agreement is not justified by any transcendental-metaphysical value, only by the individual's self-evident interest of survival. Hobbes' Leviathan has unlimited power as long as it is capable of fulfilling its fundamental role of maintaining order by monopolizing power, but collapses at the moment it fails this task (Hobbes, 1997: 82).

While Hobbes considers the hypothetical state of nature to be the most frightening possibility for any reasonable actor, Rousseau argues that the actual historical societies do not provide a more promising prospect either. The history of society is a history of various forms of inequalities and injustices, which is just partly compensated by cultural development and order. As the existing social orders have always resulted in suffering and the limitation of freedom of the majority, the task of grounding a post-metaphysical society cannot be done only by referring to the threat of war of all against all. Showing the emancipatory potential of overcoming the historically tenacious injustice is an equally important task. Only by introducing a promise of an alternative power structure, which enables actual freedom can actors being in hopelessly subordinated positions be motivated to give up the freedom of following personal interest. According to Rousseau, the stake of social contract is not only to provide order instead of the chaos of the natural state but also to create a better order in the place of the unequal *status quo* – an order, where actual freedom may rise instead of its limited or illusory version. Such transformation is based on the collective giving up of the freedom to realize individual interest in exchange for the ruling of general will. As a consequence of this self-limitation, the injustice of various privileges gives it place to the justice of equality, which is ensured by the generally applied, universal law (Rousseau, 2002: 164).

Hobbes and Rousseau elaborate two opposing bases, which are capable of motivating actors to limit their own freedom of pursuing personal goals. In a certain sense, they elaborated two phenomenological trajectories for modern societies. For Hobbes, it is the fear from the unconditionally free others, which urges the individuals to give up their own freedom along with everyone else for a monopolist of power. For Rousseau, it is the hope for the realization of latent potentials of freedom, which inspires the individual to replace the pursuit of personal interest with the subordination to general will. In this sense, the former refers to a *negative motivation for cooperation* (the fear from the deadly threat of the other), the latter describes a *positive motivation for cooperation* (the hope for realizing the lacking potentials of freedom). Based on these explanations of why any reasonable actors are interested in the self-limitation of their individual freedom, Hobbes and Rousseau elaborated contrasting typologies of social order, which can be reinterpreted as two phenomenological modalities of social integration.

Social contracts include a promise concerning the predictability of social relations: for Hobbes, it includes the relative safety from the ultimately dangerous others, for Rousseau, a constellation enabling actors to realize otherwise impossible potentials. These latent promises function as a phenomenological basis of social existence in a sense that they outline the actors' horizon of expectations. As actions based on certain expectations become general, interactive patterns are emerging around them, functioning as framework for future social action (Berger and Luckmann, 1966). In this sense, the phenomenological modalities of social contracts not only give sense to social phenomena but also institutionalize certain mechanisms of integration. This conceptual connection enables us to move from contract to integration and analyze, how mechanisms of action coordination can be differentiated according to their negative and positive modality.

While the social theoretical tradition focuses on the typology of social order in the form of integration mechanisms, it has more or less forgotten about the motivational level analyzing the fundamental reasons of cooperation. This change of emphasis resulted in the blindspot of social theories: they no longer started their investigation with the phenomenological question (why are actors motivated to choose social existence instead of dissociation?), but with the technical-functional one (which mechanisms are capable of maintaining social order?). In this sense, social contract theories provide an opportunity of expanding a horizon of social theories by recalling a forgotten level of theorizing. In case of every mechanism of action coordination, the question about their negative and positive modalities may be raised: how do they operate in those cases, where actors rely on them only because they are afraid of an alternative constellation, and in those cases, where they are considered to result in a constellation more promising than the *status quo*? Besides broadening the horizon of social theories by describing two modalities of each integration mechanisms, from the perspective of motivation for cooperation also a forgotten level of social dynamics becomes accessible. In case of every historical constellation, the question about the proportion of negative and positive modalities may be raised: are they in balance, or is one of them predominant? In the following two sections, some classic and late modern social theories are reinterpreted from this perspective.

Classical modernity: The fragile balance of negative and positive integration

Classical modernity is a retrospective term originating from the comparison with a new era characterized by the dissolution of those integration mechanisms that originally dissolved the pre-modern ones. As theological knowledge was succeeded by science, use value replaced by exchange value and the representative public sphere transformed into bourgeois, not only did uncertainties and worries emerge but also a sense of new order and security was born. Accordingly, despite its deconstructing impact, classical modernity also created its own 'tradition', which was based on formal knowledge instead of substantive dogmas, and maintained by experts instead of guardians (Giddens, 1994). The gradual dissolving of this tradition indicates the dawn of a new era, characterized not only by new mechanisms of action coordination but also by the reconfiguration of the balance of their negative and positive modalities. In the following section, Durkheim's and Weber's theories are evoked in order to describe the classical constellation while Habermas' theory helps to explain its paradoxes.

Durkheim understands modernization as functional differentiation: while archaic societies constituted of similar actors are integrated mechanically through collective consciousness, modern societies constituted mainly of specialized actors are integrated organically through the division of labour. It is important to note, however, that modern societies cannot rely solely on the contractual integration mechanisms of organic solidarity: the compliance of contracts depends on moral obligation, which can be grounded only on the level of collective consciousness. While modernization enables a new form of solidarity based on mutual dependence, the fulfilment of individual potentials and an overall increased productivity, it also creates new difficulties originating from the challenges of organizing and regulating a functionally differentiated society (Durkheim, 1997). Such social pathologies include injustice (inequalities are not the result of the difference of effort) and anomic division of labour (anomalies of job market). Furthermore, as these pathological 'social facts' are interiorized, besides social dysfunctionality, they also result in personal suffering, which could lead in the most extreme cases to suicide (Durkheim, 1951).

Weber understands modernization as instrumental rationalization in various spheres of life. Formal, calculative rationality is not only expressed in economy (capitalism) and politics (bureaucracy) but it also affects everyday life (optimized daily routines) and culture (science and modern music). On the one hand, this leads to unparalleled efficiency of social integration, which is secured by legal-bureaucratic domination (Weber, 1978: 954). Such ideal type of domination is not based on the recognition of traditions, charisma or religiously grounded values. Instead, it is based on the collective subordination to the set of universally applied laws; thus, it expresses a rational and just way of organizing social interactions. On the other hand, the disenchantment of the world also leads to the loss of those general values, which could make instrumental action meaningful. Such loss of meaning expresses the paradox of rationalization: while the particular tasks are resolved more and more efficiently, the actual meaning of action becomes less and less accessible (Weber, 1991).

From their different epistemological and methodological starting points, both Durkheim and Weber identify key integration mechanisms of modern societies and elaborate the emancipatory and pathological potentials originating from their expansion. Accordingly, in order to properly characterize the classical modern constellation, firstly the positive (motivated by a hope) and negative modalities (motivated by a fear) of these integration mechanisms need to be mapped. While the positive motivation for cooperation is expressed by the new potentials enabled by modernization, the negative one is related to the pre-modern practices desired to be transcended. Secondly, the equilibrium of positive and negative motivation for cooperation needs to be analyzed. By describing the dynamics and interactions of modern and pre-modern mechanisms, the diagnoses of times inform us about this question.

According to Durkheim, the labour market is responsible for coordinating the functionally differentiated social activities. The positive motivational basis for joining the system of division of labour is none other than the hope of being able to profit from others' expertise in exchange for one's own. Due to the collective specialization, everyone has better chances of satisfying their needs, which results in overall increase of the quality of life. In this sense, the division of labour expresses not only a private interest but also a professional vocation and an organic solidarity based on the general will. On structural level, this constellation is characterized by a fair distribution of goods, enabling actors to realize their personal goals by fulfilling their functional roles. As the functional division of labour replaces the segmental distribution of labour, its negative motivational basis is characterized by the threats originating from the latter. Order in archaic societies is maintained by repressive law, which revenges any deviations from the ritually maintained collective consciousness. From this perspective, the acceptance of an order based on restitutive law could be motivated by the fear from such rigid mechanic solidarity based on restricting the individual. Unlike in case of the positive motivation for cooperation, in this case contributing to the division of labour does not imply a vocation or an identification with an organic general will – instead, it is based on the will to keep the tyranny of a repressive order away. The institutionalization of such modality results in a system of unequal, but not completely arbitrary and unpredictable redistribution, which prevents actors from fully realizing their personal desires by contributing to collective production, but at least grants them the potential of gradual accumulation.

According to Weber, the legal-bureaucratic legitimacy is responsible for maintaining order in a rational manner. The positive motivational basis for subsuming one's will to such domination is based on the hope of realizing the rationality potential of social relationships. The capitalist-industrial mode of production, the bureaucratic organization of the state and the contractual interpersonal relations all serve the purpose of effectivity and accountability. As legal-bureaucratic legitimacy ensures the most effective technical domination of nature and the most universal normative regulation, it actually serves the private interest of every rational actor. The consequent model of integration is an inclusive rule of law, enabling the principles of justice to prevail. Such domination is the alternative of traditional, charismatic and hierocratic ones, which means that its negative motivational basis is related to fears from these forms. As these ideal types of social relationships are characterized by limited versions of instrumental rationality,[6] it may be argued that the recognition of legal-bureaucratic domination is negatively motivated by the fear from such narrow perspectives. In this case, subordination to universal legal frames is based on the fear from the purposelessness of traditions, the overwhelming nature of charismatic and the dogmatism of hierocratic domination. However, such negative legal-bureaucratic domination is not capable of providing a horizon; it is chosen as a compromise: not because of its effectivity, but because – even despite its pathologies – being less threatening than the irrational, uncontrollable alternatives. Institutionalizing such modality leads to an exclusive, potentially discriminative rule of law, which however includes the claim for rationality.

After introducing the positive and negative modalities of organic solidarity and legal-bureaucratic domination, the balance of the two can be clarified based on the diagnoses of times. Firstly, both Durkheim and Weber argue that modernization is a *fait accompli*. The predominance of organic solidarity or legal-bureaucratic domination is not only widely accepted for their potentials but also exists as an independent framework undeniable for the actors – these characteristics strengthen the positive motivation for cooperation. Secondly, both of them identify social dysfunctions and pathologies affecting the individual. The cost of anomie, injustice or loss of meaning is measured by the personal suffering caused by them – these tendencies weaken positive motivation for cooperation. Thirdly, both of them argue that modern mechanisms of integration are not exclusive. Consequently, the threats of mechanic solidarity or domination based on limited rationality remain real – these processes are responsible for the existence of negative motivation for cooperation. Based on these diagnoses, it may be argued that classical modernity is characterized by a delicate balance of positive and negative motivation for cooperation, which constitutes the phenomenological texture of the era: the former is reinforced by the results, but shadowed by the new challenges, while the latter is strengthened by the prevailing of the unwanted old mechanisms. Accordingly, such balance depends on the maintenance of the achievements, the treatment of the pathologies and the embeddedness of old practices.

Even if such fragile balance was a general experience at the beginning of the 20th century, the constellation has changed since then. Habermas is a perfect example of how these changes were interpreted by post-war social theory: not only does he develop further the ideas of Durkheim and Weber but also identifies new, irreversible dangers of modernization, which affect the balance of negative and positive motivation for cooperation. Habermas understands modernization as a rationalization of both the actors' perspectives and the institutionalized mechanisms. The former is expressed by the increasing transparency of lifeworld, which originates from the undistortedness of speech acts enabling mutual understanding. The latter is described as the functional differentiation of systems based on symbolically generalized communicative mediums (such as money or law). The communicative lifeworld and systems outline a dual model of society, where two spheres integrated by different mechanisms complement each other. However, their relation is not symmetric, as systems are dependent on the sufficient rationalization of lifeworld (that is a capability of processing disembedded, generalized mediums). Social pathologies may emerge on both levels. In case of the lifeworld, the distortions of communicative action threaten with loss of meaning, anomie and psychopathologies (Habermas, 1987: 143). In case of systems, the functional inefficiency threatens with adaptive failures potentially leading to legitimation crisis (Habermas, 1975). Besides these dangers affecting only one sphere of integration, those paradoxes of rationalization are even more serious, which threaten the whole project of modernization: as functionally differentiating systems expand due to their efficiency, mediatized communication effaces speech acts. This threatens with the dissolving of the same rationality potential inherent in lifeworld, which enables the emergence and rationalization of systems. In this sense, instrumental rationalization becomes a self-destructive 'colonizing' force (Habermas, 1987: 196).

By elaborating an improved theory of integration, Habermas provides an opportunity for analyzing the modalities of communicative lifeworld and system. The positive motivation for the former originates from the potential of undistorted communication including both moral recognition and rationality. If only the better argument determines the outcome of an interaction, then not only experiences of autonomy are born but also the accessible best answers are found. Such model of integration secures communicative action leading to mutual understanding. The negative motivation for communicative action can be explained by referring to the alternative mechanism of interpersonal integration, which is the natural attitude of lifeworld. Being unquestionable, such dogmatic horizon is maintained by explicit or latent power relations provoking endless confrontations. As the negative motivation for communicative action is based on the fear from such hopeless confrontations, it does not result in moral autonomy or a devotion to rationality, only a competence of avoiding fight through communication. On structural level, such modality is characterized by a repressed hermeneutics of suspicion, which is at least capable of preventing violence. The positive motivational basis of system integration is based on its adaptive potential. As systems enable a differentiated way of observing the environment and avoiding the potential threats, trust in them is born. The institutionalization of such practice results in the expansion of entrusted social systems. The negative motivation for mediatized communication can be explained by referring to the contingencies of linguistic communication. As lifeworld becomes fragmented, reaching mutual understanding becomes more and more difficult. Ultimately, this leads to the inability of producing meaning, establishing norms and constructing identity. If systems are based on the fear from insufficient form of communication, then they are not actually trusted, only chosen in despair. Despite such system integration is characterized by the lack of identification with the norms of efficiency, thus threatens with dysfunctionality, it is still capable of maintaining a basic predictability of interactions.

Based on Habermas' diagnosis, it seems that the fragile balance of positive and negative motivations for cooperation detected by Durkheim and Weber in the early 20th century has already started to erode in the second half of the century. On the one hand, he argues that the communicative rationalization of the lifeworld and the instrumental rationalization of the systems are undeniable but non-exclusive tendencies of modernization despite their pathologies. On the other hand, he also argues that such delicate balance is about to change: because of the conflict of the communicative and instrumental aspects of rationalization that is the colonization of lifeworld, the achievements are becoming unsustainable, the pathologies are becoming untreatable and the chance of regression to old practices increases. All in all, as a result of this paradox of modernization, the weight of negative motivation grows. In the next section, the diagnoses of late modernity will serve as the basis of analyzing the extent of such transformation.

Late modernity: The birth of negative integration

The ongoing discourse on late modernity explores various aspects of the dissolving integration mechanisms based on instrumental rationality and functional differentiation. In a certain sense, these transformations realize the destructive potential introduced by the thesis of colonization. While Habermas never provided a substantive analysis of the empirical consequences of colonization, they may be reconstructed based on Beck's and Castells' theories. The emergence of unmanageable risks and networks of global informational capitalism equally express the self-destructive potential of instrumental rationalization. As these changes progress, not only the achievements of modernization are weakened but also old and new pathologies disperse, along with regressive integration patterns. Accordingly, the transformations analyzed by Beck and Castells not only highlight how the colonization of lifeworld actually proceeds but also help to understand the reconfiguration of the balance of negative and positive motivation for cooperation.

Beck draws the line between simple and reflexive modernity, by differentiating between the logic of capitalist-industrial production and risk management. It is not risks *per se*, which are new to late modernity, rather their configuration and nature. In industrial societies, risks originating from human activity emerged (e.g. pollution, economic crises) along with attempts of handling them by experts capable of measuring and countering them (e.g. public health care, social security). However, in the second half of the 20th century, this formula changed: new risks originating from human activity appeared (e.g. nuclear energy, gene technology), which were no longer manageable by the existing procedures based on expert knowledge and insurances. Such transformation affects every level of social integration: previously expert issues become part of political debates; as national attempts of risk management became insufficient, a need for global counter-measures arises; the lines between classes or status groups are blurred; ideologies based on such distinctions lose their relevance; and patterns of individual life become unpredictable. Besides the dissolving of classical modern mechanisms of integration, new opportunities also emerge, as the weakening of social constraints enables the improvement of individual reflexivity. This competence becomes a key for the prosperity of late modern actors being left on their own to manage risks (Beck, 1992: 136). Due to its adaptive potential, reflexivity ensures the relative success of those who can rely on it – in this sense, it is capable of coordinating particular lifeworlds and local interactions. However, it does not provide a universally accessible mechanism capable of macro coordination – in this sense, it does not create a new paradigm of social integration.

According to Castells, a new era of modernity starts with the replacement of industrial mode of development (based on effective energy generation) by an informational one (based on effective processing of information). Such transformation was enabled by the parallel processes of the computing and information technological revolution and the deregulation of international financial markets. As a result of the combination of these changes, a global version of capitalism emerged, which produced surplus value by processing economical information in real time on a global scale.[7] While in classical modernity, nation states were capable of regulating their markets and decreasing the negative externalities, in late modernity, the deregulated global market is uncontrollable; thus, it enforces the adaptation of individual and organizational actors as well. The most important competence is flexibility: as global demand and supply varies unpredictably, its fluctuation needs to be followed in real time, which can be ensured by network structures enabling rapid expansion (in times of boom) and downsizing (in times of bust). Besides being the key of success in the informational global market, networks also induce several new challenges: individual and local time are adjusted to the virtual rhythm of global networks; collective representations and identities are subordinated to meanings distributed in cultural networks; and nation states lose their agency (Castells, 2010). Overall, the network as a basis of sociability is similar to reflexivity described by Beck: it provides an opportunity for the adaptation to the new constellation characterized by dissolving structures, but it does not open a new horizon of integration.

After sketching two basic types of the diagnoses of late modernity, a substantive analysis of the paradox tendencies of modernization (described by Habermas as colonization) can be elaborated. When it comes to naming the causes of the rupture in classical modernity, Beck refers to the newly emerging irreversible risks while Castells refers to the emergence of global network capitalism based on an informational mode of development. Despite their differences, at the core of both phenomena, the traces of uncontrolled instrumental rationalization are found: the new risks are born as a consequence of new technologies aiming exclusively at optimizing productivity, whereas global market is enabled by more effective information processing capabilities and deregulation is motivated by the sole purpose of profitability. In both cases, it is the uncontrolled instrumental rationalization that results in self-destructive tendencies: it equally threatens the local lifeworlds and the natural environment of human existence.

Furthermore, irreversible risks and global markets are similar, as both of them bring to life new technics, which are only partly capable of handling the late modern challenges. Reflexivity and networking provide opportunity for adapting to the increased uncertainties and to the need for flexibility. However, these technics are not capable of establishing a new paradigm of integration. On the one hand, they are fundamentally exclusive: reflexivity and networks help only those who have the necessary competences of operating them, but neglect everyone else (e.g. 'black holes' of global networks). On the other hand, they are inevitably temporary: reflexivity and networks may provide a compromising solution for a particular problem, but not a general one. As both of them were born out of the need for adaptation to an unpredictable constellation, they are reactionary instead of decisive. In this sense, the casual, particular successes of reflexivity and networking cannot be transformed into general practices: as nothing ensures their success in the rapidly changing future, they remain contingent.

Theories of late modernity inform us not only about the substantive consequences of system colonization but also about the rearrangement of the negative and positive motivation for cooperation. They describe a constellation, where the integration mechanisms based on rationality and functional differentiation dissolve and no replacements capable of providing a stable and general structure are available.[8] In this sense, late modernity is characterized by difficulties of integration and loss of hope in emancipation as well. However, that does not necessarily mean the elimination or weakening of social ties in general; rather, it expresses a reconfiguration of the modality of cooperation. Instead of relying on both hope for new possibilities and fear from threats, late modern social relations are based predominantly on the latter, resulting in a lifeworld characterized by the experience of hiatus.[9] Such constellation can be defined as *negative integration* in a sense that the way action coordination mechanisms work maintain a dominantly fearful lifeworld. On the one hand, negative integration affects the weakened, but yet to be eliminated classical modern mechanisms: their positive motivation for cooperation is diminishing, while the negative becomes predominant. On the other hand, it affects the new technics: they are exclusively based on negative motivation for cooperation.

Just as in case of classical modern integration mechanisms, where the inadequate pre-modern ones served as a negative reference point, in case of reflexivity and networking, it is the fear from the distortive, colonizing classical modern integration, which serves as the primary source of negative motivation for cooperation. In case of reflexivity, this means that the source of fear is the application of hazardous social technologies, which may be effective for their own purposes, but completely neglect the well-being of those who are affected by their negative externalities. If reflexivity is based on such motivation, then it is fuelled by suspicion not by confidence: it does not include the promise of control over one's life, only a chance for temporary harm reduction. On structural level, this constellation is characterized by reflections ultimately incapable of protecting from hazards, only locally and temporarily averting them. In case of networks, negative motivation for cooperation is related to the destructive potential of global markets. They may create previously unseen opportunities for accumulation, but at the same time undermine everyday lifeworlds. If connecting to a network is motivated by the fear from such extreme reification, then it serves the purpose of escaping: instead of handling the negative externalities of global markets on a general level, it seeks individual relief from its burdens. On structural level, these networks do not aim to control the global processes or profit from them; they only try to establish fragile spaces of familiarity.

After describing the specificities of late modern motivation for cooperation of each integration mechanism (Table 2.1[10]), an attempt can be made to summarize some theoretical conclusions. Overall, late modernity is characterized by the coexistence of mechanisms of integration maintained solely by fears from pre-modern dangers and technics of adaptation based on fears from the negative consequences of these very same emptied mechanisms. In this sense, the dynamics of late modernity depends on the equilibrium of these various fears. If the fears belonging to the former group become predominant, then pre-modern mechanisms of integration are kept at bay while modern ones are maintained with the ambivalent support of late modern technics. If the fears belonging to the latter group become predominant, then the dissolving of modern mechanisms of integration culminates, which also implies the potential return of pre-modern patterns (as the forces keeping them away disappear).

In this sense, two fundamentally different idealtypical scenarios of late modernity can be outlined. The first is characterized by the coexistence of the emptied forms of integration based on rationality and technics of adaptation to disintegration – that is the normalization of negative integration. The second is defined by the expansion of technics of adaptation completely replacing discredited mechanisms of integration and the latent re-emerging patterns of pre-modernity – that is the regressive culmination of negative integration. Like any ideal types, these scenarios should not be considered as general descriptions of the empirical tendencies, instead as tools of understanding particular constellations. In the final section, empirical analyses of the contemporary 'culture of fear' are reinterpreted in order to elaborate some of the actual consequences of negative integration.

Table 2.1 Modalities of integration in late modernity and the empirical patterns of fear

	Positive		*Negative*		
	Motivation for cooperation	*Model of integration*	*Motivation for cooperation*	*Model of integration/technics of adaptation*	*Empirical patterns of fear*
Division of labour	Hope for overall increase of quality of life	Fair distribution of goods	*Fear from repressive collective consciousness*	*Unequal, but not arbitrary distribution of goods*	*Fear from the unjust*
Legal-bureaucratic legitimacy	Hope for actualization of common interest	Inclusive rule of law	*Fear from purposelessness, uncontrollable affections and dogmatism*	*Exclusive, but not irrational rule of law*	*Fear from the irrational*
Communicative action	Hope for moral recognition and rationality	Undistorted speech acts	**Fear from confrontation**	**Distrustful, but non-violent communication**	**Fear from crimes (paranoia)**
System	Hope for controlling environment	Entrusted, adaptive system	**Fear from contingent interactions**	**Dysfunctional, but predictable system**	**Fear from the generalized other (misanthropy)**
Reflexivity	–		**Fear from irreversible risks**	**Inconclusive, but harm-reducing reflection**	**Fear from technology and science (technophobia)**
Networking	–		**Fear from global structures**	**Unpredictable, but temporarily adaptive networks**	**Fear from the alien (xenophobia)**

Negative integration and the contemporary patterns of fear

If fear is on the rise not because the world became a more dangerous place or because society is disintegrating (Elchardus et al., 2008), then the contemporary expansion of fear can be explained with a new susceptibility originating from structural transformation. Fear does not increase in general, but only in those constellations where the experiences of negative integration imply it. Empirical research about the social construction of fear helps to refine these theoretical conclusions: the substantive analyses of the culture of fear are linked to the various patterns of negative motivation for cooperation. Such synthesis provides a comprehensive understanding of how the susceptibility originating from the transformation of integration is exploited by mechanisms responsible for producing and spreading fear.

The first analyses about the social construction of fear were centred around moral panic (Cohen, 1972; Young, 1971). Such phenomenon was understood as an extraordinary outburst of fear, generated by the media. These studies described a classical modern way of constructing fear: the frightening phenomena were considered to be exceptional deviances, requiring immediate political response. However, the constellation slowly changed, as the exceptionality of moral panics was replaced by the ordinariness of news about threats, catastrophes, tragedies and dangers covered daily by the media. The popularity of frequent and dramatized media representations of dreadful events can be partly explained by their capability of orienting attention: while being occupied with extraordinary threats beyond one's responsibility, the viewers are relieved from the duty of dealing with their own pragmatic and existential problems (Glassner, 1999). The general demand for fearsome reports directing the attention away from personal issues is further intensified as late modern subject faces an extremely wide horizon of possibilities (Bude, 2017).

Such fundamental tendencies are further aggravated, as the construction of fear becomes detached from personal experiences. As scientific discourses identify more and more imperceptible threats, the actors' relation to the world transforms. The perception of environment, ourselves and the others is based more and more on the semantics of danger implying the pragmatic and moral duty of vigilance. On the one hand, this results in general distrust, that is, fear from the other in general. It concerns not only the members of the outgroup but also the members of the ingroup, who are considered to be irresponsible bystanders, potentially dangerous perpetrators or latent abusers. As danger becomes the framework of relating to the other, an alienated, misanthropic perspective is normalized (Furedi, 2006), which reduces the potential forms of interaction to mere harm reduction or potentially violent pre-emptive measures (Collins, 2008). On the other hand, generalized fears also concern the products of technology considered to be potentially health damaging. Any basic goods being industrially processed such as food is becoming the subject of continuous suspicion, which could result in technophobia (Fabiansson and Fabiansson, 2016; Ferrari, 2009).

Besides scientific discourses of environmental and social dangers, semantics of fear may also be born out of pure strategic interests. Discourses of crime function as means of 'governmentality' in Foucauldian sense: by identifying social problems as crimes, the logic of surveillance and punishment is set into motion. Through the discourse of crime, more and more areas of everyday life (such as family or school) become the subject of governance, resulting in preventive measures limiting the freedom of the actors. As a consequence, not only the willingness to give up democratic institutions in exchange for security grows but also a paranoid attitude emerges (Simon, 2007). By pointing to internal (e.g. criminals) and external (e.g. terrorists) enemies, semantics of war fulfil the purpose of pacifying class conflict: the frustrations of deprived classes are translated into hatred against deviants or foreigners. Besides the media representations, the actual countermeasures including quarantines (e.g. prisons, refugee camps, ghetto) and violence (e.g. torture, death penalty) also contribute to the reproduction of fear (Skoll, 2010). Stereotypes such as the 'flow of immigrants' fuel xenophobic fears, which result not only in hostility towards foreigners but also in the undermining of solidarity in general. By inducing recognition struggles for worthy victimhood, instead of advocating collective interest, they legitimize the weakening of welfare institutions (Linke and Smith, 2009). The cornerstones of the increase of xenophobic fears are the collective traumas caused by the acts of terror. The intensive media cover of these acts leads to a chain of events including not only the aggravation of fear but also the advocacy of securitizing political answers (e.g. increased surveillance), which contribute to further escalation of fear (Altheide, 2006).

Obviously, the above overview of empirical analyses about the social construction of fear is far from being complete. However, it covers the most significant topics appearing in the public sphere and the interferences between individuals and various institutional actors. This provides an opportunity for expanding the previous theoretical conclusions: in order to understand more precisely how the negative modality of the various integration mechanisms work, an attempt is made to link them to empirical patterns of fear (see Table 2.1). There are no considerable empirical signs of the existence of fear, which emerges as a consequence of negative modality of legal-bureaucratic legitimacy or division of labour. Neither fear from injustice nor from irrationality seems to be widespread in late modernity. Unlike them, fears originating from the negative modality of communicative action and systems could manifest in the form of paranoid fear from crimes and misanthropic fear from the other. Communication being initiated solely because of the fear from confrontation refers to the totalization of a binary distinction dividing the people into the group of aggressors and victims. Such lifeworld is strengthened by media covers and social policies centred around crime, implying the other as suspicious and the self as a potential victim. Systems relying solely on the refraining from the uncertain and contingent linguistic interactions express a distrust in the competence of others and a disbelief in the possibility of consensus. Such perception resonates to media discourses on universal corruptness resulting in a misanthropic experience of negative system integration.

Experiences originating from the negative modality of reflexivity and networks may be linked to technophobic attitudes towards artificial products and xenophobic hostility towards anything alien. Reflexivity limited to harm reduction leads to a one-sidedly worrying perception of science and technology. As a discredited image is generated in intermeshing expert and esoteric public discourses, such ambiguity is further increased, expressing how the negative modality of reflection might manifest in actual patterns of fear. Networks solely constituted as reactions to the constraints of economic and cultural globalization lead to a biased understanding of anything external. The alien is viewed as oppressive or simply threatening while the potential of learning from the other remains in blindspot. Media covers of mostly dangerous (e.g. terror) or displeasing (e.g. cultural differences) impacts of the other generate xenophobic worries, which are capable of filling the abstract experience of negative modalities of networks with substantive images.

Even if these empirical patterns of fear are just a few among many other potential manifestations of negative motivation for cooperation, they help us to picture how the phenomenology of negative integration can be used for explaining the contemporary expansion of fear. Actual patterns of fear need to be understood from the perspective of the transforming modality of integration mechanisms, as they express the fundamental social dynamics creating susceptibility to fear. Also, through a detailed conceptualization of these mechanisms, the empirical sociology of fear may find useful guidelines. It may be argued that the expansion of fear is not a general cultural transformation caused by the dissolving of social ties or the bias of the press, which is a common misconception of many empirical researchers (Tudor, 2003: 245). Instead, its various substantive forms expand in constellations constituted of different integration mechanisms, but simultaneously characterized by the predominance of negative motivation for cooperation. In this sense, if fear is on the rise, that is because more and more actors are socialized in constellations characterized by negative integration. By continuously reminding the actors of their own limitations (risks) and providing only halfway measures (networks), these spheres of action prevent identification and the comfort of an evident lifeworld – instead, they only enable the inhabiting of an inherently ambivalent, inhospitable world. At this point, fear not only becomes a frequent experience, rather a definitive one: it gradually detaches from concrete situations. As the whole lifeworld is built around it, generalized anxiety appears. The details of such experience are explored in Chapter 5.

Notes

1 In what follows, I understand social theory as a sub-discipline of sociology aiming at explaining the micro and macro levels of social integration. Based on this approach, every attempt of answering the question of 'double contingency' belongs to this sub-discipline (Parsons and Shils, 1951: 16).
2 In the same theoretical framework, anxiety is understood as a secondary emotion, characterized by the helpless generalization of fear (Kemper, 1987: 283). In this sense, understanding the emergence of fear may ground the analysis of contemporary anxiety – a topic widely discussed by sociologies of uncertainty (e.g. Beck, 1992).
3 According to classics of philosophical phenomenology like Heidegger or Merleau-Ponty, fear reframes one's relation to time, space, the other and the embodied self (Arcaya, 1979; Davidson, 2000). These observations are complemented by social phenomenology, which emphasize the intersubjective components of fear and reconstruct it as a 'relevance structure' of the lifeworld (Schütz and Luckmann, 1973).
4 Even if the chosen descriptions of social integration do not cover the whole spectrum of classical and late modern theories, they are based on a systematic selection: Weber and Durkheim introduced two contrasting forms of social integration; Habermas elaborated the most comprehensive synthesis of their models while Beck and Castells described their dissolution.
5 That is why Riley argues that the key question of classic contract theories concerns 'will': how can the actors – previously forced to subsume their will to the authorities – be motivated to willingly limit their personal interest for collective ones (Riley, 1982: 22)?
6 According to Schluchter, tradition expresses an exclusive focus on means; affectivity an unreflective following of desires; value-rationality a focus on means, ends and values independently from their consequences (1985: 134).
7 While Castells introduces a late modern version of globalization, it can be argued that it represents a sequential historical pattern, which is followed by inevitable waves of collapse (Szakolczai, 2016). This perspective may be important, when negative integration is theorized: it is a key question whether to view it as a mere step of disintegration or as a step of reconfiguration.
8 Bauman uses the term 'liquidization' to describe such process (2000), Szakolczai refers to 'permanent liminality' (2017).
9 It is important to note that such lifeworld is not simply characterized by the lack of meaningfulness, rather it is built around negativities. In this sense, it requires a new theoretical approach aiming at conceptualizing the constitutive role of nothing, its capability of organizing identities and social interactions (for such an attempt see Scott, 2017). Others are more dubious about the possibility of such exploration: if general human existence is considered to be possible strictly under conditions of stability (Szakolczai, 2015), then negativity could never provide any sort of grounds for it.
10 Those cells are boldfaced, which characterize late modernity according to both the diagnoses of times and the empirical analyses of fear. Those are put in italics, which are predicted by theories, but remain unsupported by empirical evidence. Those potentials remain unmarked, which disappear in late modernity according to both theoretical and empirical data.

References

Altheide, D. L. (2006) *Terrorism and the Politics of Fear.* Oxford: Altamira Press.

Arcaya, J. M. (1979) A Phenomenology of Fear. *Journal of Phenomenological Psychology,* 10(2): 165–188.

Bauman, Z. (2000) *Liquid Modernity*. Cambridge: Polity.

Beck, U. (1992) *Risk Society: Towards a New Modernity*. London: Sage.

Berger, P. L. and Luckmann, T. (1966) *The Social Construction of Reality*. New York, NY: Anchor Books.

Brower, S. (2011) Culture of Fear. In White, C. (Ed.), *Journeys in Social Education*. Rotterdam, Boston, Taipei: Sense Publishers, 93–110.

Bude, H. (2017) *Society of Fear*. Cambridge: Polity.

Castells, M. (2010) *The Information Age: Economy, Society, and Culture* (Volume I–III). Oxford: Blackwell.

Collins, A. (2018) *The Global Risks Report 2018*. World Economic Forum. http://www3.weforum.org/docs/WEF_GRR18_Report.pdf (last download 12/03/2019).

Collins, R. (2008) *Violence: A Micro-Sociological Theory*. Princeton, NJ: Princeton University Press.

Cohen, S. (1972) *Folk Devils and Moral Panics: The Creation of the Mods and Rockers*. London: MacGibbon & Kee.

Davidson, J. (2000) A Phenomenology of Fear: Merleau-Ponty and Agoraphobic Life-Worlds. *Sociology of Health and Illness*, 22(5): 640–660.

Durkheim, E. (1997) *The Division of Labour in Society*. New York, NY: Free Press.

Durkheim, E. (1951) *Suicide: A Study in Sociology*. New York, NY: Free Press.

Elchardus, M., De Groof, S. and Smits, W. (2008) Rational Fear or Represented Malaise: A Crucial Test of Two Paradigms Explaining Fear of Crime. *Sociological Perspectives*, 51(3): 453–471.

Fabiansson, C. and Fabiansson, S. (2016) *Food and the Risk Society: The Power of Risk Perception*. London: Routledge.

Ferrari, M. (2009) *Risk Perception, Culture, and Legal Change A Comparative Study on Food Safety in the Wake of the Mad Cow Crisis*. London: Routledge.

Furedi, F. (2006) *Culture of Fear Revisited Risk-Taking and the Morality of Low Expectation*. New York, NY: Continuum.

Giddens, A. (1994) Living in a Post-Traditional Society. In Beck, U., Giddens, A. and Lash, S. (Eds.), *Reflexive Modernization. Politics, Tradition and Aesthetics in the Modern Social Order*. Cambridge: Polity, 56–109.

Glassner, B. (1999) *The Culture of Fear: Why Americans Are Afraid of the Wrong Things*. New York, NY: Basic Books.

Habermas, J. (1975) *Legitimation Crisis*. London: Heinemann Educational.

Habermas, J. (1987) *The Theory of Communicative Action* (Vol. 2). Boston, MA: Beacon.

Hobbes, T. (1997) *Leviathan*. New York, NY: Simon & Schuster.

Kemper, T. D. (1987) How Many Emotions Are There? Wedding the Social and the Autonomic Components. *American Journal of Sociology*, 93(2): 263–289.

Linke, U. and Smith, D. T. (2009) Fear: A Conceptual Framework. In Linke, U. and Smith, D. T. (Eds.), *Cultures of Fear: A Critical Reader*. London: Pluto Press, 1–24.

Merleau-Ponty, M. (2012) *Phenomenology of Perception*. London: Routledge.

Moon, D. (2013) Powerful Emotions: Symbolic Power and the (Productive and Punitive) Force of Collective Feeling. *Theory and Society*, 42(3): 261–294.

Parsons, T. and Shils, E. (1951) *Toward a General Theory of Action*. Cambridge, MA: Harvard University Press.

Riley, P. (1982) *Will and Political Legitimacy: A Critical Exposition of Social Contract Theory in Hobbes, Locke, Rousseau, Kant, and Hegel*. Cambridge, MA: Harvard University Press.

Rousseau, J. J. (2002) *The Social Contract and The First and Second Discourses*. New Haven, CT and London: Yale University Press.

Schluchter, W. (1985) *The Rise of Western Rationalism: Max Weber's Developmental History.* Berkeley, CA: University of California Press.

Schütz, A. and Luckmann, T. (1973) *The Structures of the Life-World.* London: Heinemann.

Scott, S. (2017). A Sociology of Nothing: Understanding the Unmarked. *Sociology*, 52(1), 3–19.

Skoll, G. R. (2010) *Social Theory of Fear Terror, Torture, and Death in a Post-Capitalist World.* New York, NY: Palgrave Macmillan.

Simon, J. (2007) *Governing Through Crime How the War on Crime Transformed American Democracy and Created a Culture of Fear.* Oxford: Oxford University Press.

Szakolczai, A. (2015) Disenchantment or Irrationalisation: On Weber's Struggle to Comprehend the Dynamics of Modernity. *International Political Anthropology*, 8(1): 15–29.

Szakolczai, A. (2016) Processes of Social Flourishing and Their Liminal Collapse: Elements to a Genealogy of Globalization. *The British Journal of Sociology*, 67: 435–455

Szakolczai, A. (2017) *Permanent Liminality and Modernity.* London and New York, NY: Routledge.

Tudor, A. (2003) A (Macro) Sociology of Fear. *Sociological Review*, 51(2): 238–256.

Vannelli, R. (2015) *The Evolution of Human Sociability: Desires, Fears, Sex and Society.* Cambridge and New York, NY: Cambridge University Press.

Weber, M. (1978) *Economy and Society: An Outline of Interpretive Sociology.* Berkeley, CA: University of California Press.

Weber, M. (1991) Science as Vocation. In Gerth, H. H. and Wright, C. M. (Eds.), *From Max Weber: Essays in Sociology*, London: Routledge, 129–149.

Wilkinson, I. (1999) Where Is the Novelty in Our Current 'Age of Anxiety'? *European Journal of Social Theory*, 2(4): 445–467.

Wilkinson, I. (2001) Social Theories of Risk Perception: At Once Indispensable and Insufficient. *Current Sociology*, 49(1): 1–22.

Young, J. (1971) *The Drug Takers: The Social Meaning of Drug Use.* London: McGibbon and Paladin.

3 Power from indirect pain

A historical phenomenology of medical pain management

Physical pain is one of the most elementary human experiences. On the one hand it is a physiological state of the body, on the other hand an unignorable impression demanding countermeasures. Such dual nature locates pain at the borderland of the biological and the cultural (Schleifer, 2014: 54). Due to its uncomfortable or in some cases unbearable impact, every society develops ways to deal with it. These include interpretative frameworks about its origins, technologies of handling it and moral economies defining its normative order. However, pain is not only a pre-given phenomenon originating from external sources implying counter-measures. It is also evoked and used intentionally or unintentionally by social actors. Because of its dual nature, it is capable of mediating between the biological and the social: causing pain can destroy and rewrite elementary interpretations of the world, thus reconfiguring social relationships. That is why torture and war are considered to be the idealtypical instruments of establishing social hierarchies (Scarry, 1985: 27). A painful sensation, which is caused by another subject not only destroys the meanings of the sufferer, it also creates the experience of subordination, as the one causing the pain also has the power of stopping it. The one who hurts not only eliminates the validity of the lifeworld, but also appears as an authority of giving new sense to the world. Accordingly, the history of pain has at least two dimensions: it includes the interpretations and technologies of treatment, also the various ways of causing pain for the sake of establishing power and shaping subjectivity (Foucault, 1982). Furthermore, these dimensions are interrelated: the ontological and epistemological framing of pain outlines the available forms of causing pain; also, the power structures affect the narratives and experiences of pain itself.

Despite such fundamental interrelatedness, genealogical analyses of the treatment and the usage of pain are seldom connected to each other. The modern subject's relation to pain has been discussed mostly by those social historical and medical anthropological analyses, which are based on a comparison with either the premodern (Enenkel, 2009) or the non-Western (Throop, 2010) other. These analyses introduce discursive transformations, which resulted in the birth of a 'biomedical paradigm'. As a consequence of a positivist reframing of pain, those religious and moral connotations,

DOI: 10.4324/9781003197355-5

which dominated its non-modern understanding are eliminated. Pain is reintroduced in a reductionist framework, as a consequence of (mostly) bodily pathologies and dysfunctions. From this perspective, the modern subject's relation to pain is reduced to the attempts of eliminating its objective cause – or if this is not possible, to the decrease of the subjective suffering it causes. Based on these conclusions, several questions can be raised: what are the consequences of the disenchantment of pain for establishing power?; can modern power be engraved by pain that is perceived principally in a medical model?; how does this transformation impact the constitution of late modern subjectivities?

The transformations of pain as a basis of power can be reconstructed from the historical analyses focusing on violence. They argue that the overall level of violence has been decreasing drastically in modernity (Muchembled, 2012). Due to the 'civilizing process' physical hurting has been banned from both public and private spaces, while being replaced by subtler ways of maintaining hierarchies (Elias, 2000). These conclusions also lead to several questions: how does modern power (greatly disassociated from violence) contribute to the subject's relation to pain?; what kind of mechanisms substitute the intentional use of physical violence in the grounding of power; what are the consequences for 'subjectification' (Foucault, 1982)?

In order to answer these questions, a historical phenomenological analysis is conducted. Firstly, a phenomenological reconstruction of pain is elaborated. Based on Husserl's and Merleau-Ponty's analyses, the experience and the embodiment of pain is discussed, which is complemented with Scarry's analysis on the constitutive role of pain in the process of engraving power. This framework is applied in the second and third sections, while the idealtypes of early and late modern pain management are elaborated based on historical and medical anthropological sources. The historical comparison of the technologies of pain management and the political usage of violence outline a genealogy of a power, which is intertwined with the hegemonic biomedical paradigm. In the last section, an attempt is made to critically engage with Foucault's concept of biopower: the historical phenomenological analysis of pain complements his diagnoses of times by introducing the concept of 'power from indirect pain'. Such power is not based on directly hurting the subordinated ones, but relies on the withheld potential of treating pain. The pain, which is not caused intentionally, but simply allowed to subsist – despite the promised biomedical solution – becomes a modern equivalent of hurting. As a consequence, not only an obscure, inaccessible power is engraved, but also self-objectifying subjectivities emerge being susceptible to addictive behaviour patterns.

A social phenomenology of pain

Most theories of pain attempt to clarify the ontological status, which proves to be a controversial task: on the one hand, it seems to be localizable in the body; on the other hand, it may be experienced without any obvious organic cause or bodily locus, which implies a psychic origin. According to Husserl's phenomenological analysis, in order to solve this dilemma, a differentiation is needed between the living-body (*Leib*) and the body as object (*Körper*). Pain cannot be explained by solely relying on either of these aspects, as its existence is related to both of them. While in the 'natural attitude' the body is a pre-given constituent of the (embodied) self (Husserl, 1989: 159), in pain a distance is born between the (disembodied) self and the body. The body in pain is transformed into an object: not anymore the instrument of free will, but a thing determined by external forces (Geniusas, 2017). In this sense, pain is a transformative experience: it reframes the relation to the self and the world as well (Husserl, 1989: 160). Husserl's analysis has been complemented by Merleau-Ponty in several ways (Carman, 1999). According to him, the body and the world constitute an undividable complex (Merleau-Ponty, 1962: 206). This means that pain is not simply a new experience among others, instead it transforms how the world is inhabited: what used to be full of potentials is now full of obstacles. In this sense, severe pain does not simply transform the lived-body into an object, while resulting in new experiences, but turns the world into a burdensome or unbearable totality (Svenaeus, 2015).

Even though philosophical phenomenology laid down the bases for the social scientific analysis of pain, it was Scarry's seminal book, which opened the path for a fundamentally social approach. It helps us to move away from the purely epistemological approach characterizing philosophical phenomenologies towards the analysis of the political dimension of pain. Scarry chooses an atypical starting point: instead of focusing on accidental injury or illness, she focuses on wounds inflicted in the process of torture or war (which are *par excellence* social phenomena). Such choice has consequences for the whole phenomenology of pain, as it provides access to those aspects, which remain in the blindspot of epistemological approaches.[1] According to her, even if pain is a pre-linguistic experience, it is capable of affecting the existing meanings by erasing them and providing a new framework for rewriting (Scarry, 1985: 27). This destructive capacity is used in the process of torture: the continuous invasive pain gradually fills up the horizon of lifeworld, until the point the victim is reduced to a bare body in pain. The overwhelming experience of pain overwrites both memories, personality traits and dispositions. The one being responsible for such agony is not just an average other, but a quasi-omnipotent agent, who has not only the power to destroy the world, but also to give it back. Therefore, torturers always aim at presenting themselves as obvious sources of the pain: this causal relationship engraves their unquestionable authority in the victim. Their goal is to reduce the world into the opposition of a bare body in pain and an omnipotent (bodiless) will determining the fate of the former (Scarry, 1985: 57).

However, the mere facticity of the unlimited power of hurting is not sufficient on its own for the long term establishment of power. For this purpose, the victim has to be alienated from themselves on the most elementary level of their body functions: the capacities previously serving as the source of enjoyment are transformed into the places of agony (e.g. eating is replaced by starving, free movement by uncomfortable postures). As the body is taken over, it is not merely reduced to be an object, but rather a living-body (*Leib*) turned inside out: on the one hand it still belongs to the victim, while being completely controlled by the torturer (Scarry, 1985: 51). This elementary experience of embodied subordination grounds the linguistic reinterpretation of the whole lifeworld. Torture is never only about causing harm; it includes the element of speaking as well. While the seeming function of asking questions during the process is to gather information, the actual purpose is the gradual reconfiguration of the victim's lifeworld. It is through the conversation that the bodily subordination is translated into a mutual interpretation of the world originating exclusively from the torturer (Scarry, 1985: 49).

Even though torture is an extreme situation of experiencing pain, the processes identified by Scarry have general relevance. The structure of torture not only highlights the destructive and constitutive aspect of pain, but at the same time reveals how the experience of subordination is born in the act of causing harm. Of course, in case of pain, which is not inflicted by a recognizable agent (i.e. not the result of harming or torture), the impression of authority does not emerge explicitly. However, that does not make it non-existent: the experience of pain implies the seeking of answers to the questions concerning its causes and the related responsibilities.[2] Thus, even in case of a seemingly non-social pain, questions, such as 'why is it happening?' and 'who or what is responsible for the agony?' are inevitable. A need for interpretation arises, which is never a neutral explanation, but includes the element of a latent subordination (to the presumed source pain). In other words, pain implies power attributed to its source, even if the cause is unidentifiable. In this latter case, power is delegated to those, who provide the dominant interpretative narratives and the related treatments. This conclusion opens the path for a social phenomenology of pain in modernity. Making sense of pain is a historically contingent process involving not only interpretative frameworks, but also those structures, which implicitly or explicitly maintain them. This social phenomenological approach is applied in the following sections, while attempting to answer the questions: what kind of interpretations of pain are born in early and late modern constellations?; what sort of power is grounded by the praxes based on them; and how does this effect late modern subjectivities?

Early modern pain: Between transcendental and medical

In order to reconstruct how pain is used and interpreted in contemporary societies, a comparison with the direct social historical antecedents proves to be useful. Early modernity is a liminal constellation characterized by gradual departure from medieval civilization to the secularized modern form of life. The transforming interpretative frames of pain can be reconstructed from social historical sources focusing on the attitudes of everyday actors; the emerging medical discourses; and the reconfiguration of violence. Of course a comprehensive overview of such vast literature is an impossible task within a book chapter, so the aim of the present analysis is humbler: an attempt is made to elaborate an idealtypical model of how pain has been interpreted, treated and used in the transforming early modern Europe.[3]

The most important transformation affecting the everyday relation to pain can be described as a reluctant secularization. In medieval civilization pain was inseparable from the transcendental: at the most fundamental level it implied a godly punishment, which had to be endured for the sake of salvation. Pain of labour, illness or injuries were equally treated as inevitable consequences of the original sin (and also personal sins), so their reduction was not considered to be a legitimate goal (Le Goff, 1992: 235). Within this context pain was either cultivated as a means to salvation (e.g. the flagellant movement), or accepted as a necessary element of human existence (e.g. the neo-stoic reinterpretation of pain as something beyond our control – Enenkel, 2009). In early modernity, such religiously grounded moral economy of pain was gradually complemented by an instrumental paradigm: pedagogy started to use corporal punishment in order enhance learning skills, based on a theory linking pain and memory (Traninger, 2009); the bourgeoisie started to rely on self-exploitative work ethics (exchanging personal suffering for profit – Weber, 2005). These examples of instrumentalized pain did not follow anymore a transcendental logic. Instead they followed a calculative logic: pain was viewed as a necessary means to an end. As a consequence, the medieval unconditional acceptance of agony was gradually complemented with the intention of differentiating between useful and useless pain (Moscoso, 2012: 84). Enduring agony was not anymore a religious-moral obligation, but depended on the evaluation of its usefulness. If it did not serve any purpose, its elimination remained the only logical way to relate to it.

Early modern medicine was not independent from the transformation of these theological-moral frames. For a long time, pain was not at the centre of medical attention, it was rather treated as an inconvenience (e.g. it made surgical interventions difficult). It was localized it in the body, while being framed as a fundamentally mechanical question (Schoenfeldt, 2009). While lay and expert discourses on painkillers were not separated throughout the early modern era, gradually an autonomous medical discourse emerged. It interpreted pain as a phenomenon, which should be measured objectively by medical science (Tousignant, 2014). Later on, this unique access granted the monopoly of knowledge about pain to doctors, while excluding the subjects in pain themselves from the process of interpretation. Nevertheless, the monopolization of pain management was not a sudden transformation, as it is expressed by the diffuse usage of the first painkillers. They were used as a multifunctional tool for preventing or treating just about any negative conditions ranging from depressed mood, exhaustion, anxiety or physical pain. In this sense these drugs were treated as general countermeasure to the various forms of suffering of modernizing life (Culley, 2014). In this sense, painkillers were born as alternatives – and later on, rivals – of the religious narratives and rituals of pain management.

The discovery of technologies capable of reliably eliminating pain indicates the end of early modernity in the history of pain management. The real capacity of eliminating pain became undoubtable with the birth of anaesthesiology. While previously the surgical interventions reproduced the pain of the martyrs, these new technologies transformed the clinic into the sterile, supervised space, as it is known today (Moscoso, 2012: 114). Of course, as the efficiency of controlling pain remained contingent for a while, the neurological interpretation describing it as a bodily function, which can be turned on or off, did not become hegemonic until the perfection of biomedical painkillers. It was challenged throughout the whole era by several approaches: Protestantism argued that suffering still carries a religious meaning, which has to be revealed in the worldly existence (Korsten, 2009); romanticism and sentimentalism defended the necessity of pain for human existence, thus continued a medieval interpretation even if in a secularized manner (Moscoso, 2012: 84); theories of hypnosis questioned the bodily nature of pain (Moscoso, 2012: 127).

In this sense early modernity is characterized on the one hand by the weakened, but persisting theological-moral framing and the emerging, but not hegemonic medical framing of pain. Such ambiguity characterized the transformation of the technologies of hurting as well. The 'civilizing process' fundamentally reconfigured the role of physical violence in social relationships: while in medieval times the ones in power (i.e. the nobility) had the privilege of act according to their affections (even in a violent way), gradually self-restraining became a virtue, resulting in the banishment of violence from public interactions (Elias, 2000). This transformation of manners was enabled by the emergence of several new praxes capable of setting boundaries for those young, unmarried men, who were responsible in the biggest number for the various forms of violence. These praxes included not only the perfection of the policing technologies of the state monopolizing violence, but also the increased surveillance of adolescents considered to require 'special attention' (Muchembled, 2012). In parallel with the civilization of manners and the pacification of potential perpetrators, the system of justice also transformed: the spectacle of public torture and execution was replaced by the logic of prison aiming at disciplining instead of publicly demonstrating revenge and deterrence (Foucault, 1977. These transformations were complemented by the increase of the sensitivity of the spectators: as compassion became an imperative, pain was not perceived anymore as an educative punishment, but as an uncomfortable spectacle, which – unless being justified by a rational goal – needs to be eliminated, minimalized or hidden (Moscoso, 2012: 70). Even though these parallel processes tended to the same direction of the overall decrease of violence, such transformation was not linear and general at all. Based on the long-term homicide rates, it seems that instead of a general decrease, it is more valid to refer to the marginalization of violence: instead of disappearing completely, violence was banished to the social and spatial peripheries (Mc Mahon et al., 2013).

Overall, the early modern treatment and usage of pain outlines an ambiguous picture. The passive, undifferentiated medieval interpretation (originating from a theological grounding) was complemented with an instrumental one; the ignorant medical practice was complemented with more and more effective treatments of pain and a consequent instrumentalist discourse; violence as unconstrained privilege was banished from the public sphere to the margins of society. However, none of these tendencies became exclusive, as the earlier practices survived even if in a weakened form. In this constellation the main characteristics of pain became its contingency: it was not anymore defined by premodern frames, not yet by modern ones. Unlike in medieval times, when pain implied guilt, while strengthening the worldly and transcendental power relations, the early modern construction of pain ceased to be a definitive experience. The space opened up for interpreting pain from the interchangeable perspectives of transcendental and naturalizing semantics: if either of them proved to be inefficient, the other could have been used as a substitute. This also affected the structure of power, which could be built upon it: it was neither an unquestionable heavenly order, nor an undeniable natural order, but a non-hegemonic constellation based on the oscillation between these two realms.

In this sense, in early modernity the question of pain was opened up, without any conclusive answers. As a consequence, the very fabric of power was weakened. As violence was banished from the public sphere and the control over pain was yet to be established, authority as such became contingent. In a certain way, these transformations contributed to the expansion of freedom both on individual (i.e. personal autonomy) and collective levels (i.e. political revolutions). As traditional power was weakened due to the temporary vacuum of both transcendental and naturalized paradigms of pain and violence, actors had the opportunity of reconfiguring themselves autonomously. Contemporary power can be understood from a comparison with such liminal constellation: the elimination of its contingency did not only result in the emergence of a hegemonic interpretation of pain, but also the birth of a new power structure.

Late modern pain: The consequences of hegemonic medicalization

Even though the transcendental and naturalizing paradigm was coexisting for a few centuries, their rivalry concluded as modern medicine became more efficient. The new technologies capable of not only decreasing pain, but also treating its biological causes provided an unquestionable authority for medical discourse claiming to represent the objective truth of nature. Such authority relies on the aura of efficiency, which is supported by the statistical charts of decreasing mortality rates (Woods, 2007) and also by everyday experiences. Previously risky life events (such as giving birth) and infections (such as tuberculosis) became manageable (McKeown, 2004), while the public awareness of healthy environment (hygienic and unpolluted working and living areas) and lifestyle (appropriate health behaviour) was raised (Madsen, 2017). Due to these tendencies, not only the life expectancy, but also the health quality was improved, which greatly contributed to the legitimacy of the biomedical paradigm. Despite the inarguable success, its blindspots and paradoxes also became more and more visible, which resulted in the emerging criticism of biomedicine.[4]

The expansion of medical knowledge is at the centre of many of these criticisms: by stepping out from the clinical context to the realm of everyday life, it provides normalizing technologies of the self, which are fixated on the narrow criteria of hygiene, physical and mental health (Rose, 1999a: 74). These transformations complement the continuation of the civilizing process[5]: since violence has been sanctioned by law, its prevention gradually became a priority. At this point, the previously parallel histories of biomedical expansion and the civilizatory reduction of violence become intertwined. Standardized models of 'normal behaviour' and 'personality development' are elaborated by psy-sciences, which reinterpret violent behaviour as a deviation from the normalcy. Such models influence not only the public sphere, but also ground the operation of state institutions and social policies (Rose, 1999b: 123). As a result of all these efforts combined, violence was not only expelled from the public, but its reframing by the psycho-medical discourses also led to its legal persecution in the private sphere (Clark, 2011). Overall, in its mature form, the broad medical discourse became a key constituent of interpreting and handling every forms of pain including illness and violence. Such hegemony represented the dawn of a new power structure relying on discourse and discipline instead of direct violence. According to Foucault, this is the basis of modern 'biopower', which is capable of establishing control over the elementary aspects of life (such as nurture or sexuality) through technologies of 'governance' (Foucault, 1997).

Many analyses of the construction of pain in contemporary societies rely on these diagnoses as a theoretical background. However, if we take seriously Scarry's social phenomenological analysis and the early modern history of pain management (discussed in the first two sections), then Foucault's concept of discursive biopower proves to be one-sided. Even if the secularization of pain and the parallel decrease of violence undoubtedly contributed to the emergence of a new logic of power, that does not make pain irrelevant for the modern engraving of authority. Even if discursive technologies of governance are capable of structuring one's behaviour through normalizing self-discipline, from a phenomenological perspective it may be argued that subordination still depends greatly on the experience of pain. As Foucault focuses fundamentally on the interrelatedness of subjectivation and power (Foucault, 1982), pain appears on his horizon as a subsidiary problem being relevant for the social history of both medicine and punishment, but not an indispensable element of explaining power. That is why he considers the experience of pain to be relevant for power mostly in premodern times, while the praxis of grounding of power through pain becomes obsolete in modernity. Accordingly, Foucault and those who follow his footstep miss the chance of raising the question of modern power from the perspective of the medicalized experience of pain.

In order to investigate this question, I suggest to take the phenomenology of pain as the starting point: according to these analyses, pain inevitably implies the experience of subordination, even if its source is not trivial. As pain is not eliminated in modernity by far, it may be argued that its experience still contributes to the engraving of a certain from of power, even if in an indirect way. This means that medicalization and civilization do not simply establish a new discursive logic of power, which replaces the traditional one (directly relying on causing pain). Instead, my hypothesis is that the biomedical paradigm of pain management can be reinterpreted as a new, indirect source of power, which is nevertheless still a power from pain.

The power from medicalized pain complements the theory of biopower in several ways: it focuses on the failures of medical knowledge resulting in the persisting experiences of pain, instead of its success resulting in normalizing self-governance; it takes into consideration the hegemony of medical discourse as a special burden (making helpless those, who cannot be treated within its frames), instead of viewing it solely as a technology of control; it understands power as being constituted in a negative way (through the missing treatment of pain), instead of a positive way (through the expansion of normalizing discourses justified by their painkilling potential). In order to empirically describe power from medicalized pain, those anthropological case studies can be overviewed, which analyze medical practice dealing with pain in contemporary societies. Their insights help to understand not only how the hegemonic paradigm can fail in treating pain, but also the consequences of a pain, which is not supposed to exist.

In order to understand the consequences of the medicalization of pain, firstly those mechanisms need to be taken into consideration, which disqualify alternative interpretations. Foucault connects the birth of modern 'clinical gaze' to a fundamental transformation: while the 18th century doctors asked the patient 'What is the matter with you?', the clinicians relying on biomedical discourse do not focus anymore on the whole subject, only on the symptoms indicating a disease (Foucault, 2003: xviii–xix). Medical discourse is organized in opposition to what is considered to belong to the realm of 'belief': it is strictly based on measurable bodily parameters, while anything outside of them is defined as superstition.[6] In this sense, medical discourse considers irrelevant – or explicitly denies – those cultural constituents of pain, which are responsible for making it comprehensible beyond its sheer facticity (Good, 1994). This exclusivity creates an aura of omnipotence: even if medical paradigm explicitly does not claim to be able to treat every condition, by disapproving all alternatives, it ends up implying that if a treatment exists, it is possible only within its framework. This conviction justifies the practice of automatically translating any lay description of pain to naturalizing language games, without attempting to understand them in their original cultural context (Good, 2007; Kleinman and Kleinman, 1991). The technical reduction of the patients' narratives does not mean that the interpretation of pain becomes irrelevant for the experience *per se*, instead it contributes to the alienation from its cultural background, which encloses the patient in a passive and helpless role (Kleinman, 1973). In this sense, medical practice not only denies the relevance of cultural and subjective constituents of pain, but also creates an alienated discursive framework.[7]

The patients being deprived of the narrative competence about their own experiences find themselves in a precarious situation. As medical discourse is hegemonic, the only way to find solution to agony is following the expert instructions. However, if these praxes turn out to be inefficient, instead of reflecting on its own method, medical discourse tends to question the credibility of the patient. Many patients suffering from chronic pain report the experience of being doubted by the doctors claiming that the pain exist only in their heads (Jackson, 1992; Snelgrove, 2017). In some cases, those, who cannot be treated within the medical paradigm are moved to more and more marginal institutions, which are not operating with the promise of finding solutions, but as final depository for the hopeless patients (Biehl, 2010). In other cases, the medical discourse hides its failures by delegating pain untreatable by biological means to the competence of psy-sciences. They are supposed to reinterpret pain as a consequence of a distorted personality, maladaptation, traumas or mental disorders, also they are entitled to provide treatment (Goesling et al., 2018). Such tendency highlights not only how medical discourse can protect the image of its omnipotence by re-labelling the failures, but also how pain unfitting to the biological framework can be addressed in a seemingly legitimate way. By reinterpreting it as mental disorder (e.g. depression, anxiety), it can still be placed in the medical universe, even if under a non-bodily label. As a consequence of such practice, the dividing line between physical pain and other forms of suffering becomes blurred.[8] Accordingly, medical paradigm of pain maintains its hegemonic status either by blaming the victims, by marginalizing them or by redirecting them to psy-therapies.

While medical discourse promises a general solution to various forms of pain, it is often incapable of fulfilling such promise. Pain and unbearable mental distress does not occur randomly: they burden disproportionately the members of disadvantaged social groups. People working in physically demanding positions cannot choose between pain and comfort, as the former is a constitutive element of their tasks. Thus they turn to technologies of 'bricolage' including elements of expert medicine (e.g. prescribed painkillers) and lay treatments (e.g. alcohol as painkiller), while inhabiting a fundamentally painful world (Das and Das, 2007). Pain does not only affect those who work in physically demanding positions: in the world of global capitalism, the flexibility demanded by market is burdened on the employee, who experience it as a constant mental stress (Boltanski and Chiapello, 2005), or as actual pain due to the fragmentation of biological cycles of regeneration (Castells, 2010: 468). Beside of work related burdens, pain also originates directly from inequalities: the experience of exclusion or deprivation from recognition is a painful one, not only in metaphorical sense. These forms of agony show that in many cases, it is the social structure being responsible for pain, not any particular institutions or actors (Macdonald and Leary, 2005; Singh, 2017). These variants of 'social suffering' reveal a hidden 'politics of life'. Beside governing the subjects, medical practice also produces inequalities: as any particular intervention (or its denial) involves a decision about worthy and unworthy life, the way certain pain is treated expresses the status of social recognition of the sufferer (Fassin, 2009).[9]

The paradoxes of a hegemonic medical model become the most visible in case of disability, which is a *par excellence* untreatable condition. The 'long shadow of eugenics' over disability reveals the extreme dangers of a purely medical paradigm: if the only acceptable relation to pain is its elimination, in case of untreatable pain, the logical solution is the exclusion – or in the worst case, the elimination – of the sufferer. Even though this latter option may seem to belong to totalitarian regimes such as the Nazi Germany, as the development of new medical technologies such as pre-natal diagnostics prove it, the boundaries of indispensable lives are still challenged in various contexts (Ginsburg and Rapp, 2016). Even if eugenics is an extreme example, there are subtler mechanisms dealing with various forms of pain untreatable by the medical paradigm. The overuse of painkillers or antidepressants indicate a strategy relying on the obscuring of the source of pain, while partially supressing it or suspending the interest in it (Hardon and Sanabria, 2017). By sedating the actors, the medical paradigm may prolong the existence of a hegemonic façade. However, it is rather the postponing of the facing with its controversies, not a solution to the pain itself: lives spent in partially supressed pain are still lives in pain. Counter-discourses such as anti-psychiatry (Double, 2006) or anti-pharma movements (Weber et al., 2009) attempt to reveal these paradoxes by blaming the medical paradigm for causing harm instead of treating it.[10]

Beside these subtler dysfunctions of the biomedical framing of pain, there are several examples of explicit agony created or maintained by new technologies and interventions. On the basic level of the political economy of biomedicine lies the negotiation of deservingness. As the bodily facticity of pain becomes the objective truth of suffering, it is also the final source of legitimizing solidarity claims and political struggles of redistribution. This motivates actors to translate all of their suffering to a biological language game: as poverty, unemployment or persecution are unaccepted claims for support, being the victim of pollution, industrial accidents (Petryna, 2004), or illness and injuries (Ticktin, 2006) are applied. Despite the sufferers' attempts to gain recognition through pain, mechanisms of exclusion still prevail and deprive those, who are considered to be unworthy (e.g. the poor, the unemployed, the immigrant) of treatment (Nguyen and Peschard, 2003). In these situations, the very price of the treatment is often paid in biological commodity: either by participation in medical testing in exchange for treatment (Inhorn, 2010) or money (Rajan, 2007), or by selling one's organs on the grey market of transplantation (Cohen, 1999). In these cases, the medical paradigm explicitly contributes to the reproduction of already existing inequalities: by opening new territories of the body for exploitation, it intensifies former types of subordination.

Power from indirect pain: The emergence of self-objectifying subjectivities

Based on the comparison of the early and late modern construction of pain, it may be concluded that the biomedical paradigm monopolizes not only the interpretation of pain originating from illness, but also the framing of violence (which became related to affective and personality disorders). Within this constellation, the medical discourse gains the exclusive right of differentiating between (superstitious) beliefs and (scientific) truth. Those experiences of pain, which cannot be handled within the medical framework are either marginalized or reinterpreted as mental disorders. Despite the claim of having exclusive access to reliable treatments, the medical paradigm is incapable of handling various forms of pain (e.g. pain reproduced by unhealthy living or working conditions), while also being responsible for generating new types (e.g. pain caused by addiction to painkillers and antidepressants). Furthermore, the medical paradigm ignores those original inequalities, which affect the process of pain management (e.g. exclusion from treatment, medical exploitation). All in all, these transformations affect not only the medical sphere, they are also responsible for reconfiguring the relation of power and pain.

Instead of causing harm in a recognizable act, medical pain management has the potential of letting pain subsist by not intervening, despite claiming to have exclusive expertise of treatment. These elements are equally important for understanding the birth of a power, which is not directly established by any authority figures, but emerges as an unintended consequence of inadequate or negligent medical praxes leaving those patients to suffer, who has no choice, but to put their trust in the hegemonic biomedical institutes. As such power – lacking any intentional agents or goals – is born from indirect pain, it results in the experience of insecurity or helplessness. These impressions are complemented with the consequences of the biomedical 'hubris': discrediting every alternative treatment, while insisting on its own validity, a failed biomedical intervention may imply the experience of betrayal. As there are no alternatives on the horizon of the sufferer (due to the hegemonic status of biomedical discourse), the representatives of the failed biomedical paradigm appear as agents capable of treating pain, but denying the remedy. By not eliminating pain despite their self-declared competence, from the phenomenological perspective of the sufferers, the agents of the medical paradigm are perceived as the indirect cause of pain. In the eyes of the disappointed patients left on their own, they commit violence – even if in a negative way. Consequently, they unintentionally generate a certain form of power, a 'power from indirect pain'.

Such power differs from both its medieval and early modern antecedents. In the former case pain was attributed to a non-empirical, but omnipotent God, whose worldly and church representatives wielded the power. They were mostly capable of causing, not actually handling pain, but at least they provided transcendental narratives of relief, which enabled the birth of the experience of a paternalistic subordination. In early modernity, such model was complemented by the emerging medical paradigm promising to treat pain, instead of merely justifying it. In case of success, medical technologies provided escape from the religious authority; in case of failure, redemption still could be used to give sense to the inescapable pain. Such potential of experimenting with alternatives resulted in the experience of a less deterministic subordination including the element of the relativism of authorities that is a form of freedom.

In late modernity, once again the chance for such freedom is missing due to the hegemony of biomedical paradigm. However, such exclusivity leads to paradoxes in case of the inevitable failures. The option of handling persisting pain by non-medical methods, which give transcendental sense to the suffering is extremely limited,[11] as such methods are considered to be superstitious or simply unscientific. Thus, persisting pain becomes an anomaly in the frames of biomedicine, a phenomenon which is obscured for not being supposed to exist. This anomaly is either pushed around within the medical complex (e.g. the overuse of painkillers and antidepressants, marginalization) or excluded from it (e.g. blaming the victim of chronic pain) – but in the end, it remains a burden on the subjects. As no alternatives are present on their horizon, sufferers might attribute the responsibility to those actors, who are supposed to fulfil the promise of biomedicine and provide treatment. Their denial of doing so may lead to the experience of a malevolent power, which is characterized by the capability of healing and the withholding of such capability.[12] The representatives of such power may include not only those, who have the right to give or deny treatment, or supress pain (i.e. the broad medical staff); but also those who maintain painful living conditions (e.g. employers, managers, family members, traditions); who gain profit on others' pain (e.g. medical companies, exploitative usurers); who are differentiating between worthy and unworthy pain (e.g. social policies, social workers, NGOs). In various constellations, any of their combination can be perceived to be responsible for the denial of treating pain or the miserableness of a sedated life.

Indirect pain results in the experience of a power, which is not causing suffering because of an unknowable, but assumable transcendental intention, but out of pure negligence – simply because it is not motivated enough to end the agony.[13] The representatives of such power do not cause pain because of their personal cruelty. They are often insensible operators of the medical paradigm, which is not only intolerant to any alternative discourses, but at the same time incapable of treating many kinds of pain, while potentially causing pain itself. However, it is the same negligence, which makes such power so frightening: if one cannot fit into the medical framework, then there are hardly any alternative ways to make a difference, which leaves the sufferer lost in a space inhabited by indifferent and uncomprehending others. In this constellation, the subject has no choice, but adapting to the constraints: individuals affected by indirectly induced pain relate themselves through the same objectifying gaze, which is applied by the hegemonic biomedicine.

The experience of being subordinated to biomedical power reconfigures late modern subjectivities.[14] Power structures play a key role in the process of 'subjectification': the actors do not simply internalize an external normative structure, rather they work on themselves according to the related 'technologies of the self' (Foucault, 1982). This has special consequences for the objectifying and negligent biomedical power. Not only does it threaten with the increase of helplessness, anger and frustration, but even more importantly, it provides self-objectifying technologies of the self. According to the biomedical complex, pain and suffering originates from disturbed bodily functions. In order overcome them, one needs to self-experiment, until a new homeostatic balance is reached. This means the finding of an optimal combination of medications and bodily practices, which are implemented on a regular basis. As the actors start to relate to their embodied existence as an object-body (*Körper*), which needs to be controlled and fine-tuned (instead of being inhabited), an objectifying technology of the self is cultivated. The potential consequence of such self-objectification is addictive behaviour: as pain (and pleasure) is interpreted as a manageable sensation, the actors become dependent on the tools securing their painless existence. Hybrid subjectivities are born, constituted of human and non-human components. These possibilities are explored in Chapter 6.

Notes

1 Of course, Scarry's approach also has blindspots of its own: it has been criticized both for the over-emphasizing of the unsharability of pain (Fannin, 2019) and the reintroduction of the body-mind dualism (Dawney and Huzar, 2019).

2 Bendelow and Williams argue that the experience of pain implies a question of theodicy (1995: 93). Scarry also explains the emergence of belief (that is the establishment of a transcendental authority) by pointing to the ontological difference between the immaterial (thus invulnerable) God and the vulnerable human, which grounds an unquestionable subordination (1985: 183).

3 The historical sources referred below identify early modernity as a period roughly between the 15th and 18th centuries characterized by the parallel existence of non-secular worldviews and social structures, which are complemented by phenomena questioning their validity, such as reformation, the exploration of the new world, the birth of empiricist science, commercialization, political revolutions (Enenkel, 2009).

4 Needless to say, most of the below analyzed reflections are not moral in their approach (i.e. they do not question the general benevolence of modern biomedicine), but rather structural: by highlighting the unintended consequences, they reveal the distortive potentials of healing and pain management independently from the intention of the practitioners.

5 Of course that does not mean the elimination of violence as such: its exported or marginalized forms not only exist, but also flourish with the introduction of new technologies of hurting (McSorley, 2019).

6 Even though attempts of expanding the horizon of the biomedical approach, such as 'holistic medicine' or the 'biopsychosocial model' are not unknown, their impact still remained marginal compared to the mainstream positivist paradigm. The former approach is usually criticized for not being scientific enough (Kopelman and Moskop, 1981), the latter is considered by many to be 'vague, useless, and even incoherent – clinically, scientifically and philosophically' (Bolton and Gillett, 2019).

7 Of course, the criticism of these reifying tendencies is not completely unknown for the medical paradigm. Recently, reflections advocating the further need of improvement towards a client centred, reflexive medicine became more frequent (Prilleltensky, 2005) – however, they are still far from becoming the mainstream approach.

8 Some even argue that in modernity, the experience of pain caused by chronic illness and suffering originating from depression becomes phenomenologically undistinguishable (Ratcliffe, 2015: 87).

9 In different ways similar diagnoses appear in theories on 'bare life' (Agamben, 1998) and 'necropolitics' (Mbembe, 2003).

10 The most obvious recent example is the discourse on 'opioid epidemics', which reveals the paradox of medical paradigm uncritically mishandling any forms of suffering through the logic of painkilling, thus causing further pain (Netherland and Hansen, 2016).

11 That does not mean such praxes are completely unknown. In liminal situations, such as palliative care, the biomedical paradigm may be complemented with existentialist counselling or even with religious support (Steinberg, 2011). However, these praxes represent rather the exceptions, then the usual praxes.

12 The phenomenological interrelatedness of pain and the experience of evil can also be analyzed from the meaninglessness of pain: if it proves to serve no purpose, it implies a negative answer to the question of theodicy (Dahl, 2017). From this perspective, the power from indirect pain represents a social structure responsible for 'useless suffering' (Levinas, 2002).

13 Accordingly, power from indirect pain is related to solidarity: it is the result of dysfunctional or lacking social support. These issues are further explored in Chapter 8.

14 It should be emphasized that the extent of such impact does not depend on the frequency of those who have first-hand experience about the unintended consequences of a failing biomedical complex. As the biomedical model is in a hegemonic position, it expresses the 'final truth' of pain, which has consequences for the 'final truth' of power as well. Accordingly, it establishes an idealtypical horizon of expectations.

References

Agamben, G. (1998) *Homo Sacer: Sovereign Power and Bare Life*. Stanford, CA: Stanford University Press.

Bendelow, G. and Williams, S. (1995) Pain and the Mind-Body Dualism: A Sociological Approach. *Body and Society*, 1: 83–103.

Biehl, J. (2010) Human Pharmakon Symptoms, Technologies, Subjectivities. In Good, B., Fischer, M. M. J., Willen, S. and Good, M. J. D. V. (Eds.), *A Reader in Medical Anthropology: Theoretical Trajectories, Emergent Realities*. Malden, MA: Wiley-Blackwell, 213–231.

Boltanski, L. and Chiapello, È (2005) *The New Spirit of Capitalism*. London and New York, NY: Verso.

Bolton, D. and Gillett, G. (2019) *The Biopsychosocial Model of Health and Disease*. Cham: Palgrave Pivot.

Carman, T. (1999) The Body in Husserl and Merleau-Ponty. *Philosophical Topics*, 27: 205–226.

Castells, M. (2010) *The Information Age: Economy, Society, and Culture* (Vol. 1). Oxford: Blackwell Publishers.

Clark, A. (2011) Domestic Violence, Past and Present. *Journal of Women's History*, 23(3): 193–202.

Cohen, L. (1999) Where It Hurts: Indian Material for an Ethics of Organ Transplantation. *Daedalus*, 128(4): 135–166.

Culley, S. (2014) Killing Pain? Aspirin, Emotion and Subjectivity. In Boddice, R. (Ed.), *Pain and Emotion in Modern History*. London: Palgrave Macmillan, 130–147.

Das, V. and Das, R. K. (2007) How the Body Speaks: Illness and the Lifeworld Among the Urban Poor. In Biehl, J., Good, B. and Kleinman, A. (Eds.), *Subjectivity: Ethnographic Investigations*. Berkeley, CA: University of California Press, 66–97.

Dahl, E. (2017) The Inner Tension of Pain and the Phenomenology of Evil. *International Journal of Philosophy and Theology*, 78(4–5): 396–406.

Dawney, L. and Huzar, T. J. (2019) Introduction: The Legacies and Limits of the Body in Pain *Body and Society*, 25(3): 3–21.

Double, D. B. (2006) *Critical Psychiatry*. London: Palgrave Macmillan.

Elias, N. (2000) *The Civilizing Process. Sociogenetic and Psychogenetic Investigations*. Oxford: Blackwell.

Enenkel, K. (2009) *The Sense of Suffering Constructions of Physical Pain in Early Modern Culture*. Leiden: Brill Academic Publishers.

Fannin, M. (2019) Labour Pain, 'Natal Politics' and Reproductive Justice for Black Birth Givers. *Body and Society*, 25(3): 22–48.

Fassin, D. (2009) Another Politics of Life Is Possible. *Theory, Culture & Society*, 26(5): 44–60.

Foucault, M. (1977) *Discipline and Punish: The Birth of the Prison*. New York, NY: Random House.

Foucault, M. (1982) The Subject and Power. *Critical Inquiry*, 8(4): 777–795.

Foucault, M. (1997) *Society Must Be Defended: Lectures at the Collège De France. 1975–1976*. New York, NY: St. Martin's Press.

Foucault, M. (2003) *The Birth of the Clinic. An Archaeology of Medical Perception*. London: Routledge.

Geniusas, S. (2017) Phenomenology of Chronic Pain: De-Personalization and Re-Personalization. In van Rysewyk, S. (Ed.), *Meanings of Pain*. Dordrecht and New York, NY: Springer, 147–166.

Ginsburg, F. and Rapp, R. (2016) Not Dead Yet' Changing Disability Imaginaries in the Twenty-First Century. In Das, V. and Han, C. (Eds.), *Living and Dying in the Contemporary World: A Compendium*. Berkeley, CA: University of California Press, 525–542.

Goesling, J., Lin, L. A. and Clauw, D. (2018) Psychiatry and Pain Management: At the Intersection of Chronic Pain and Mental Health. *Current Psychiatry Reports*, 20(2): 12–20.

Good, B. (1994) *Medicine, Rationality and Experience: An Anthropological Perspective*. Cambridge: Cambridge University Press.

Good, M. J. D. V. (2007) The Medical Imaginary and the Biotechnical Embrace: Subjective Experiences of Clinical Scientists and Patients. In Biehl, J., Good, B. and Kleinman, A. (Eds.), *Subjectivity: Ethnographic Investigations*. Berkeley, CA: University of California Press, 362–381.

Hardon, A. and Sanabria, E. (2017) Fluid Drugs: Revisiting the Anthropology of Pharmaceuticals. *Annual Review of Anthropology*, 46: 117–132.

Husserl, E. (1989) *Ideas Pertaining to a Pure Phenomenology and to a Phenomenological Philosophy – Second Book: Studies in the Phenomenology of Constitution*. Dordrecht: Kluwer.

Inhorn, M. C. (2010) Quest for Conception Gender, Infertility, and Egyptian Medical Traditions in Good. In Fischer, B., Willen, M. M. J. and Good, S. (Eds.), *A Reader in Medical Anthropology: Theoretical Trajectories, Emergent Realities*. Malden, MA: Wiley-Blackwell, 319.

Jackson, J. (1992) 'After a While No One Believes You' Real and Unreal Pain. In Good, M. J. D. V., Brodwin, P., Good, B. and Kleinman, A. (Eds.), *Pain as Human Experience: An Anthropological Perspective*. Berkeley, CA: University of California Press, 138–168.

Kleinman, A. (1973) Medicine's Symbolic Reality: On a Central Problem in the Philosophy of Medicine. *Inquiry*, 16(1–4): 206–213.

Kleinman, A. and Kleinman, J. (1991) Suffering and Its Professional Transformation: Toward an Ethnography of Interpersonal Experience. *Culture, Medicine and Psychiatry*, 15(3): 275–301.

Kopelman, L. and Moskop, J. (1981) The Holistic Health Movement: A Survey and Critique. *Journal of Medical Philosophy*, 6(2): 209–235.

Korsten, F. W. (2009) Bodies in Pain and the Transcendental Organization of History in Joost Van Den Vondel. In Enenkel, K. (Ed.), *The Sense of Suffering Constructions of Physical Pain in Early Modern Culture*. Leiden: Brill Academic Publishers, 377–403.

Le Goff, J. (1992) *Medieval Civilization: 400–1500*. Oxford: Blackwell Publishers.

Levinas, E. (2002) Useless Suffering. In Bernasconi, R. and Wood, D. (Eds.), *The Provocation of Levinas: Rethinking the Other*. London: Routledge, 156.

Macdonald, G. and Leary, M. (2005) Why Does Social Exclusion Hurt? The Relationship between Social and Physical Pain. *Psychological Bulletin*, 131: 202–223.

Madsen, W. (2017) Early 20th Century Conceptualization of Health Promotion, *Health Promotion International*, 32(6): 1041–1047.

Mbembe, A. (2003) Necropolitics. *Public Culture*, 15(1): 11–40.

McKeown, T. (2004) Medical Issues in Historical Demography. *International Journal of Epidemiology*, 34: 515–520.

McSorley, K. (2019) Predatory War, Drones and Torture: Remapping the Body in Pain. *Body and Society*, 25(3): 73–99.

Mc Mahon, R., Eibach, J. and Roth, R. (2013) Making Sense of Violence? Reflections on the History of Interpersonal Violence in Europe. *Crime, History & Societies*, 17(2): 5–26.

Merleau-Ponty, M. (1962) *Phenomenology of Perception*. London: Routledge & Kegan Paul.

Moscoso, J. (2012) *Pain: A Cultural History*. Basingstoke: Palgrave Macmillan.

Muchembled, R. (2012) *A History of Violence: From the End of the Middle Ages to the Present*. Malden, MA: Polity Press.

Netherland, J. and Hansen, H. (2016) The War on Drugs That Wasn't: Wasted Whiteness, 'Dirty Doctors' and Race in Media Coverage of Prescription Opioid Misuse. *Culture, Medicine, and Psychiatry*, 40(4): 664–686.

Nguyen, V. K. and Peschard, K. (2003) Anthropology, Inequality, and Disease: A Review. *Annual Review of Anthropology*, 32(1): 447–474.

Petryna, A. (2004) Biological Citizenship: The Science and Politics of Chernobyl-Exposed Populations. *Osiris*, 19(1): 250–265.

Prilleltensky, I. (2005) Promoting Well-Being: Time for a Paradigm Shift in Health and Human Services. *Scandinavian Journal of Public Health*, 33(suppl 66): 53–60.

Rajan, K. S. (2007) Experimental Values: Indian Clinical Trials and Surplus Health. *New Left Review*, 45(3): 67–88.

Ratcliffe, M. (2015) *Experiences of Depression*. Oxford: Oxford University Press.

Rose, N. (1999a) *Powers of Freedom: Reframing Political Thought*. Cambridge: Cambridge University Press.

Rose, N. (1999b) *Governing the Soul: The Shaping of the Private Self*. London: Free Association Books.

Scarry, E. (1985) *The Body in Pain: The Making and Unmaking of the World*. New York, NY and Oxford: Oxford University Press.

Schleifer, R. (2014) *Pain and Suffering*. London: Routledge.

Schoenfeldt, M. (2009) Aesthetics and Anesthetics: The Art of Pain Management in Early Modern England. In Enenkel, K. (Ed.), *The Sense of Suffering Constructions of Physical Pain in Early Modern Culture*. Leiden: Brill Academic Publishers, 19–39.

Singh, R. (2017) The Pain: How Does Anthropology Look at It? Suffering of Body and Mind. *Ethnologia Actualis*, 17: 123–139.

Snelgrove, S. (2017) An Interpretative Phenomenological Analysis of Non-Malignant Chronic Low Back Pain. In van Rysewyk, S. (Ed.), *Meanings of Pain*. Dordrecht and New York, NY: Springer, 129–147.

Steinberg, S. M. (2011) Cultural and Religious Aspects of Palliative Care. *International Journal of Critical Illness and Injury Science*, 1: 154–156.

Svenaeus, F. (2015) The Phenomenology of Chronic Pain: Embodiment and Alienation. *Continental Philosophy Review*, 48(2): 107–122.

Throop, C. J. (2010) *Suffering and Sentiment: Exploring the Vicissitudes of Experience and Pain in Yap*. Berkeley, CA: University of California Press.

Ticktin, M. (2006) Where Ethics and Politics Meet: The Violence of Humanitarianism in France. *American Ethnologist*, 33(1): 33–49.

Tousignant, N. (2014) A Quantity of Suffering: Measuring Pain as Emotion in the Mid-Twentieth-Century USA. In Boddice, R. (Ed.), *Pain and Emotion in Modern History*. London: Palgrave Macmillan, 111–129.

Traninger, A. (2009) Whipping Boys: Erasmus' Rhetoric of Corporeal Punishment and its Discontents. In Enenkel, K. (Ed.), *The Sense of Suffering Constructions of Physical Pain in Early Modern Culture*. Leiden: Brill Academic Publishers, 39–59.

Weber, M. (2005) *The Protestant Ethic and the Spirits of Capitalism*. New York, NY: Routledge.

Weber, K., Thomas, L. G. and Rao, H. (2009) From Streets to Suites: How the Anti-Biotech Movement Affected German Pharmaceutical Firms. *American Sociological Review*, 74(1): 106–127.

Woods, R. (2007) Medical and Demographic History: Inseparable? *Social History of Medicine*, 20(3): 483–503.

Part II

Networks of depression, anxiety and addiction

The idealtypical transformations introduced in the first part explore a process, which can be best described as the emptying of suffering. The first dimension originates from the promise of overcoming suffering through ownership: if this potential remains untapped, the subjects are left perplexed, while missing any reliable alternative interpretative frameworks (such as a religious one) – that is the experience of depression. The second dimension originates from the lost horizon of positive integration – that is the experience of a constant, diffuse fear or anxiety. The third dimension originates from the discrepancy between the hegemonic, yet objectifying biomedical technologies – implying the experience of ignorance and potentially addictive behaviour patterns related to reification. Although, these social historical transformations differ in many sense, they still point to the same direction of emptying suffering by gradually depriving it from meanings. The horizon of control through property is based on the assumption that suffering is meaningful only if endured as an investment, in exchange for future profit. The experience of depression indicates the trap of this tendency: in case of the suffering is not controllable, or the countermeasures are not acquirable, then the vacuum collapses on the subject, resulting in hopelessness. The experience of anxiety related to negative integration indicates the isolation of the sufferer: as collective countermeasures are not considered to be possible anymore, exclusively individual strategies are pursued, which are not capable of ensuring any sense of security (a possibility depending on trustful intersubjectivity). As the horizon of biomedical pain management reduces suffering into its bodily dimension, it blocks those interpretative processes, which could integrate the experience into one's identity. Without such consolidation, the only way of relating to suffering is to rely on the repeating of physical treatment, that is, to become dependent on pain killing technologies.

Based on the first part, it may be concluded that the modern forms of suffering are equally related to the phenomenological process of emptying. In the second part, the sociological consequences of such constellation are mapped. While emptying suffering on the level of available meanings, mechanisms of integration and power structures opens the path for the emergence of depression, anxiety and addiction, solely these long term transformations

DOI: 10.4324/9781003197355-6

are not suitable to explain mental disorders. For this purpose, comprehensive sociological models are needed, which are capable of establishing a connection between distorted forms of micro and macro social integration and distressed phenomenological patterns. Chapters 4–6 elaborate such models, while relying on various social theoretical tools. Depression is analyzed as a social suffering related to the distorted communicative and competitive mechanisms of action coordination. Anxiety is explained as a detachment of fear from concrete events, which phenomenological narrowness is related to insecure and untrustworthy networks, incapable of narrating and managing fear in a reassuring manner. Addiction is reinterpreted as a partly self-objectified, hybrid subjectivity, which is related to the emergence of acceleration and information society. While the first part outlined the general structural transformations resulting in empty suffering, the following analyses explore those particular social constellations, where actors become susceptible to its consequences, namely depression, anxiety and addiction.

4 Depression as social suffering

Distortions of communicative and competitive interactions

From a genealogical perspective, it may be argued that the prevalence of depression increases due to complex transformations adjusting time consciousness, intersubjectivity and everyday agency to the logic of absolute dominion (see Chapter 1). In order to refine this general conclusion, those social spaces have to be explored, where the potential distortions are actualized. These include the fields of material and symbolic struggles (Bourdieu), along with the linguistic and mediatized cooperative interactions (Habermas). Based on these premises, the following chapter aims at identifying the integration mechanisms actualizing the distortive potential of absolute dominion by combining the psychopathology of depression with critical social theories.

However, such synthesis has its own challenges: the relationship between critical theories and psy-sciences has always been a controversial one. Following classic approaches like those of Goffman (1961) and Foucault (2006), social theories tend to look at the knowledge provided by psychiatry and psychology as epistemologically problematic.[1] Such suspicion resulted mostly in the negligence of psychopathological knowledge. In order to overcome the disciplinary distance, a common ground needs to be established: the concepts of mental disorders and social suffering have to be linked.

Suffering is a common field of interest of psy-discourses (seeking therapeutic treatments) and critical theories (seeking a normative basis[2]). Yet, the latter have developed an overly narrow approach to suffering: instead of analyzing its wide empirical spectrum, only those aspects are taken into consideration, which are compatible with one or another sociological framework and the related concept of political mobilization (Renault, 2010).[3] Being preoccupied with its particular forms, critical theories never undertook the task of systematically mapping the various phenomenological forms of suffering. This task was delegated to psychopathology aiming at lessening or eliminating them. The arbitrary negligence of critical theories can be corrected by rehabilitating psy-knowledge in the eyes of critical theory: explanatory models of mental disorders have to be reinterpreted as empirical descriptions of extreme suffering (characterized not only by distress, but also the inability of overcoming it), which can be used for grounding a normative basis. However, such rehabilitation should not imply the uncritical acceptance of psychopathological

DOI: 10.4324/9781003197355-7

explanations. According to sociological criticism, psychopathological models tend to ignore the broader social component of suffering. In order to avoid such shortcoming, the limited or latent social components of psychopathological explanations need to be elaborated. These considerations outline the ground of a synthesis: mental disorders can be reinterpreted as social suffering by complementing the psy-models with the related latent structural distortions.[4]

The following chapter demonstrates how such a synthesis can be elaborated: Bourdieu's and Habermas' critical theories are complemented with clinical descriptions of depression. In the first section, the most important ideas contained in these influential theories are reviewed, with special emphasis on how they understand the personal consequences of the distorted patterns of social integration. The aim is not only to introduce the individual experiences of social suffering as understood by these theories, but also to highlight their limitations, and thus indicate those points where the theories require complementing. In the second section, the clinical understanding of depression is summarized as it appears in diagnostic manuals and textbooks (that express a falsified 'minimal consensus' of psy-discourses). Besides characterizing the symptoms and the most common causal models, an attempt is also made to highlight those points of argumentation where, implicitly or explicitly, a social element appears, as these intersections provide an opportunity to connect psychological and sociological models. In the third section, Bourdieu's and Habermas' critical theories are combined with the psychological explanations of depression. The aim of this synthesis is to specify those social constellations which threaten with a depressive pattern of suffering.

Distortions of integration and experiences of suffering

According to Horkheimer, the most significant characteristic of critical theories is their attempt to understand existing forms of society from the perspective of potential ones (1976). In this sense, critical theories include both the elements of theory of society ('how are societies integrated?') and utopia ('how could societies be integrated in a less distorted way?'). These two components define critical theories as an autonomous subfield of sociology, distinguishing them from both other forms of social criticism that lack a specific theory of integration (e.g. gender-based or postcolonial criticism) and social theories that lack a normative grounding (e.g. system or network theory). The most important contemporary critical theories differ along these two dimensions: they may rely on alternative normative bases, and they may also explain the processes of integration by referring to different concepts of action coordination. In what follows I choose two authors from this rich tradition. The opinions of Bourdieu and Habermas represent probably the two most influential – but fundamentally different – solutions at both of these levels (Susen, 2007). While Bourdieu focuses on the multi-dimensional space of inequalities, Habermas is concerned with the moral and democratic quality of interactions. Even if their theories do not cover every aspect of social life, together they provide a comprehensive approach that is appropriate for demonstrating the argument presented in this chapter. Both authors provide a model of how social integration may become distorted and what type of social suffering emerges as a result. However, as they approach them from the perspective of integrational dysfunctions, they work with an overly narrow set of sufferings, which needs to be complemented.

At the heart of Bourdieu's theory lies an extended concept of capital. Material and symbolic capitals structure social actions by differentiating between the possible and the impossible. Around each capital a field emerges in which actors compete for the same goals with the help of accessible resources. As capitals determine the sphere of possibilities, they outline structural positions characterized by similar potentials. The relationship between the former is fundamentally conflictual: as they compete for the same resources, they are inevitably involved in a zero-sum game (Bourdieu and Wacquant, 1992: 97). Despite this latent conflict of interest, the everyday operation of the fields is usually pacified, as ensured by illusion-framing competition as a meaningful and fair activity. Even if actors in different positions have unequal chances of accumulating capital, this illusion is capable of legitimizing hierarchies by obscuring prevailing class differences (Bourdieu, 1998). Maintaining a legitimate order depends on success with naturalizing inequalities: i.e. the reinterpretation of social inequalities as natural differences (e.g. meritocracy claiming class differences are the consequence of variation in talent and effort). Such naturalization of existing class relations can be understood as symbolic violence in the sense that it relies on the interiorization of arbitrary meanings and evaluations that ground one's relation to the world. Besides the implications at the level of the intentionality of actors, such a process also affects one's corporeal and dispositional level, creating various forms of class habitus. Habitus expresses one's position in the multidimensional space of fields by determining the horizon of aspirations and the accessible strategies of acquisition (Bourdieu, 1990: 53).

According to Bourdieu, as the legitimacy of interpersonal relationships depends on the symbolically violent veiling of actual class interests, the very act of doing sociological analysis is inherently critical. Furthering an understanding of what holds together social units is inseparable from unveiling hidden class interests, the limitations of habitus, and the arbitrariness of naturalizing illusions. According to Bourdieu, the naturalized reproduction of class positions ultimately results in life strategies built around various patterns of misery, such as the anxiety of the precarious worker whose factory has closed, or the resignation of the immigrant who is on the one hand exploited on job markets, and on the other is faced with prejudices (Bourdieu et al., 1999). While such miseries are related to the latent reproduction of inequalities, this does not mean that a subordinated class position in itself implies the experience of suffering. In many cases, deprived structural positions are complemented with strategies aimed at breaking out from the given constraints (de Certeau, 1984; Rafieian and Davis, 2016). Therefore, it is rather argued that inequality is one among many dimensions which results in individual suffering only in conjunction with other distortions of social and interpersonal relationships. In order to specify the cases in which a deprived field position results in an unbearable life, the perspective of capitals needs to be complemented with the systematic analysis of empirical forms of suffering.

Habermas differentiates between two levels of social integration: the lifeworld reproduced by a series of speech acts, and systems maintained by communication through symbolically generalized mediums. The former refers to the natural understanding of a world that is an unquestioned horizon of social action. As long as naturalized meanings secure the frames of achieving instrumental goals and coordinating interactions, a lifeworld may function as an unreflected-on set of assumptions that serve as a recipe for everyday life. However, when such meanings become problematic and stop enabling everyday practices, actors start reflecting on them. Such reflection takes place not only in the realm of consciousness, but also in speech acts oriented at mutual understanding. By renewing the interpretation of the world through a communicative process, a genuinely shared horizon is born which is capable of not only orienting actors in an instrumental way, but also of integrating social units (Habermas, 1984: 329). However, complex societies cannot solely rely on linguistic interactions. As a result of functional differentiation the mutual lifeworld has shrunk, giving way to alternative mechanisms of integration. Instead of communicatively renewed shared meanings, these mechanisms rely on automatized means of action coordination enabled by symbolically generalized mediums such as money or law. Unlike the communicatively reproduced lifeworld, these mediums enable the cooperation of actors belonging to incommensurable lifeworlds, as long as they both comply with the related semantics and logic. Around such mediums subsystems emerge (e.g. economies and administration) which create their own realities. These are given to actors as a secondary nature with special rules and constraints (Habermas, 1987: 155).

At the heart of Habermas' social criticism is the potential for undistorted communication based on a pure exchange of arguments, and leading to a consensual interpretation of the world. Obviously, such a utopian scenario is endangered by many factors, such as intentional manipulation or unintentional dogmatic speech acts (Habermas, 1990: 166–167). Besides these intersubjective factors, systems also threaten communicative action by gradually replacing them (colonization). As a consequence of the distortion of communicative action, crises emerge at the level of culture, integration and personality in the form of loss of meaning, anomie and psychopathologies (Habermas, 1987: 143). In this sense, Habermas directly links social- and psychopathologies. However, lacking further attention to this issue, the author's theoretical gesture can be interpreted rather as an indication of an open question, not as an elaborated part of the theory. The connection between distortions of social integration and actual suffering is further complicated by the fact that even Habermas refers to certain communicative distortions as justifiable. By rehabilitating systems as functional necessities, he tries to locate a social sphere wherein reification is legitimate, and criticizes only the unlimited expansion of such a sphere as self-destructive (Honneth, 2006: 126–127). According to Habermas, the distortion of speech acts on its own does not automatically imply suffering. As in many cases, the limitation of communicative action is inevitable, the normative content of the notion requires further analysis: the exact relation between types of distortion at the level of communicative action, lifeworld, system and the patterns of suffering that result in psychopathologies needs to be elaborated.[5]

The theories of Bourdieu and Habermas differ both at the level of the conceptualization of social integration and the normative basis of social criticism, while covering some of the most important logics of action coordination and normative bases. However, my argument is that, despite their strengths, they fail to reach their goal of providing a universal means of criticizing social phenomena. The fact that Bourdieu and Habermas do not link distortions of social integration to the empirical variety of suffering causes problems not only because it makes falsification of the theories difficult, but also because the lack of elaboration on this level undermines the critical potential of the theories. Referring to sufferings of social origin without taking into consideration the fullest available list of empirical forms of personal suffering threatens to create both theoretical blindspots and false conclusions. By arbitrarily excluding some forms of suffering from the horizon of social criticism, on the one hand potentially widespread or devastating ones are ignored, while on the other important theoretical potential remains untapped. The empirical spectrum of suffering could orient critical theories in the sense that it implies the reverse task: instead of deriving forms of suffering from philosophical constructs (as current critical theories do), a typology of the distortions of social integration can be elaborated based on the various empirical patterns of suffering. In case of every specific extremities of suffering, the following question can be posed: what kind of distortion contributes to their occurrence in the differently integrated social spheres? In what follows, this question is analyzed with the help of psychotherapeutic descriptions of depression.

Psy-discourses of depression

Although therapeutic descriptions of individual suffering provide the most complete list of the empirical forms of suffering, this does not mean that these descriptions are free from theoretical limitations of their own. Therefore, it requires clarification how critical theories may relate to them. To answer this question those reflections need to be taken into consideration which attempt to clarify the epistemological and ontological nature of psychopathologies. The biological positivism of psychiatry is located at one endpoint of the spectrum in explaining psychopathologies as bodily illness. The opposite of this approach is expressed by the various, mostly incompatible theories labelled 'anti-psychiatry' (Double, 2006). On the one hand, this broad category includes those opinions which deny the existence of mental illness either by arguing that only organs can suffer disease, not patterns of behaviour (Szasz, 1961), or argues that psychopathologies are actually deviant behaviour patterns arbitrarily labelled with the essentializing stigma of abnormality (Scheff, 1999). On the other hand, anti-psychiatry advocates also include those who think of mental illness as a comprehensible response to an insane world, resulting in the disassociation of the individual (Laing and Esterson, 1964), or reactions to the alienating nature of capitalism (Cooper, 1980; Deleuze and Guattari, 1977). While all of these criticisms challenge the biomedical paradigm, their radicalism has led to their gradual marginalization compared to the content of positivist psychiatry.

In place of anti-psychiatry, new, less radical approaches have emerged in sociological discourses of mental health. 'Social realism' indicates a stance of maintaining a distance from both a biologically reductionist view of mental illness and radical constructivism. Instead, it views mental illness as having a biological and psychological causal structure which is also embedded in a socially constructed setting (Rogers and Pilgrim, 2014: 12–14). Advocates of the sociology of mental disorders complement this approach by defining their subject as 'harmful dysfunctions' (Wakefield, 1992). As any distress can be functional (e.g. sadness experienced as a result of loss), only those forms should be understood as disorders which emerge without 'adequate' reason (e.g. sadness experienced without loss). In this sense, a mental disorder is always the result of incompatibility between agent and environment, opening up the possibility of understanding it from the perspective of the distortions of the latter (Busfield, 2011: 145).

These various approaches provide an opportunity for translating psy-discourses of depression into objects of use in critical theories. Psychotherapy and psychiatry come into contact with various extreme cases of suffering which emerge during the life course, rendering both actors and their social environment helpless. While these therapeutic practices may differ in many aspects, they still share a set of basic assumptions covering both the viewpoint of diagnoses and explanations. I refer to this set as the minimal consensus of psy-discourses that functions as mutually accepted core knowledge as appears in diagnostic manuals and widely accepted educational textbooks. In what follows, I will reconstruct the basic features and explanations of depression based on such sources. As the aim of the reconstruction is to inform critical theories, I focus on those models which include social components such as interaction patterns, collective routines and representations or structural positions. I view these psy-models as social realist descriptions of harmful dysfunctions. This means that while giving credit to the explanations appearing in them, I also modify their emphases by reinterpreting the identified inner dysfunctions as social distortions.

According to the most recent edition of the American Psychiatric Association's diagnostic manual, depression is characterized by the following chronic symptoms: depressed mood, diminished interest in activities, drastic change of weight and appetite, sleeping disorder, permanent fatigue, feelings of worthlessness, inappropriate guilt, incapability of concentrating, recurrent thoughts of death. If at least five of these symptoms are present within a two-week period, while a depressed mood is present throughout most of the day, nearly every day, psychiatry talks about major depressive disorder (APA, 2013: 160–164). Even if the diagnostic manual strictly limits itself to the most basic information, it still provides some general guidelines about the social components of the emergence of depression. Depression is a phenomenological horizon, characterized by an inability to find pleasure in the world. Placing this observation in a sociological framework, we may argue that experiencing pleasure may be blocked not only by inner constraints, but also social ones. Those who are persistently excluded from pleasant activities by concrete 'others' (e.g. over-regulating norms) or structural effects (e.g. a lack of resources) are actually exposed to experiences resembling a depressed mood. Such deprivation from pleasure, if maintained for a longer period, may slowly deconstruct the various components of agency, as expressed in the experiences of superfluity (guilt, worthlessness), disturbances of basic routines (eating and sleeping problems) and diminishing capacities (concentration and motivation-related problems). Similarly to the inability to experience pleasure, the deconstruction of agency may be the result of social factors, in addition to having internal causes. If one is persistently deprived of recognition (e.g. belongs to a minority group), has their most basic bodily functions disturbed (e.g. works according to unpredictable timeframes) or is excluded from engaging in autonomous action (e.g. has a precarious or automated job), her agency is actually dissolved by the social environment. In this sense, depression could be interpreted as a result of the interiorization of a distorted social constellation.

These correspondences can be further elaborated with the help of dominant psychological explanations of depression. Early psychoanalysis-themed literature argued that symptoms of depression are similar to grief in many ways: the loss of a loved one in many cases results in regression to a state when one cannot differentiate oneself from another. While such process of grief is widespread in its temporary form, in certain cases it may become chronic and turn into depression. Individuals whose needs were inadequately dealt with during childhood (either insufficiently satisfied, or over-nurtured) remain dependent on the loved other, making them incapable of dealing with their loss (Freud, 1917). Similar processes of regression apply to symbolic or imagined losses as well, explaining the emergence of depression without actual death. Object relation theory advances these observations in the direction of understanding depression as a consequence of relationships that make one feel insecure. Separation or loss in early childhood has significant potential to contribute to the emergence of depression (Beidel et al., 2012: 223–224; Comer, 2010: 251–255).

Behaviourist approaches describe the emergence of depression as a process of maladaptation: if positive feedback becomes scarce, one loses the motivation to engage in socially acclaimed action, resulting in even fewer rewards, leading to completely giving up on activity. In this sense, the loss of social rewards plays a key role in the emergence of depression (Lewinsohn et al., 1979). Cognitive theories provide an alternative explanation by arguing that, instead of a lack of social incentives, negative thoughts that lead to gradual isolation are responsible for loss of agency. Children who acquire maladaptive patterns of attribution and attitudes during interaction with their environment will underestimate the importance of joyful events and their contribution to them, while overestimating the significance of joyless events and their own responsibility in their occurrence. These errors of thinking function as automatic thoughts. They are responsible for a one-dimensional, negativistic perception of the world, which makes the individual feel depressed (Beck, 1967). The theory of learned helplessness complements these observations by highlighting the importance of the experience of losing control. According to this theory, deprivation of rewards or negative attribution patterns alone are not responsible for depression, but a specific combination of the two may be. Depression arises when individuals feel that they are losing control over achieving positive feedback, and blame themselves for this failure (Seligman, 1975). If the experience of not being able to affect what may or may not happen is paired with the lack of any explanation other than one's own inability, then the scope in which to make a difference is destroyed, rendering acting futile (Beidel et al., 2012: 225–227; Comer, 2010: 255–259).

Sociocultural approaches emphasize the interpersonal and structural factors contributing to the emergence of depression. Considering communication and social skills, depression is more prevalent among people who have difficulty expressing themselves and require above-average social reassurance, which both increase the chance of isolation. A lack of social support in relationships with trustworthy or intimate others also plays a significant role, as without them there is no one to help with overcoming losses or failures (Barlow and Durand, 2009: 231–237). Gender differences are also decisive, which is a result of the coexistence of multiple factors: if vulnerability factors (e.g. the lack of a confiding relationship) are complemented with provoking agents (e.g. bereavement) and symptom-formation factors (e.g. previous episodes of depression) women become especially susceptible to depression (Brown and Harris, 1978). Structural explanations focus on ethnic and social differences: belonging to ethnic minorities and to deprived social classes are considered to be risk factors as they suggest social positions where both recognition and control are scarce, while negative, blaming judgments are frequent. In these disadvantageous social positions, learned helplessness is the consequence of social effects that include deprivation of control and self-blaming narratives (Comer, 2010: 259–263).

With the help of these various psychological theories, a more detailed picture of the emergence of depression can be drawn, helping us outline those social mechanisms and environments which threaten to deprive of pleasure and dissolve agency. Psychoanalysis calls attention to the question of dependence on actual others and symbolic tokens. While this approach understands dependence as a result of under- or over-nurture, from a sociological point of view we may argue that dependence is inseparable from social life. Everyone is dependent on either concrete others (e.g. caretakers) or abstract institutional entities (e.g. social insurance) which are responsible for their material and nonmaterial reproduction. If these entities are lacking (e.g. during periods of unemployment) and material or nonmaterial needs remain unfulfilled, then a depressed mood will be the expression of an actual state of helplessness instead of one of regression. These observations can be further clarified by referring to the focus of object relation theory on insecurity. Feeling secure or insecure is characteristic of any social constellation, depending on others' willingness and capability to provide help in times of need. Accordingly, it is not only early childhood experiences but any sustained experience of insecurity (e.g. employment in a precarious job) that can contribute to depression.

Based on the behaviourist approach, sociological explanations can thus refer to those social constellations where positive feedback is rare. Beside those few identified in previous research (gender, race and class inequalities), social theory may provide a systematic framework for conceptualizing the deprivation of various forms of recognition (e.g. Honneth, 1996). Cognitive theory draws attention to those processes of socialization which result in maladaptive attitudes and attributions. From a social theoretical point of view, such patterns of relating to the world are dependent on those interactions where they are reconstructed. In this sense, they are rooted in actual social networks which devalue joy (e.g. puritan traditions), idealize suffering (e.g. ideologies of martyrdom), question the significance of the individual (e.g. collectivist cultures), or over-emphasize personal responsibility (e.g. milieu in which protestant ethics abound). In such networks negative automatic thoughts are not errors of individual thought processes but involve a socially transmitted framework of understanding the world. The theory of learned helplessness refers to social constellations where, on the one hand, one is deprived of control, while on the other hand no other explanations for failure are accessible than personal inadequacy. This happens in those subordinated social constellations where opportunities are extensively determined by structural positions, while inequalities are successfully legitimized (e.g. neoliberal markets).

From this review of the most widely accepted psy-discourses about depression (with the exception of biological explanations) it is clear that they have a wide role to play in informing critical theories. In the case of every social theoretical framework the following questions might be raised. Under what circumstances do the various mechanisms of action coordination strengthen the sentiment of insecurity by endangering key resources? Is positive, reinforcing feedback missing? Do the collective representations emphasize the significance of negative events and burden the individual with responsibility, while devaluing the importance of positive events and reducing the contribution of the individual? Are individual actors deprived of control over their action, while also lacking the potential for revolting against subordination? On the one hand, these dimensions highlight the social factors involved in the emergence of depression: if one's social environment is constituted of relationships characterized by the conjunction of such distortions, then a depressed mood will appear as a phenomenological consequence of the social constellation. On the other hand, these distortions are capable of grounding the normative basis of critical theories: as their conjunction results in extreme suffering, they can be evaluated as pathologies of integration. In the following section we return to Bourdieu's and Habermas' theory and complement them with these insights.

Depressive distortions of social integration

The first question that needs to be answered concerns the location of the psychological dimensions of depression in the different conceptual levels of the various social theoretical frameworks. In social theoretical terms, insecurity can be understood as the unpredictability of social constellations. If the outcomes of either instrumental activities or interactions are contingent, then instability becomes a dominant experience. To prevent this, every society develops mechanisms responsible for minimizing contingency, which are conceptualized differently by each theory. Bourdieu refers to the logic of fields as the structure that brings stability to society (even if an unequal one): by outlining a naturalized framework of goals and means, they define the space of possibilities, thus coordinate everyday action. Habermas argues that the backbone of functionally differentiated, complex societies is systems coordinated by generalized mediums: by providing an automatized process of communication, they manage interactions even between incommensurable lifeworlds.

The psychological notion of positive feedback can be translated into social theoretical terms as a resource provided by others through a rewarding mechanism. Such conceptualization highlights the fact that every society applies standards of worthiness and ways of redistributing collectively produced resources. Bourdieu refers to the logic of capitals, which expresses the mutually desired goals within each field: their distribution expresses the potential for positive feedback. In the Habermasian approach, the most important resource is the communicative competence relating to the ability to shape the lifeworld. Accordingly, recognition can be located on the level of speech acts.

In the social theoretical approach, negative and self-blaming representations can be understood as elements of a socially constructed reality. They can be conceptualized as parts of a wider semantic universe which is continuously renewed in various network constellations. In Bourdieu's theory, illusions represent the semantic level of social integration: this is where legitimizing narratives are elaborated, reinterpreting inequalities as natural differences. Habermas refers to the notion of lifeworld as a self-evident, meaning structure shared with others: until becoming problematic, this serves a recipe for everyday action.

The psychological concept of learned helplessness can be grasped by social theories as limitations to one's agency. Thus it can be conceptualized as a social obstacle that limits one's autonomy and prevents attempts at change. Bourdieu refers to the notion of habitus being responsible for organizing action: autonomy and the initiation of change can be grasped as part of a set of dispositions. In Habermas' approach the level of speech acts offers the chance to express autonomy: change can be initiated by arguing and convincing others.

After linking the psychological dimensions of depression to the social theoretical concepts of integration, the distorted social forms which are responsible for the emergence of such patterns of suffering can be mapped within each theoretical framework. From Bourdieu's perspective, social suffering can be explained by referring to the veiled, unequal reproduction of capitals. To further specify his diagnosis, we need to reintroduce insecurity and deprivation from positive feedback as manifesting on the level of field and capital; negativistic and self-blaming collective representations on the level of illusions; and legitimized loss of control on the level of habitus. Insecurity could appear at the level of fields as a lack of stability involving acquired capitals. This could happen both as a consequence of either the competitiveness of a contest (so capital has to be reinvested over and over again, without a chance of securing it), or the impossibility of its conversion to more stable capitals (so a portfolio cannot be diversified). In these – and other similar – cases, the actor can never be sure if the accumulated capitals will fulfil their original goal (i.e. secure the future space of possibilities) but is instead continuously exposed to the potential of losing the fruits of their efforts. Furthermore, the insecurity of capitals can be complemented by the difficulties of acquiring them. This could be the consequence of either the scarcity of resources (when the desired capitals are rare), or bias in the competition (some actors are in a disadvantaged position). In both cases the rewards of the field are accessible only to the few luckiest or most powerful, leaving others with the experience of constant deprivation.

Negativistic, self-blaming narratives may emerge on the level of illusions as part of the discourses explaining and legitimizing existing social differences. The over-emphasizing of negative events may be the consequence of either a traumatized collective memory (rendering those affected unable to cast off memories of violence, hardship or catastrophes), or a belief system focusing on a transcendental sphere instead of mundane pleasures (resulting in puritan norms and values). In both cases, negative events are naturalized as either highly probable or inevitable, which means that suffering is not only legitimate, but a widespread moral obligation. Worldviews that blame individuals for their failure may be the consequence of either hubris (overestimating one's capacity to affect fate), or a lack of solidarity (ignorance concerning the suffering of others). In these cases, individuals are considered to be responsible for themselves, thereby not only legitimizing leaving individuals on their own, but also excluding any interpretation that sees failure as anything other than deserving of self-blame.

Getting used to not having control and giving up the potential for revolting against such constellations may be described on the level of habitus. Giving up claims to autonomy may be the consequence of either growing up in subordinated field positions (getting used to not having a decisive word in defining valuable goals and approved ways of reaching them), or identifying with a strictly hierarchic field logic (interiorizing an authoritarian way of organizing social life, where a chain of command is beyond criticism or doubt). In both of these cases, every action is initiated by external agents, resulting in the basic experience of being controlled by others. Giving up willingness to revolt against personal lack of control may be the consequence of either experiencing deterrent sanctions (being punished severely for the slightest deviation from norms), or exposure to extremely effective techniques of surveillance (detection of every single deviation). In these cases, revolt against the existing constellation may seem to be either too risky or futile, leading to the preservation of the defenceless position.

After reintroducing the preconditions of depression (such as insecurity, lack of reward, negativistic, self-blaming semantics, loss of control) at the level of fields, illusion and habitus, we may continue elaborating an appropriate normative basis. Depression emerges in those constellations in which competitive, unconvertable, resourceless or biased fields are combined with traumatized, unworldly, arrogant or ignorant illusions, and segregated, authoritarian, frightened or overseen patterns of habitus. If the distortions of the fields, illusions and habitus point in the direction of a similar pattern of suffering, then they produce a coherent social reality, trapping the individual. As they provide the same experience of the impossibility of pleasure without enabling the emergence of alternative experiences, together they contribute to the dissolution of agency. However, if fields, illusions and habitus do not constitute a coherent pattern of distortion, the chance of an extreme form of suffering being invoked (taking the shape of depression) gradually decreases. If similar distortions do not characterize all three levels, the compensatory effects of either fields, illusions or habitus may provide solutions to problems arising on the other levels. Accordingly, critical theory inspired by Bourdieu should focus on the conjunction of these independent distortions, instead of simply referring to the general tendency of the veiled reproduction of inequalities.

From Habermas' perspective, social suffering can be explained by referring to the intentional, unintentional or systematic distortions of communicative action. To better specify his diagnosis, we need to reintroduce insecurity as manifesting on the level of system; negativistic and self-blaming collective representations on the level of lifeworld; and deprivation from positive feedback and legitimized loss of control on the level of communicative action. In this theoretical framework insecurity can be interpreted as the underperformance of systems based on symbolically generalized communicative mediums. This could be the result of either an increase of system complexity beyond control (making the actor disoriented), or the loss of credibility of the mediums and semantics that organize the system (making the actor suspicious). Due to these dysfunctions mediatized interactions become unpredictable, which contingency is experienced by the actors as general insecurity originating from social action.

A lack of rewarding experiences can be grasped on the level of communicative action as the incapability of contributing to the construction of a mutual reality. This could be the consequence of either a role characterized by stigma (preventing the actor's opinion from being taken seriously), or the lack of meaningful knowledge or adequate competence of argumentation (preventing the defence of validity claims). In communicative processes characterized by such deficits, actors are excluded from influencing others, which results in a loss of motivation. In some cases, a lack of rewards is replaced by a permanent feeling of having lost control over interactions and the giving up of hope regarding the opportunity to change the distorted formula. The experience of losing control over speech acts can be the result of an extreme divergence of basic assumptions (fragmented lifeworld), or the violation of the logic of validity claims (opinions are sustained without being justified). In both cases, reaching mutual understanding seems to be an impossible task, leaving actors with the sentiment of helplessness. Losing faith in changing the *status quo* could be the consequence of either withdrawal from interaction (being afraid of failure and humiliation), or exclusion from the public sphere (being refused cooperation by others). In both of these cases, actors lose their opportunity to practice speech acts, resulting in the naturalization of communicative incompetence.

Negativistic, self-blaming collective representations could be described on the level of lifeworld as elements of the natural everyday interpretation of the world. The exclusive focus on ominous events may be the consequence of either frequent failures to realize goals (dysfunctions of instrumental rationality), or harsh social and natural conditions (difficulties with satisfying basic needs). In both of these cases, the success of everyday action is highly contingent, which leads to the emergence of exaggerated precautions as the basis of the horizon of expectations. Self-blaming explanations of failure may appear either because of a strong sense of duty (a feeling that one's mistakes endanger the whole community), or a high level of professionalization (believing that success depends on one's expertise). In both cases, failure is interpreted as the responsibility of the actor, who also views negative outcomes as a result of breach of duty, or insufficient expertise.

This reinterpretation of the preconditions of depression with the notions of system, communicative action and lifeworld enables us to return to the issue of identifying an appropriate normative basis. Depression emerges in those constellations where overly complex or discredited systems are combined with stigmatized, incompetent, fragmented, incoherent, isolating or exclusive communicative action and unsuccessful, endangered, moralizing or functionally differentiated lifeworlds. If the distortions of the system, communicative action and lifeworld point to the same pattern of suffering, then a coherently distorted social reality is born, causing a homogenous experience of suffering. Without the parallel distortion of lifeworld and system, the negative consequences of an unequal pattern of communication may be compensated for. Accordingly, critical theory inspired by Habermas should focus on combining these various distorted mechanisms of integration, instead of simply referring to the limitations of communicative action.

Towards a comprehensive model of depression as social suffering

The reinterpretation of the same dimensions of suffering from the perspective of various critical theories has the potential for not only expanding the horizon of each theory, but also combining them. As the same patterns of suffering that originate from insecurity, deprivation of positive feedback, negativistic, self-blaming collective representations and legitimized loss of control may emerge in social spheres organized by different mechanisms of social integration, there is no reason to limit the scope of critical theories to either the dimension of the reproduction of inequality (Bourdieu) or the distortion of communication (Habermas). Instead, critical theory grounded on the level of actual suffering which combines both of these social theoretical insights needs to be elaborated. Table 4.1. illustrates how such a task may be envisaged.

Depression as social suffering emerges if distortions of social relationship – organized by either the logic of field, illusion and habitus, or the logic of system, communicative action and lifeworld – create a coherent constellation realizing the potential of empty suffering.[6] All of these variously distorted social spheres can contribute simultaneously to insecurity, deprivation of positive feedback, negativistic, self-blaming collective representations and legitimized loss of control. In other words: when it comes to depression, it is not the logic of integration, but the related social suffering, which matters. Structurally mixed, but phenomenologically coherent patterns of empty suffering (e.g. when competitive fields combine with stigmatized communicative action, unworldly illusion, moralizing lifeworld and authoritarian habitus in case of a fundamentalist constellation) are just as dangerous as structurally homogenous ones. Table 4.1. outlines alternative structural pathways leading to similar experiences of suffering. If any combination of these distorted paths creates a coherent social environment, the individual is trapped in a social constellation, resulting in the emergence of a depressive pattern of suffering. Accordingly, an appropriate target of social criticism is the predominance of distorted relationships in one's social network.

Even if this theoretical conclusion is yet to be tested by empirical research, numerous previous results indirectly support its relevance. Sociological studies of depression identify several constellations which are characterized by complex patterns of insecurity, deprivation of positive feedback, negativistic, self-blaming collective representations and legitimized loss of control

Table 4.1 Social factors of depression based on the social theoretical models of Bourdieu and Habermas

Logics of social integration/preconditions of depression	*Insecurity (psychoanalysis)*	*Deprivation of positive feedback (behaviourism)*	*Negativistic collective representations (cognitive)*	*Self-blaming collective representations (cognitive)*	*Loss of control (learned helplessness)*	*Incapability of revolting (learned helplessness)*
Logic of competition (Bourdieu)	Competitive, unconvertable fields	Resourceless, biased fields	Traumatized, unworldly illusions	Arrogant, ignorant illusions	Segregated, authoritarian habitus	Frightened, overseen habitus
Logic of cooperation (Habermas)	Overly complex, discredited systems	Stigmatized, incompetent communicative action	Unsuccessful, endangered lifeworld	Moralizing, functionally differentiated lifeworld	Fragmented, incoherent communicative action	Isolating, exclusive communicative action

emerging in variously integrated social units. While economic hardship in itself is among the most important factors that contributes to such experiences, specifying its variations provides for a more in-depth understanding of the social preconditions of depression. For example, some studies emphasize the effect of debt, which contributes to the emergence of depression as an independent factor (Drentea and Reynolds, 2015). To be a debtor is to be connected to overly complex systems (the global financial sector, with its complicated rules of banking) which is often complemented with non-communicative institutional practices and ignorant illusions (as banks may not explain every relevant detail of transactions), resulting in a functionally differentiated lifeworld and frightened habitus (originating from concerns about incapability to pay off loans). In this sense, such social constellations evoke a pattern of distortions which create a coherent experience of suffering that threatens to result in depression.

Gender differences of depression are also well mapped: women are over-represented as patients in general (Roberts, 1985) and as patients treated with psychotropic drugs (Ettore and Riska, 1993). Feminist social criticism explains these differences on the basis of the cultural and structural inequalities that condemn women, whose experiences filling subordinated roles and positions can be expressed only through the 'voice of unreason' in a Foucauldian sense (Busfield, 1996). The model introduced above may help to further elaborate such observations by identifying those social mechanisms which are responsible for maintaining a depressive phenomenological horizon. In this sense, the question for feminist criticism of mental disorders is whether women are more exposed to the type of social distortions which are indicated in Table 4.1.[7]

While the main goal of this chapter was to describe those social constellations, which contribute to the emergence of depression, it also has some consequences for the conclusion of Chapter 1. The logic of absolute dominion pervades primarily those fields, which are characterized among other by unconvertable capitals, biased challenges and exclusive consequences. In these constellations the – inevitable, but not necessarily distortive – struggle for material and symbolic capital occurs in a dehumanizing fashion, as the rivals subordinate every moral obligation to the promised personal success. Losing in a competition like this implies not only a particular failure, but the undermining of the totality of lifeworld. Failing within these fields, after interiorizing the collective illusion of absolute dominion implies not only the inability of treating sufferings, but also the secondary suffering caused by the totalizing experience of personal incompetence and helplessness. This conclusion may also be complemented from the perspective of various forms of communication. The logic of absolute dominion pervades primarily those interactions, which rely on either overly complex, discredited mediums, or incompetent, fragmented, exclusive speech acts in order to optimize the cooperation according to the logic of personal interest. In both cases, the actors lose the chance of mutual understanding despite seemingly continuing an interaction. As the communication transforms into pseudo-understanding, the occasional failure of instrumental goals results not only in the experience of distrust, or disorientation, but also a general sense of inadequacy and loss of hope.

Notes

1 Most social theories treat the causal models of psy-sciences only as the *subject* of criticism instead of a potential tool of criticism (e.g. Cohen, 2016; Flick, 2016).

2 As Adorno puts it: 'The need to lend a voice to suffering is a condition of all truth. For suffering is objectivity that weighs upon the subject; its most subjective experience, its expression, is objectively conveyed' (1973: 17–18).

3 In classic sociology, Marx emphasized the bodily hardship of the exploited proletariat, Weber the loss of meaning of the rationalized actor, Durkheim the emotional burden of disintegration (Wilkinson, 2005: 76–78). Later, these mundane forms of social suffering were complemented with the extreme experiences of world wars, totalitarianism and the Holocaust (Arendt, 1951; 1963). Recently, those forms of social suffering have received attention which are responsible for the dehumanizing experience of superfluity: unemployment, homelessness and illegal immigration are just the few most visible expressions of social constellations in which actors are continuously deprived of their human dignity (Bourdieu et al., 1999; Das et al. 1997). These various types have become important because of their particular potential for political mobilization: by revealing the hidden patterns and mechanisms of social suffering, not only criticism may be grounded, but also solidarity fostered in the mediatized public sphere (Boltanski, 1999; Renault, 2010).

4 Even though attempts to connect critical theories with psy discourses are not completely unknown, they usually aim at providing new perspectives for therapy (e.g. Gruber and Böhm, 2012; Whitley, 2008). The grounding of the normative basis of critical theories with therapeutic insight remains unprecedented.

5 Habermas made some attempts to causally link pathologies of communication with psychopathologies by referring to the pattern of 'double bind communication' that is applied to describe the socialization background of schizophrenic inpatients (Habermas, 1998). However, as later research showed, even if such correlation exists, it cannot be characterized as causation in the strict sense (Chaika, 1990).

6 Similar conclusions are drawn by Rosa, while analyzing various social distortions from the perspective of late modern construction of temporality. He argues that depression is a 'pathology of time' in at least three senses: it is related to the unbearably fast pace of change implying unpredictability; the lack of utopic timeframes implying futurelessness; and the impossibility of grounding a temporally coherent identity due to the ephemerality and fragmentation of life events (Rosa, 2010: 248). While the parallelisms are obvious (e.g. between overly complex systems and unpredictability; traumatized illusions and futurelessness; or fragmented, incoherent self and the ephemeral life events), the preconditions and the scope of the two analyses differ. Even if distorted intertemporality is a key element of depression (Fuchs, 2013a), it is not the only relevant factor: other aspects of intersubjectivity, including interaffectivity or intercorporeality cannot be reduced to it (Fuchs, 2013b). Accordingly, not only those distortions of social integration contribute to depression, which disturb intertemporality (as reconstructed by Rosa), but also those, which affect other aspects of intersubjectivity (as reconstructed above).

7 Similarly, the critical explanations regarding class, age (Bierman and Pearlin, 2011) and racial or ethnic differences (Miller et al., 2013) in depression may also be deepened by the model described in this chapter by analyzing whether members of these groups are exposed to a greater extent to the suffering that arises in the constellations summarized in Table 4.1.

References

Adorno, T. W. (1973) *Negative Dialectics*. New York, NY: Seabury Press.

American Psychiatric Association (2013) *Diagnostic and Statistical Manual of Mental Disorders* (5th edition). Washington, DC: American Psychiatric Publishing.

Arendt, H. (1951) *The Origins of Totalitarianism*. New York, NY: Harcourt, Brace and Co.

Arendt, H. (1963) *Eichmann in Jerusalem: A Report on the Banality of Evil*. New York, NY: Viking Press.

Barlow, D. and Durand, M. (2009) *Abnormal Psychology: An Integrative Approach*, Belmont, CA: Wadsworth Publishing.

Beck, A. T. (1967) *Depression: Clinical, Experimental and Theoretical Aspects*. New York, NY: Harper & Row.

Beidel, D., Bulik, C. and Stanley, M. (2012) *Abnormal Psychology* (2nd edition). Cambridge: Pearson.

Bierman, A. and Pearlin, L. I. (2011) SES, Trajectories of Physical Limitations, and Change in Depression in Late Life. *Society and Mental Health*, 1(3): 139–152.

Boltanski, L. (1999) *Distant Suffering: Morality, Media and Politics*. Cambridge: Cambridge University Press.

Bourdieu, P. (1990) *The Logic of Practice*. Cambridge: Polity.

Bourdieu, P. (1998) Is Disinterested Act Possible? In *Practical Reason – On the Theory of Action*. Stanford, CA: Stanford University Press.

Bourdieu, P. et al. (1999) *Weight of the World: Social Suffering in Contemporary Society*. Cambridge: Polity.

Bourdieu, P. and Wacquant, L. J. D. (1992) *An Invitation to Reflexive Sociology*. Cambridge: Polity.

Brown, G. W. and Harris, T. (1978) *The Social Origins of Depression: A Study of Psychiatric Disorder in Women*. London: Tavistock.

Busfield, J. (1996) *Man, Women and Madness. Understanding Gender and Mental Disorder*. London: Palgrave Macmillan.

Busfield, J. (2011) *Mental Illness*. Cambridge, UK and Malden, MA: Polity.

de Certeau, M. (1984) *The Practice of Everyday Life*. Berkeley, CA: University of California Press.

Chaika, E. O. (1990) *Understanding Psychotic Speech: Beyond Freud and Chomsky*. Springfield, IL: Charles C Thomas.

Cohen, B. (2016) *Psychiatric Hegemony A Marxist Theory of Mental Illness*. London: Palgrave Macmillan.

Comer, R. J. (2010) *Abnormal Psychology*. New York, NY: Worth Publishers.

Cooper, D. (1980) *The Language of Madness*. Harmondsworth: Pelican.

Das, V., Kleinman, A. and Lock, M. M. (Eds.) (1997) *Social Suffering*. Berkeley, CA: University of California Press.

Deleuze, G. and Guattari, F. (1977) *Anti-Oedipus: Capitalism and Schizophrenia*. New York, NY: Viking Press.

Double, D. B. (2006) Historical Perspectives on Anti-Psychiatry. In Double, D. B. (Ed.), *Critical Psychiatry*. London: Palgrave Macmillan, 19–41.

Drentea, P. and Reynolds, J. R. (2015) Where Does Debt Fit in the Stress Process Model? *Society and Mental Health*, 5(1): 16–32.

Ettore, E. and Riska, E. (1993) Psychotropics, Sociology and Women. *Sociology of Health and Illness*, 15(4): 503–524.

Flick, S. (2016) Treating Social Suffering? Work-Related Suffering and Its Psychotherapeutic Re/Interpretation. *Distinktion: Journal of Social Theory*, 17(2): 149–173.

Freud, S. (1917) Mourning and melancholia. In *Collected Papers* (Vol. 4). London: Hogarth Press and the Institute of Psychoanalysis, 152–172.

Foucault, M. (2006) *History of Madness*. New York, NY: Routledge.

Fuchs, T. (2013a) Temporality and Psychopathology. *Phenomenology and the Cognitive Sciences*, 12(4): 75–104.

Fuchs, T. (2013b) Depression, Intercorporeality and Interaffectivity. *Journal of Consciousness Studies*, 20(7–8): 219–238.

Goffman, E. (1961) *Asylums: Essays on the Social Situation of Mental Patients and Other Inmates*. New York, NY: Doubleday.

Gruber, D. and Böhm, M. (2012) Pierre Bourdieus Soziologie: Ein Wegweiser Für Die Sozialpsychiatrie? *SWS Rundschau – Die Zeitschrift der Sozialwissenschaftlichen Studiengesellschaft*, 12(1): 19–37.

Habermas, J. (1984) *The Theory of Communicative Action Vol. 1*. Boston, MA: Beacon.

Habermas, J. (1987) *The Theory of Communicative Action Vol. 2*. Boston, MA: Beacon.

Habermas, J. (1990) *Moral Consciousness and Communicative Action*. Cambridge: MIT Press.

Habermas, J. (1998) Reflections on Communicative Pathology. In *On the Pragmatics of Social Interaction*. Cambridge: MIT Press.

Honneth, A. (1996) *The Struggle for Recognition: The Moral Grammar of Social Conflicts*. Cambridge: Polity.

Honneth, A. (2006) *Reification: A Recognition-Theoretical View*. The Tanner Lectures on Human Values. http://tannerlectures.utah.edu/_documents/a-to-z/h/Honneth_2006.pdf.

Horkheimer, M. (1976) Traditional and Critical Theory. In Connerton P. (Ed.). *Critical Sociology: Selected Readings*. Harmondsworth: Penguin.

Laing, R. D. and Esterson, A. (1964) *Sanity, Madness and the Family*. London: Penguin Books.

Lewinsohn, P. M., Youngren, M. A. and Grosscup, S. J. (1979) Reinforcement and Depression In Depue R. A. (Ed.), *The Psychobiology of the Depressive Disorders*. New York, NY: Academic Press.

Miller, B., Rote, S. and Keith, V. M. (2013) Coping With Racial Discrimination: Assessing the Vulnerability of African Americans and the Mediated Moderation of Psychosocial Resources *Society and Mental Health*, 3(2): 133–150.

Rafieian, S. and Davis, H. (2016) Dissociation, Reflexivity and Habitus. *European Journal of Social Theory*, 19(4): 556–573.

Renault, E. (2010) A Critical Theory of Social Suffering. *Critical Horizons*, 11(2): 221–241.

Roberts, H. (1985) *The Patient Patients*. London: Pandora.

Rogers, A. and Pilgrim, D. (2014) *A Sociology of Mental Health and Illness*. Maidenhead: McGraw-Hill Open University Press.

Rosa, H. (2010) *Social Acceleration. A New Theory of Modernity*. New York, NY: Columbia University Press.

Scheff, T. J. (1999) *Being Mentally Ill: A Sociological Theory.* New York, NY: Aldine de Gruyter.

Seligman, M. E. P. (1975) *Helplessness.* San Francisco, CA: Freeman.

Susen, S. (2007) *The Foundations of the Social: Between Critical Theory and Reflexive Sociology.* Oxford: The Bardwell Press.

Szasz, T. (1961) *The Myth of Mental Illness.* New York, NY: Harper & Row.

Wakefield, J. C. (1992) Disorder as Harmful Dysfunction: A Conceptual Critique of DSM-III-R's Definition of Mental Disorder. *Psychological Review*, 99(2): 232–247.

Whitley, R. (2008) Postmodernity and Mental Health. *Harvard Review of Psychiatry*, 16(6): 352–364.

Wilkinson, I. (2005) *Suffering: A Sociological Introduction.* London: Polity.

5 Networks of anxiety

From the distortions of late modern societies to the social components of anxiety

From a modernization theoretical perspective, it may be argued that fear becomes a common experience in contemporary societies due to the emptying of the actors' motivation for cooperation (see Chapter 2). In a constellation characterized by negative integration fear is not only experienced more frequently, but it also becomes the general texture of the lifeworld – thus anxiety arises. While such diagnosis focuses on the reconfiguring of social structures, it ignores the micro level social mechanisms constituting an anxious lifeworld. In order to fill this gap, anxiety needs to be reintroduced on the fundamental level of intersubjectivity, as a consequence of distorted social interactions. The theoretical strategy of this chapter is similar to the one applied in Chapter 4: following a psychological clarification of anxiety and the sociological clarification of the related forms of distorted intersubjectivity, an attempt is made to link the two approaches. Anxiety is reinterpreted as a form of social suffering originating from social relationships reinforcing a detached, generalized pattern of fear.

In the first section, an attempt is made to identify the key phenomenological constituents of anxiety based on psychoanalytic, cognitive and existentialist descriptions. These theories explain anxiety by referring to a non-reactive, non-targeted fear, which results in the unconditional, diffuse and general expansion of worry. In the second section, those social constellations are reconstructed, which may be related to the emergence of an anxious phenomenological horizon. Based on the conclusions of Chapter 2, those forms of sociability are chosen, which are related to negative integration, while playing a decisive role in the adaptation to the flexibility requirements of late modernity. White's network theory is chosen as a primary sociological tool: it focuses on the non-stop dynamics of identity and control struggles originating from the perpetual connecting and disconnecting. The formal network theory is complemented by substantive analyses focusing on ontological security (Giddens) and trust (Honneth), which are equally threatened by the emergence of negative integration. These insights are combined into a critical 'network phenomenology' capable of describing those social distortions, which contribute to the emergence of anxiety as a late modern social suffering.

DOI: 10.4324/9781003197355-8

Detaching fear: Psychological and existential accounts of anxiety

Generalized anxiety can be explained from the perspective of several psychological traditions. Among these, three are particularly important for a phenomenological overview: psychoanalysis is capable of highlighting the unconscious, pre-intentional aspects, cognitive theory can help to explore the intentional level and existentialism highlights those elements, which are related to general human experiences. A classic psychological analysis of generalized anxiety can be found in the works of Freud, who differentiated between realistic (facing actual danger), neurotic (systematic prevention of acting out id impulse) and moral anxiety (punishment for expressing id impulse). Generalized anxiety is the result of being exposed to the latter two: if children are prevented from or punished for their id impulses, they learn to relate to them as being extremely dangerous. As even experimenting with them is considered to be too risky, any empirical contact is avoided – thus, the experience of a terrifying object is born, which is disconnected from the logic of trial and error (Freud, 1933).

The psychoanalytical approach is complemented in many ways by the cognitive, which focuses on irrational automatic thoughts exaggerating the threat of negative events, social devaluation or personal incompetence. Even ordinary situations can be perceived as dangerous, which leads to overcautious defence strategies (Beck et al., 1985). Often unpredictable negative events are the formative force behind such irresistible automatic thoughts: being irregular and uncontrollable, they motivate suspicion and overprotective attitudes. Recent theories emphasize that both positive and negative reinforcements of worrying may result in continuous, undifferentiated fear. Mere precaution is considered to be the sign of responsibility, an attitude approved by the community – however, if such normative pressure increases, it may be turned into obsessive preoccupation with threats. As exaggerating precaution is disapproved by the others, it may lead to the birth of meta-worry – the actors oriented to avoid it start monitoring themselves, that is to worry because of worries. In sum, several tracks may lead to continuous, diffuse worrying, that is the generalization of anxiety (Wells, 2005). Behaviourist theories complement these argumentations by showing that rituals of worrying may provide comfort for people having increased basic level of bodily arousal: as discomforting situations are handled by reorienting one's attention to the well-known attunement of worry, such practice is reinforced and becomes a general attitude (Borkovec et al., 2004).

Beside clinical psychology, anxiety has been analyzed by various existentialist approaches as well. Although, the demarcation line between normal and pathological existence is never unambiguous, in case of anxiety it is especially blurred (López-Ibor and Zappino, 2019). While clinically oriented theories tend to view anxiety as an eliminable form of suffering, philosophical analyses highlight its functional role in existential self-fulfilment: they argue that anxiety is a reaction to the experience of meaninglessness. Kierkegaard analyzed anxiety as a central phenomenon of human existence: unlike fear, which has a definitive object, anxiety is a fear without exact target. It emerges in those moments, when aesthetic or ethical existence proves to be paradox. Accordingly, despite having any concrete goals, anxiety is not purposeless: it motivates the pursuing of self-fulfilment. The discomfort related to anxiety urges the actors to move beyond the horizon of the material (pleasure) and social world (norms) and seek a transcendental purpose by relying on a 'leap of faith' (Kierkegaard, 1980).

While most existentialist thinkers refuse Kierkegaard's conclusion, which points to faith, as the final destination of anxiety, the functionality of anxiety in the process of self-fulfilment is widely approved. According to Heidegger, anxiety as a mood refers to the exposedness to death: it implies a sense of insignificance. This experience is not only a desperate one; it is also an opportunity for relating to the self in a new way. Anxiety confronts the subject with an existential decision: if it is averted by escaping to uncritical identification with the others, then inauthentic existence is chosen; if it is taken seriously, a development towards authentic existence (based on the constant facing with nothingness) may begin (Heidegger, 2012). According to Sartre, anxiety is also closely related to the perception of the others. It informs the subject about the threat posed by the others to one's freedom and agency. Facing these trials has a constructive potential: they may help to find meaningfulness, without falling into the trap of becoming the hostage or the enemy of the others (Sartre, 1984).

While most existential theories agree on defining anxiety as an objectless fear, some counterarguments are also known. Lacan argues that instead of understanding anxiety as completely objectless, it should rather be seen as targeting an object outside the realm of things. The distinctive feature of anxiety is the incomprehensibility of the object of fear, which is not the equivalent of the lack of any concrete objects. Anxiety motivates the subject to discover its source, which is a process of giving sense to an unusual, haunting impression (Robertson, 2015: 11). However, contrary to the existentialist arguments, according to Lacan this process does not point to any particular directions: neither faith, nor authenticity, nor the other. Anxiety raises a personal challenge, which is always embedded in the particular life of the subject. These challenges are usually related not only to the inner cognitive and emotive processes, but also to the interpersonal relations. The incertitude of anxiety is often evoked by the 'voice' or the 'gaze' of the other, who is capable of reframing everyday situations in an unexpected way, thus questioning ontological security (Robertson, 2015: 187).

Based on these analyses we may argue that the phenomenological structure of generalized anxiety is characterized by the detachment of fear from the concreteness of actually dangerous events. On the one hand, such process can be related to distorted socialization that is the enforcement of supressing one's fear and the denial of sharing them. If the parents forbid their children to experiment with their id impulses or express them, a zone of taboos is born, which is terrifying and empirically inaccessible at the same time. On the other hand, the emergence of anxiety could be understood as a result of maladaptative self-discipline: either because of the exposure to unpredictable events, or because of the ritualization of worrying, constant fear may seem to be an adequate general strategy of distancing the self from the world. As fear is disconnected from empirical feedback, it loses its concrete boundaries and starts to expand unlimitedly. Finally, the whole life is built around it, especially after one becomes immune to opposing impulses: as too much worry leads to meta-worries, there seem to be no easy way out from the spiral of generalization. At this point fear starts to exist on its own: it no longer operates as a reaction to negative events, but as the basis of the horizon expectations. A third way to detach fear from concrete events is to be exposed to challenges not having a defined, recognizable source, nevertheless concerning the subject: having a surfeit of pleasures, being oppressed by norms, facing the possibility of death, being judged by the others – these are just a few examples to such experiences.

While these descriptions explain anxiety mainly as an inner process, it is worthy to note, that an implicit element of the social appears in them: in case of psychoanalysis, the impact of the other is explicit (they motivate the suppression of id impulses); in case of cognitive-behaviourist theory, it is implicit (anxiety originates from the lack of collective interpretations providing alternative for the ritualization of worry) and explicit (anxiety implied by unpredictable, insecure social world); in case of existentialism, it is related to the cultural context, which may constitute a hedonistic, moralizing, nihilistic or stigmatizing environment, equally exposing the subject to anxious experiences. This provides an opportunity for bridging individualistic and social phenomenologies of anxiety. While psy-discourses describe a distorted pattern of relating to the world with a vague reference to the social, sociological theories provide opportunity for elaborating this crucial aspect by adding network phenomenology to the formula. In the next section the following question is raised: how do distorted social networks contribute to the emergence of a non-reactionary, non-targeted pattern of fear? Those social theories are taken into consideration, which have the potential of highlighting the various constitutive factors of anxiety: tabooing interactive patterns, unpredictable social constellations, missing interactive processes of dealing with worry, cultural patterns implying incomprehensible fears.

Networks of ontological security and trust

According to social theories of classical modernity, mechanisms of social integration are responsible for solving the challenge of 'double contingency', that is the mutual unpredictability inherent in every social interactions (Parsons and Shils, 1951: 16). From this perspective, modernization is an evolutionary process enabling the emergence of new mechanisms capable of coordinating social action. Since the birth of sociology, social theories attempted to conceptualize the substantive and formal characteristics of action coordination: while classical theories tended to focus on specific levels (e.g. the markets in case of Marx, or the system of division of labour in case of Durkheim, or the actors' motivations in case of Weber), contemporary theories elaborate a more comprehensive approach. According to them, double contingency inherent in every social situation is handled on pre-intentional level, by mutually shared or compatible motivations unreflected by the actors; on intentional level, by collective interpretations of the world; and on structural level, by social constraints reproduced as unintended consequences of social action.

In late modernity these mechanisms of action coordination are reconfigured: as concepts such as the common habitus, the shared narratives of legitimacy or the stable social systems became equally replaced by temporary, flexible mechanisms of action coordination. These new forms of sociability require new integration models: White's network theory (2008) provides such an alternative. From the perspective of his theory, the general mechanisms of action coordination elaborated by classic social theories (such as lifeworld, system or field) can be rebuilt from below, based on the close observation of how actors and institutions connect to each other (Fuhse, 2015). From this perspective, the morphological characteristics of the network, the structure of ties, the position within a network, the dynamism of connecting and disconnecting gets special attention, as they determine the frame and extent of social action.

According to White, the basic social dynamic is the attempt of gaining control over a given situation. The control may be established differently by actors in varying positions. The way of securing control outlines the identity of the actors, in a given network configuration. If the network is expanded or reduced, the former balance gives place to uncertainties implying the formation of new identities elaborated through new ways of control. In this sense, interconnected actors ceaselessly adapt to the continuously changing network environment: they are immersed in an endless attempt of controlling new configurations by connecting to or disconnecting from them, while constructing new identities. Based on these premises, the task of social theory is to identify those mechanisms, which are capable of stabilizing control patterns (creating 'network domains') and consequent identities (White, 2008: 2).

The most basic form of such mechanisms are 'stories' exemplifying the ordinary patterns of control. These narratives constitute the basis of networks, as they thematize controversial issues and identities as well. Beside general stories, the stabilization also relies on 'disciplines', which are responsible for outlining various rules of connecting and disconnecting. Different sets of rules – grounding an interface (based on instrumental logic), a council (based on deliberative logic) or an arena (based on competitive logic) type of network – provide opportunities for different control attempts, thus enable different identities (White, 2008: 63). Disciplines are complemented by 'styles' – such as the concept of 'rationality' – providing detailed paradigms of identities and types of control. Stories, disciplines and styles are fundamental in networks constituted of direct ties – however, they are not capable of explaining the stabilization of indirect networks. The latter configurations rely on institutions legitimized by a certain 'rhetoric' and 'control regimes' regulating hierarchical interactions (e.g. expert-client, patron-employee – White, 2008: 171).

White proposes a paradigm shift: instead of focusing on the question of double contingency inherent in every social action, he focuses on an extended space of contingencies inherent in the networks. In this sense, he does not attempt to model mechanisms capable of solving double contingency, but mechanisms capable of solving 'network contingency'. This paradigm shift reveals the limitedness of classic integration models: as social actions are embedded in a network, their coordination depends on the interference of every involved actor, not only those who are directly contributing to an interaction. Those models of action coordination, which neglect the network embeddedness of social action, inevitably miss a fundamental element of explanation: in their eyes the always changing, complex web of interactions, which directly or indirectly affects action situations is considered to be driven by a homogenous logic of integration. The basic difference between the interaction and network based approaches is the extent of social relations taken into consideration: network theory replaces any singular logic of action coordination with a multi-dimensional space of integration logics, which compete or reinforce each other according to the momentary network constellation.

Such paradigm shift also has implications for social phenomenology aiming at analyzing social suffering. While most theories of classic modernity postulate general mechanisms of meaning construction and consequent definitive frameworks of relating to the world (such as Durkheim's collective representations, or Weber's types of legitimacy), they fail to operationalize the coexistence of various integration mechanisms within the same network. By reintroducing theories of action coordination as mere ties within the fragmented, diffuse world of networks, these shortcomings can be overcome. A social phenomenology becomes available, which can handle the shifts and discrepancies of various integration logics within the same network. Such network phenomenology provides a conceptual horizon fitting the special requirements of late modern negative integration. It can grasp the characteristics of those flexible social entities, which are ceaselessly expanding and shrinking; connecting and disconnecting; reconfiguring and maintaining a pattern.

Despite these advantages, White's theory has little to offer, when it comes to the substantive questions of anxiety. Even if networks constitute an unpredictable social world, which is one of the most important precondition of a disquieting environment, on their own they are not capable of explaining every constituent of anxiety (including the mechanisms of tabooing, social reinforcement or worrying cultural patterns). In order to cover these aspects, those specific network constellations need to be elaborated, which play a key role in constituting the sense of security and trust, while controlling everyday interactions. For this purpose, Giddens' theory of reflexive modernization and Honneth's theory of recognition is called upon: the formal model of networks is complemented with their substantive conclusions.

From Giddens' perspective, action coordination can be understood through the notions of routines, and the reflexivity of the actors and institutions. According to his concept, the fundamental level of social action is constituted of those routines, which are developed in the everyday life by the actors themselves. These unreflected routines are responsible for ensuring 'ontological security' (that is the familiarity of the inhabited world) by maintaining the regularity of everyday praxis. Routines not only fulfil the existential needs of preventing anxiety, but also contribute to the emergence of institutions in the process of 'structuration' (Giddens, 1984). While in traditional societies the institutions were controlled by 'guardians' (who linked collective memories and everyday challenges), in late modernity institutions are operated by 'experts'. Their authority is not based on a distinguished role, but on formal training – thus they are not capable of orienting actors in general, only in specific contexts belonging to their expertise (Giddens, 1994). Even if modern institutions are 'disembedded' from the concreteness of face to face familiarity, the integration they provide is never an automatized, 'systematic' process: both the individual and the institutional actors reflect on themselves and their environment, while trying to influence the processes. This monitoring becomes especially important in late modernity, as the trust in expert knowledge weakens (Giddens, 1990). Reflexivity becomes a basic element of both individual action (such as the construction of identity, the planning of individual life paths, the management of consumption and the intimate relationships) and institutional procedures (such as life politics or generative politics). While this transformation opens new horizons, it also contributes to the rise of new challenges: ontological insecurity, distorted identity construction and unreflective institutions mismanaging risks may occur as a consequences of insufficient application of the individual and institutional reflexive potentials (Giddens, 1991).

These insights provide the first theoretical tools for complementing the network models with substantive elements, in order to identify distortions. Based on Giddens' conclusions, routinized and reflexive networks may be differentiated. The former ones organize social practices by repeating patterns of connecting and disconnecting. They are independent from reflexivity, but ensure ontological security. In routinized networks, the actors do not seek individual ways of connecting, instead follow the authority of a quasi-guardian figure positioned at the centre, while controlling the repeated patterns of connecting and disconnecting. As opposed to the routinized logic of action coordination, reflexive actors consider more than one point of view during their interactions: these networks are integrated through reflexive evaluation of multiple (expert) interpretations. This means that ties are constructed freely, in a decentralized structure, not being controlled by any single, central actor. Accordingly, these networks are free from dogmatisms and repetition, which makes them more decentralized and flexible compared to other constellations. In reflexive networks, the relationship between lay and expert actors tends to be two-way: interactions based on expert semantics are complemented with responsiveness of the actors.

In Honneth's approach, action coordination can be understood through the various forms of recognition: love, solidarity and rights. According to this theory, on the fundamental level of interactions a wish to be recognized can be found: the emergence of an autonomous, confident, morally competent, trustful self depends on the recognition of the other. However, acknowledgement is rarely given for free: in most cases it has to be earned or competed for. This struggle for recognition, wherein the constitution of the self is at stake, frames the mechanisms of action coordination (Honneth, 1996: 82). Despite this general stake, recognition appears in various forms. Love is the recognition of the individual qualities by the concrete other – it plays central role in intimate relationships by grounding basic confidence and trust in the other. Solidarity is the recognition of the individual merits by the community – it plays central role in everyday relationships by maintaining self-esteem and grounding trust in the collective of a status group. Rights are the recognition of the universal humanness by the community – it plays a central role in the formal relationships by enabling self-respect and moral autonomy and trust in the society as a whole. The deprivation from these various forms of recognition results in different forms of suffering, such as physical violence, denigration or discrimination. On the one hand, these are individually experienced, on the other hand, they express potentially collective traumas. Accordingly, they may equally provoke individual or collective attempts of (re)gaining recognition (Honneth, 1996: 135). These struggles are constitutive elements of the interactions: directly or indirectly they contribute to the processes of action coordination. From this perspective, it may be argued that the network distortions can be described as various forms deprivation from recognition resulting in the limiting of an autonomous self and a distrustful relation to the concrete and generalized others.

These insights provide further theoretical tools for complementing the network models with substantive dimensions. As love and intimacy orients social action by the logic of mutual disclosure and emotional support, the networks integrated according to this logic are characterized by the disconnection from the institutional levels of sociability. In this constellation actors focus exclusively on each other with the sole purpose of maintaining their relationship. These distinct 'cliques' are capable of reinforcing confidence and trust by providing an intersubjective space, which is controlled solely by the few involved. Solidarity refers to networks integrated by the rewards based on achievements or status. As the rewards are not local, but approved widely, these networks are based on indirect ties. Another important characteristic of these ties is the horizontal extension: they connect actors in similar structural position, sharing similar experiences within their own particular networks. If these tokens provide a stable, predictable horizon of control in various, independent networks, they are capable of grounding identities and establish trust, even in an ever-changing environment. The third network type is the legal, which is characterized by universality that is the independence from any particular attributes. The promise of rule of laws is to constitute 'control regimes' valid in every social situation by subordinating everyone to a certain set of formal rules. Networks based on rights have the potential of constituting basic trust in the general others, unless the rules are characterized by arbitrary misinterpretations. Within this setting, social distortions may originate from networks depriving the actors from love, lacking solidarity, or misusing universal laws.

A network phenomenology of anxiety

After overviewing the phenomenological description of anxiety and the appropriate social theories, an attempt can be made to combine the two. In what follows, those distortions of routine, reflexivity and recognition based networks are identified, which hold the potential of tabooing, unpredictable, unsupportive social relations or worrying cultural patterns. These could be viewed as various factors pointing to the same direction: the more of them are present in one's social environment, the higher is the chance of the emergence of anxiety (see Table 5.1). While only a few distortive ties may not have significant impact, if one's ego-network is constituted mostly of distorted ties, a social world emerges, which traps the actor: fear becomes detached from concrete events and transforms into an untargeted, diffuse general worry.

As networks of routines are characterized by the repeating of the same logic of connecting and disconnecting surveilled by a central figure of authority, unpredictability is incompatible with them. The first potential distortion originates from the rigidity of repetition: if it becomes an exclusive logic, then alternative network configurations may not emerge, which reduces the chance of the emergence of new identities along with new interpretations of the world. Such limited space of interactions increases the chance of further silencing those issues, which are incommunicable in the existing framework. As a result, a set of taboos is born in the routinized network, which cannot be discussed despite being considered to be dangerous – this is a tabooing element of an objectless fear. The second potential distortion is related to the speed of repetition: if the pace of routinized connecting and disconnecting is too fast, the actors do not have time to foster those traditions, which are responsible for providing reassuring narratives. Without narratives anchored in collective memories, actors following routines are left on their own with overwhelming fearful experiences – this is an unsupportive element of an

Table 5.1 Networks of anxiety

	Tabooing	*Unpredictability*	*Lacking support*	*Culture (hedonist, nihilist, moralizing, stigmatizing)*
Networks of routines	Rigid patterns of connecting and disconnecting (no space for alternative ties)	–	Overly busy network dynamics (no time to create additional ties of understanding)	Overly centralized control paired with dense ties of surveillance (moralizing as the other is judged according to their normality)
Networks of reflexivity	–	Lack vertical ties (missing hierarchy of expertise)	Reciprocity of ties is low (connecting is initiated by one side)	Overly decentralized control regimes (nihilism as a consequence of lacking any regular patterns)
Networks of love	Lacking ties between members of cliques (exchange of intimate experiences is low)	Formation of cliques only between far ties (the other is unknown)	–	Cliques are temporary (hedonist as the network exists only during the time of desire)
Networks of solidarity	Low network heterogeneity (worthiness is attributed to a majority)	Fragmented structure of ties (lack of any structure prevents collective experiences)	–	Segregating network dynamics (stigmatizing as difference is excluded)
Networks of rights	–	Frequent change of control regimes (lack of stability of indirect ties)	Low density of vertical ties (low chance of relating to adequate expert support)	Dead zones in the reach of control regime (stigmatizing as certain members are discriminated)

uncontrollable fear. The third potential distortion is related to the overly centralized structure of the network: if the guardian figures maintain a strict control by establishing exclusively vertical ties, then everyone is subject to their surveillance. In this constellation, the pressure of being morally judged may increase to a level, where it causes constant fear from inadequacy – this is a moralizing element of generalized anxiety.

Networks of reflexivity constitute a contrasting constellation, as they are based on the logic of decentralization and experimenting with new configurations, which are both preventing the logic of tabooing. The first potential distortion originates from the complete lack of vertical structures: even if expertise is based on the chance of a universal claim of criticism implying horizontal ties, it still relies on hierarchies based on knowledge. If not even such hierarchies can be institutionalized, then the lay actors lose orientation points required for grounding ontological security in a reflective manner (even reflexivity needs a set of certainties provided by experts). In a completely free floating configuration, there is no chance differentiating between relevant and irrelevant fears – that is a contingency element of reflexive networks. The second potential of distortion is related to the reciprocity of ties: while reflection may seem to be the task of the individual actors, it also depends on a deliberative process, where the lay and expert knowledge is combined in a fruitful way. If the element of mutual understanding is missing and the communicative ties are initiated solely from one direction, then the chance of discussing fears in a reassuring way is low – thus actors within certain network positions remain alone with interpreting and handling them. The third potential distortion is related to the extreme decentralization of control: as a consequence, the networks may become so fragmented that any sort of mutual background knowledge is missing. In this constellation, the complete lack of collective interpretations of the world reinforces the actors about the impossibility of a meaningful shared framework, which is the expression of a nihilistic culture – that is a nihilist source of ontological insecurity endangering reflexive networks.

Intimate networks are built around the logic of mutual disclosure, support and responsibility within cliques (networks characterized by high density of inner and scarce density of outer ties). The first possible distortion of these networks originates from the complete isolation of such cliques. If actors do not have a chance of sharing their experiences with others in similar position from a different network, then they are closed in a single interpretative framework elaborated in their particular context. In these configurations the chance of tabooing grows high, as isolating intimacies intensify the fear from inexplicable dangers. The second type of distortion is related to the distant origins of the members of the intimate relationship. If the actors' background networks do not overlap at all, then their identities diverge, so they become mutually unpredictable for each other (especially in those situations, which depend on the initial socialization process). The experience of continuous hindrances not only undermines ontological security, but also trust in the other as well – that is a contingency related source of diffuse fear. The third type of distortion originates from the misuse of the intimacy clique in a hedonistic way: if the ties are maintained only during the time of enjoyment, while being dissolved right after satisfaction, the actors cannot rely on them. In this sense, the ephemerality of cliques constitutes a distrusting social environment: as even those relations fail, which supposed to establish confidence and trust, the actors face a profoundly unpredictable world – that is a hedonistic source of diffuse fear.

Solidarity networks are characterized by a horizontal structure, which is responsible for both the recognition of worthiness by the peers and the consequent support. The first type of distortion in these constellations originates from the homogeneity of ties: if the members of a network are constituted of similar actors, then the chance of naturalizing the attributes of the majority as the criteria of normalcy or adequacy grows high. In this constellation alternative paradigms of worthiness remain not only unrecognized, but also viewed with suspicion and prejudices – consequently, the actual or imagined minorities become the sources of undefined, yet frightening preconceptions, which are evoked by their actual or potential connecting. The next type of distortion is related to the fragmentation of horizontal ties: if the collective experiences are missing due to the low density of ties between actors in similar structural position, then not only collective action becomes improbable ('class consciousness' remains latent), but also the rivalries between actors in the same status are sharpened ('false consciousness'). As a consequence, solidarity is replaced by the atmosphere of generalized suspicion concerning the peers, who are considered to be not only unpredictable, but also potentially hostile – that is a general, undefined form of fear from the other. The third type of distortion is connected to segregating dynamics: if horizontal connecting is related to the attribution of sameness, then those who perceived to be different may find themselves in an isolated position preventing any further chance of integration. In such stigmatizing cultural framework, the processes of 'othering' establish an irreversible distinction between the 'us' and the 'others', thus threatens the subjects with the potential of a final exclusion – this results in a permanent insecurity of identity and a diffuse fear from the gaze of the others.

Networks of legal recognition are based on the attempt of making normative decisions in a transparent way by grounding them on the level of basic principles and well-defined procedural mechanisms (accordingly, legal networks exclude the possibility of tabooing). The first type of distortion is related to the pace of changing those basic principles and procedures, which are responsible for orienting the actors: if the changes are too fast, the logic of connecting and disconnecting is not adjustable by anyone. Such failure of those control regimes, which are supposed to organize overlapping networks creates not only insecurity about what is possible and impossible, but also fear from the expectable. The second type of distortion originates from the low density of vertical ties. In this case, the control regime is dysfunctional in a sense that it is not capable of realizing its intentions: without proper network embeddedness, even the most refined principles may become corrupted in the process of their application. As a consequence, the trust towards these institutions deteriorates until the point of giving its place to a diffuse fear of the impossibility of order. The third type of distortion is related to the potential of discrimination: if there are 'dead zones' within the networks integrated by universal rights, this means that certain groups are excluded from the protection of the law. The violation of the universality principle undermines the possibility of rights in a profound way: as the security of laws relies on universality (on the promise of being applied to everyone without exception), the experience of discrimination damages the overall trust (as no one can be sure, if they are not to be discriminated next). Accordingly, discriminative laws contribute to the general insecurity of social order – relating rights to a fearful horizon of expectations.

Of course these various networks affect the actors not separately, but in parallel. This means that the social constituents of generalized anxiety are present in those situations, where both the routine and reflection based networks, plus the love, solidarity and rights based networks are distorted the same way. Fear is detached from frightful events and becomes a generalized worry, if routines are distorted by rigidity, too fast pace, over-centralization; reflectivity is hindered by lack of hierarchies, reciprocity or stability; love is distorted by isolation, social distance or temporariness; solidarity is limited by exclusivity, fragmentation or segregation; rights are distorted by instability, ineffectivity or selectivity. From social phenomenological perspective it may be argued that anxiety is born when the very social basis of giving sense to the world occurs in homogenously distorted networks, which create a uniformly distressing horizon.

References

Beck, A. T., Emery, G. and Greenberg, R. L. (1985). Differentiating Anxiety and Depression: A Test of the Cognitive Content Specificity Hypothesis. *Abnormal Psychology*, 96(3): 179–183.

Borkovec, T. D., Alcaine, O. M. and Behar, E. (2004) Avoidance Theory of Worry and Generalized Anxiety Disorder. In Heimberg, R. G., Turk, C. L. and Mennin, D. S. (Eds.), *Generalized Anxiety Disorder: Advances in Research and Practice*. New York, NY: Guilford Press, 77–108.

Freud, S. (1933) *New Introductory Lectures on Psychoanalysis*. New York, NY: Norton.

Fuhse, J. A. (2015). Theorizing Social Networks: The Relational Sociology of and Around Harrison White. *International Review of Sociology Revue Internationale de Sociologie*, 25(1): 15–44.

Giddens, A. (1984) *The Constitution of Society. Outline of the Theory of Structuration*. Cambridge: Polity.

Giddens, A. (1990) *The Consequences of Modernity*. Cambridge: Polity.

Giddens, A. (1991) *Modernity and Self-Identity. Self and Society in the Late Modern Age*. Cambridge: Polity.

Giddens A. (1994) Living in a Post-Traditional Society. In Beck, U., Giddens, A. and Lash, S. (Eds.), *Reflexive Modernization. Politics, Tradition and Aesthetics in the Modern Social Order*. Cambridge: Polity, 56–109.

Heidegger, M. (2012) *Being and Time*. Cambridge: Cambridge University Press.

Honneth, A. (1996) *The Struggle for Recognition: The Moral Grammar of Social Conflicts*. Cambridge: Polity.

Kierkegaard, S. (1980) *The Concept of Anxiety*. Princeton, NJ: Princeton University Press.

López-Ibor, M. and Zappino, J. P. (2019) Vital anxiety. In Stanghellini, G., Broome, M., Raballo, A., Fernandez, A., Fusar-Poli, P. and Rosfort, R. (Eds.), *The Oxford Handbook of Phenomenological Psychopathology*. Oxford: Oxford University Press.

Parsons, T. and Shils, E. (1951) *Toward a General Theory of Action*. Cambridge, MA: Harvard University Press.

Robertson, B. (2015) *Lacanian Antiphilosophy and the Problem of Anxiety*. New York, NY: Palgrave Macmillan.

Sartre, J. P. (1984) *Being and Nothingness*. New York, NY: Washington Square Press.

Wells, A. (2005). The Metacognitive Model of GAD: Assessment of Meta-Worry and Relationship With DSM-IV Generalized Anxiety Disorder. *Cognitive Therapy and Research*, 29(1), 107–121.

White, H. C. (2008) *Identity and Control: How Social Formations Emerge*. Princeton, NJ: Princeton University Press.

6 Actor-networks of addiction

From reification to the emergence of a late modern hybrid subjectivity

Similarly to the increasing prevalence of depressive mood and anxious relation to the world, the generalization of addictive behaviour patterns is also closely related to late modernity. Even if substances altering the state of mind (for either ritual, medical or recreational purpose) have been consumed in most known human civilizations (Crocq, 2007), the misuse of these substances has become a public concern only since early modernity (Hirschfelder, 2014). Addiction has been framed in various ways throughout the period: it was either interpreted in a religious, moral, criminal or biomedical framework (Lynn, 2009). Although, gradually the biomedical interpretation became dominant, addiction never ceased to be a complex, controversial phenomenon having moral and existential connotations as well. Accordingly, in its case, the dividing line between normalcy and pathology remained a blurred one: the moral judgments referring to the weakness of will were never completely replaced by narratives of bodily illness.

Even if addiction has been viewed throughout early and classic modernity mostly as an individual or social anomaly, recently its discourse has been transforming: a parallel narrative emerged reinterpreting addiction as an inevitable element of late modern existence (Brodie and Redfield, 2002). Such shift of emphasis is indicated by the sudden explosion of the new forms of addiction: it is not anymore related to specific substances (e.g. alcohol, nicotine, coffee or drugs), instead almost any particular form of behaviour can be turned into addiction (e.g. playing, watching series, eating, sexual behaviour, etc.). This boom indicates the birth of what can be called a 'culture of addiction' (Shelby, 2016). Such culture is based on an objectifying relation to the self: the claim for controlling pleasure and pain – originally characterizing external representatives of biopower – is applied by the actors on themselves. They start to manage their mood in an instrumental way – even at the cost of self-destructive consequences. According to several analyses, the culture of addiction culminates in the 'pharmacological revolution' expanding the landscape of substances by introducing several new legal drugs (e.g. Prozac, Xanax, etc.). These technologies serve the same purpose as the traditional drugs: absorbing suffering. However, unlike their predecessors, they

DOI: 10.4324/9781003197355-9

are approved by biomedical authority, thus become normalized technologies of the self (Golub et al., 2015).

Based on these observations, it may be argued that addiction is becoming a twofold phenomenon: it is not simply a pathology or a challenge, but a way of life deeply related to the late modern condition. Despite this transformation, most contemporary analyses of addiction do not take into consideration both of these aspects: they either try to explain the causes of addiction as a self-destruction behaviour pattern, or the cultural practices normalizing an obsessive relation to the world. In order to avoid one-sidedness, in the following chapter an attempt is made to reconstruct addiction as a late modern phenomenon, which is equally related to the specific social distortions of the era and the ways late modern actors attempt to solve them. It is argued that addiction is related to a 'hybrid subjectivity', including the element of reification and an ambiguous attempt of transcending such deprivation from agency.

For this complex purpose, a social phenomenological analysis is conducted, which is capable of covering the questions of responsibility, agency, social distortions and technologies of pleasure and pain management at the same time.[1] In order to map those social constellations, which play a constitutive role in the emergence of addiction, several dimensions need to be taken into consideration. Despite the various attempts of establishing 'addictology' as an interdisciplinary enterprise, most analyses still focus solely on either the biological, psychological or social dimensions, while ignoring the others (Rhodes et al., 2010). This dividedness results not only in blindspots, but also 'antinomies': on the one hand, biomedical approaches focusing on physiological processes forget about the cultural constituents of the body itself, which does not simply exist in a cultural setting, but rather built around social structures; on the other hand, social scientific approaches tend to end up in a 'disembodied cognitivist' position ignoring the possibility of a non-symbolic meaning operating on the pre-reflective physiological level (Weinberg, 2002). Furthermore, as the disciplinary dividedness has far reaching consequences for social policies and therapeutic praxes, the reductionist models threaten with the limited efficiency or complete misguidedness of the interventions. In order to avoid these traps, a proper model of addiction is needed, which is capable of moving forward from the traditional ontological distinctions, such as the material and immaterial, the body and mind, or the object and subject. As it has been suggested by others as well (Fraser et al., 2018), actor-network theory may provide a suitable basis for such enterprise.

In the first section, various phenomenological descriptions of addiction are overviewed in order to reveal the idealtypical inner mechanisms maintaining the pathology of the 'motivational system'. According to these analyses, the dynamics of addiction is fundamentally related to the distortion of being in the world: a subjectivity based on immersing in an object by relating to it solely on the basis of 'passive synthesis'; incapability of relating to the others as 'faces'; 'inauthentic existence'. While trying to find a solution to this condition, the actor turns to those technologies, which are provided as means of managing pain and pleasure. However, as these technologies are not suited to treat the existential source of the distortion, only the experienced symptoms, they trap the actor, who can choose between the original suffering and the dependence on the temporary solutions. In the second part, various social theories are overviewed, which provide conceptual tools for elaborating the late modern social factors of addiction: Latour's actor-network theory, Honneth's theory of reification, Lash's theory of information society and Rosa's theory of acceleration. In the third part, the results of these reconstructions are combined into a social phenomenology of addiction: the original distortion of existence is conceptualized as a consequence of reification, that is being stuck in intermediator position of actor-networks; the technologies promising escape are reinterpreted as mediators enabling the temporary shift between mediator and intermediator roles; the normalization of the usage of these technologies is interpreted through the models of information and acceleration society (both of them exemplify the normalization of hybrid subjectivities balancing on the border of mediator and intermediator roles). Based on these analyses, it is concluded that in late modernity addiction becomes a naturalized form of existence: it originates from empty suffering related to reification, which is handled by mediators promising a relative improvement in the form of a hybrid subjectivity (characterized by partly mediator and intermediator roles).

Balancing on the verge of subjectivity: Phenomenological descriptions of addiction

Even though addiction has many faces depending on the activity or substance being at its core, yet there are several fundamental characteristics, which are present in most of its occurrences. Furthermore, even if it is impossible to talk about a unified description of addiction (as psychological, biological and social scientific approaches develop their own variants focusing on different elements), yet a general phenomenological description may be elaborated. In what follows, an attempt is made to provide such idealtypical model.[2] This could help identifying the latent social distortions related to addiction, which is understood as a dimension of empty suffering.

As a meta-analysis of psychological studies argues, addiction is a pathology of the 'motivational system': it originates from the dysfunctions of the response, impulse-inhibition, evaluation and planning subsystems (West and Brown, 2013: 8). These elements express the gradual levels of consciousness in the process of the birth of motivation as a starting point of action: what is perceived by the actors as an intent implying a certain behaviour pattern is constituted of both conscious (e.g. evaluation) and unconscious (e.g. impulse-inhibition) elements interacting with each other (e.g. certain impulses are considered to be useful, while others are to be repressed, which is both shaped by individual responses and the social environment).

The motivational system is unstable by design: it needs to remain flexible in order to secure adaptation to varying environments. Addiction is characterized by the loss of this flexibility: if the feedback mechanisms (being responsible for preventing the exclusivity of any particular form of motivation) are suspended, either because of inner or environmental causes, the actor becomes fixated on a single behaviour pattern, which starts to dominate their horizon (West and Brown, 2013: 9).

Various theories of addiction explore the causes of this dysfunctionality. The incomplete list of the available explanations include learning theories (referring to positive and negative reinforcing mechanisms), drive theories (referring to particular unconscious motivational forces), inhibition dysfunction theories (referring to the inability of resisting certain impulses), imitation theories (referring to the interiorizing of social practices), choice theories (referring to rational and biased decision of the costs and rewards of certain behaviour), positive reinforcement theories (emphasizing the extreme form of pleasures implying the craving for repetition), need theories (referring to either pre-existing or acquired necessities), identity theories (emphasizing the lifeworld built around certain objects of dependence), biological theories (referring to dysfunctional or modified brain processes) and social theories (emphasizing the role of the relevant others in the social network, the supply-demand balance, the marketing and communicating elements or the organizational elements – West and Brown, 2013: 153). Such overview reveals the wide range of – unconscious, conscious, social and biological – factors contributing to the emergence of the distortion of the motivational system. However, in order to move towards a unified model capable of synthesizing these results, a common denominator is required.

For this purpose, a phenomenological model is elaborated, which is capable of integrating the conclusions of the divergent researches by translating their results to a common pre-disciplinary language. From a Husserlian perspective it may be argued that addiction impacts the subject at the fundamental level of giving sense to the world. Construction of meanings occurs through passive synthesis (i.e. the functioning of idealizations and schemas) and active interpretation (i.e. turning the attention towards prominent objects). While most acts of perception include both elements, in case of addiction the former becomes dominant. The addicts do not simply turn towards a certain object, while keeping a distance needed for reflection; instead they are completely immersed in the object, which becomes the sole source of sense for them, while their ego is silenced (Copoeru, 2014). Accordingly, the basic phenomenological sense of addiction is the complete dependence on the object as a source of meaning: the subjects subordinate themselves to it by resolving from taking actively part in the construction of its meaning. This one-sided unification with the object results in the elimination of the boundaries between the ego and the thing: the subject becomes fixated on the object, thus starts to live for it. Gradually the whole lifeworld is constituted around the object of addiction, which is now at the centre of the world, the one and only reference point of measuring any other persons and things. In sum, addiction is characterized by the giving up of the active role in the process of interpreting the world – the subject is restricted to passive synthesis with an object, which becomes the sole source of meaning.

From the perspective of Levinas' ethical phenomenology, these observations may be complemented at important points. According to him, not every type of fixation leads to addiction: this is a particular danger emerging in interactions with objects (or objectified subjects). The world is constituted of two types of entities according to the capability of contributing to the process of giving sense: 'things' cannot interpret themselves, while 'faces' are capable of denying the interpretation of the subject by giving sense to themselves (Levinas, 1969). Unlike in case of things, which do not imply any sort of relationship, least of all fixation, the noticing of face implies an absolute ethical responsibility, that is a complete devotion to the other.[3] However, interaction with the face and the consequent responsibility differs from addiction: the other constitutes an ever-changing horizon, which can be approached in a hermeneutic way (with the intention of mutual understanding), not instrumentally (with the purpose of consumption or usage). Accordingly, fixation on the other does not imply the giving up of agency – this occurs only in case of subject-object relations. As the ethical relating to the face is prior to any ontological relating to things (Levinas, 1969), it may be argued that the addictive phenomenological structure originates from a distortion of intersubjectivity (Peperzak, 2009). It occurs if a category mistake is made: a subject relates to an object in an absolute way, which is originally applicable only to other subjects. The object of addiction is none other than the missing face, which is mistakenly treated by the subject with absolute, undivided attention (that is a passive synthesis replacing mutual understanding). As this category mistake inevitably fails, the substantive responsibility (i.e. the engagement with the needs of the face) is transformed into an empty fixation on the non-existing needs of the object.

Intersubjectivity is not only the birthplace of ethical commitments, but also of the self, which is constituted as an autonomous subject in the ethical process of taking responsibility for the other. Consequently, the replacement of the union with the other by the union with an object reconfigures the whole lifeworld, which is divided into three interrelated modalities. The 'high' is characterized by the complete immersion in the object: autonomous consciousness is suspended, as the subject is reduced to an attachment of the object. The end of high is followed by the emergence of 'craving', which is characterized by a sense of disorientation and the desire of filling the vacuum created by the passing experience of immersion: thus, in this phase the goal of repetition becomes exclusive. Unless, this drive succeeds, 'deprivation' begins, which is characterized by a frozen, depressive world: no activities seem to be meaningful anymore, while superfluity becomes a dominant experience (Di Petta, 2018). Together, these phases indicate the distortion of the plasticity of time consciousness. The subject loses the capability of inhabiting an open horizon of future including the potential of aiming at distant goals, while shaping the world according to them. In case of an addict lifeworld, such horizon is inaccessible, as the subject is lost in the continuous present organized by the drive for the high. While the horizon of craving and high includes a short term, temporal horizon of future, as the cycle is restarted over and over again, the constitution of linear time is ultimately suspended. The addict is dropped out of time, which is fragmented into continuously repeated cycles (Kemp, 2009).

Based on these observations, it may be argued that addiction originates from the potential of subjects becoming objects by letting themselves being absorbed in the engagement with things. Accordingly, addiction depends not only on the horizon of the subjects, but also on the space of possibilities outlined by the used or consumed things (Schalow, 2017). In order to understand the impact of this space, the phenomenological role of technology as the instrument of socially reconfiguring nature has to be clarified. According to Heidegger's analyses, technology has become the fundamental element of modern existence, as more and more aspects of everyday life are intermediated by functionally differentiated objects designed to manipulate nature in a specific way (Heidegger, 1977). These technological instruments promise control in those interactions with nature, which are originally characterized by contingent outcomes – that is a prospect of control over pleasure and pain.[4] As such control becomes a possibility, pleasure and pain depends – beside the availability and accessibility of the technologies – solely on the subject's will.[5] Therefore, in the age of technology, the real question is not, why do actors become addicted to certain objects ensuring pleasure; instead, why is not everyone addicted (Schalow, 2017: 32)?[6]

Even if it may seem to depend on the choice of the actors, the immersion in technologically controlled, pleasant sensations is seldom based solely on the decision of the individual. It is always embedded in a social and cultural context defining the frames of relating to such technologies. In modernity, the dividing line between nature and technology is blurred, which implies the naturalization of the instruments at hand: they are not anymore perceived as targets of moral or ethical evaluation, but as the extensions of nature, that is evidently given usable things. As the mere existence of a technology implies a general encouragement of using it, the critical reflection on whether it should be used or not becomes the exception. Relying uncritically on technology is the feature of the 'they' (*das Man*), which means that the addiction originating from such relation is an expression of 'inauthentic existence' (Schalow, 2017: 38). The only way of escaping the allurement of technologies providing control over pleasure is the escape from the influence of the 'they' and the aim for an authentic way of being characterized by voluntarily abstaining from the instrumental governance of sensations.

However, such abstinence is particularly difficult not only because of the peer pressure of the 'they', but also because of the strength of the sensations enabled by the technologies.[7] The moments of 'high' are ecstatic in a sense that they may provide the unique experience of complete carelessness and security, which is in sharp contrast with the careful and insecure experience of everyday life (Leneghan, 2011). Due to these experiences, the objects of addiction are reinterpreted as fetishes: even if they are not influencing the actor at a particular moment, they are desired as the sole keys to a pleasant or pain-free existence. Accordingly, the technology turned into fetish completely fills the temporal horizon of the addict (either as an actual or a missing sensation), whose whole world starts to be built around it (Schalow, 2017: 52). As a result, the potential of control, which was originally the promise of the technology turns out to be the cause of actually losing control. If technologies of pleasure and pain are used uncritically, in an inauthentic way, the subjects lose their autonomy of organizing time or engaging intersubjective relationships. They become part of a strictly functional order, where pleasure and pain may be controlled, but only in a confined space, which is indifferent to the needs of the subjects. Through the technology used, the subjects are integrated in a broader functional order, where their pain and pleasure exist as part of the infrastructure. Therefore, the naturalized consumption of the pain and pleasure management technologies ultimately results in the helplessness of the subject, who becomes controlled by those instruments, which were originally used in the promise of providing control. However, such danger is not new: it is revealed by the earliest criticisms of modernity, namely by Marx's analyses of capitalism (Schalow, 2017: 62).

As a consequence of the capitalist logic of reproduction, the workers become objects (due to their workforce being treated as commodity). Their enjoyment and suffering is also commodified: it has a technology, a price and a place (i.e. 'free time'), which are all dependent on the functional order of the market.[8] In this constellation there is no need for transcendental legitimacy of power (which is expressed in the phrase: 'religion is the opium of the people') – power is justified directly by the technologies of pain and pleasure (which is expressed by the paraphrase: 'opium becomes the opium of the people' – Schalow, 2017: 63). This broader social context is a central element of the social phenomenology of modern addiction: an inauthentic existence relies on a reinforcing self-delusion, which is responsible for naturalizing the cycle of highs and cravings. As the acquired technologies of pain and pleasure enable the temporary overwriting of 'moods', they create not only the experience of being in control, but also the impression of living a meaningful life and an identity built around the consumed goods. However, these interpretations are tenable only as long as the consuming is practiced ceaselessly. The instruments of control do not have any inherent, substantive impact, which would last after their consumption. Accordingly, the impression of being in control proves to be an illusion veiling the existential trap of continuous consumption. By acquiring technologies of mood, the existential challenges are not resolved, rather postponed – only to return in an even severer form right after the pain-killing effect is gone (Schalow, 2017: 72). These analyses highlight the broader consequences of futile ownership and power trough indirect pain, elaborated in Chapters 1 and 3.

Addiction relies on the illusion of control, which is reinforced by the social practices and institutions of capitalist production and consumption. The structural pressure is so strong, that addiction is one of those rare mental disorders, which is often not perceived as problematic by the affected persons. As relating to things and the others according to the logic acquiring and consuming is culturally approved in modernity, addiction also becomes a normalized being in the world (Schalow, 2017: 77). It is perceived to be problematic only in those cases, where it threatens the very foundations it is built on: if the technology of pleasure and pain management is used in such a great extent that it becomes unsustainable (either because their acquisition is not affordable or because the consumption becomes unrewarding). In these cases, the existential challenges postponed by the technologies become visible, along with the consequences of the unsatisfied desires. Accordingly, addiction is never solely a mental disorder of the individual, but also a symptom of a cultural crisis (Schalow, 2017: 117). Consequently, the treatment of addiction cannot be based only on individual therapeutic praxes. It is a paradox of biomedical paradigm how to treat distortions originating from the emergence of technology (and capitalism) with further technologies (see Chapter 3). Instead, a phenomenologically informed intervention needs to start with the basic structures of being in the world including the distortions of intersubjectivity, time consciousness, horizon of control and culture (Schalow, 2017: 162).[9]

A common denominator of these various approaches is the reconfiguration of agency: unlike many mental disorders (such as depression or anxiety), addiction is not a form of helplessness (resulting from either a dispirited distortion of mood or a paralysing misinterpretation of the future), but an ambivalent limitation of agency. Those, who suffer from addiction are just as assertive as any other subjects: they focus on goals to be reached by the most efficient way possible. The main difference is the level of obsession: in case of an addict lifeworld, one central goal completely fills the horizon overwriting any other considerations. As the addicts lose the ability of deliberately choosing from a set of potential goals, their autonomy is limited to the differentiation of means. Accordingly, the addict is in ambiguous position: on the one hand maintains agency (by aspiring for a certain goal), on the other hand suffers from losing it (by not being able to choose from alternative goals). As modern subjectivity is based on the assumption of freedom of will, this paradox condition questions the foundations of the self: as the loss of autonomy is experienced, subjectivity itself becomes contingent. In this sense, the stakes of addiction concern the ontological status of the actor: depending on the outcome of the struggle, they may either regain their subjectivity or be reduced to a mere extension of an object. As the subject-object metamorphosis is at the centre of addiction, it is not surprising that it emerges around those situations, where such transformation is not a mere accident, but a functional necessity (e.g. constellations unbearable as a subject, but temporarily survivable as an object; or liminal conditions and rites, where the status of the subject is reconfiguring).

These phenomenological analyses complement those various psychological models, which describe addiction as a pathology of the motivational system. Addiction emerges in those situations, where becoming or being a subject is difficult (see social and imitation theories), thus the self is modified: instead of engaging in reassuring intersubjective relationships, a technology is used for inhabiting the world (see choice theories). While this creates a temporary solution for controlling pleasure and pain (see reinforcement and learning theories), an illusion of constructing a meaningful identity is born (see identity theories). The subjects are trapped in this situation, as they rely on the supplementary technology (see need and biological theories). As a result, the actors not only lose their autonomy (and the prospect of authenticity), but as they inhabit a world adjusted to an object, they cease to be subjects (see drive theories). By following the perpetual cycles of high and craving, they move in unchangeable tracks, as if being turned into automatons. All in all, the various scientific theories highlight particular elements of a general phenomenological reconstruction of addiction. These correspondences not only reinforce the reliability of the idealtypical phenomenological description, but also provide insight for the further development of the model into a sociological direction.

Addiction emerges in social constellations, which are characterized by an initial difficulty forcing the actor of giving up its authenticity and autonomy. If technologies providing escape from the difficulty by enabling the immersion in an object are available, the actors may use this option. If the usage is socially supported or simply remains unchecked, while the difficulties persist, then the escape becomes a habit. Consequently, the actor is trapped in the cycle of seeking the redeeming technology and facing the dread of its lack. Gradually, this exposedness transforms them: as the technology, which used to be a temporary solution to difficulties becomes the basis of existence, the actors lose the ability of shifting between the passive and active modalities of engaging the world – they become passive extensions of the applied technology. Therefore, in order to reconstruct the social constituents of addiction as a distorted phenomenological pattern, three factors need to be mapped: the ones related to the difficulties of existing as a subject and constructing intersubjectivity; the technologies promising control over lost authenticity; and the everyday practices, the cultural and structural components of the normalization of a partly objectified existence.

Actor-networks of reification, information and acceleration

In case of depression, the most relevant social theories are related to material or symbolic capitals and to the linguistic or mediatized communication, as these highlight the late modern characteristics of the transforming ownership and intersubjectivity (see Chapter 4). In case of anxiety, the most relevant social theories refer to networks of ontological security and trust, as these explain the late modern aspects of negative integration (see Chapter 5). In case of addiction, those social theories are relevant, which explain the objectifying consequences of an indirect biomedical power (see Chapter 3). As most social theories focus on the actors' motivations and interpretation of the world or their structural and institutional environment, material things appear on their horizon as theoretically marginal entities adjusting to the instrumental goals of the subjects. This general blindspot prevents the adequate analysis of those social phenomena, which are characterized by the blurring of the boundaries between objects and subjects and the back and forth shift of the actor's ontological status. In order to overcome this sociological short-sightedness, firstly Latour's actor-network theory is overviewed, which aims at criticizing the immaterial focus of social theories, while introducing an alternative approach. Even if the sociological analyses of addiction rely on various theoretical sources, a common feature characterize most of them: because of the inevitable normative connotations of the topic, they share some sort of critical stance (Netherland, 2012). However, Latour's approach is not providing any normative basis – therefore, it has to be complemented with further theories, such as Honneth's, Lash's and Rosa's reflections on late modernity.

According to Latour's approach, mainstream sociology has been following a misleading track since the triumph of the Durkheimian tradition, which understands 'social forces' (e.g. norms or collective representations) as immaterial causes explaining the integration of social units and the coordinated action of the individuals. Consequently, universal models of integration were postulated, resulting in the ignorance of the material components of sociability. In order to overcome this blindspot, an artificially naïve approach needs to be elaborated, based on the principle of 'follow the actors!' (Latour, 2005: 30). From this perspective, networks of subjects and objects appear, whose complex interactions result in those phenomena, which are over-simplified by the categories of the 'sociology of the social'. Notions like action, society, community, values or norms narrow the complexity of social phenomena, thus prevent proper understanding. They presuppose some sort of immaterial social facticity, which is followed, approved or incorporated by the actors, therefore explains the phenomena themselves. Even if the theories of the social played a key role at the time of grounding sociology, since then they became counterproductive. By postulating the existence of universal social forces integrating interactions in the same fashion, they ended up in empirically unsustainable over-generalizations (Latour, 2005: 9).

In order to overcome the limitation of these generalizing models, the way the social is understood needs to be rephrased. Instead of viewing it as a solid structure capable of imposing itself on the individual, it should be viewed as a temporary assemblage of human and non-human 'actants' (that is subjects or objects holding the potential of becoming causes). In the constantly changing configurations, human and non-human entities may equally play an active or a passive role. In this sense actor-networks are hybrid configurations, which do not adjust to any universal schema: instead they are built up from the interactions of the actants adapting to the broader environment and each other at the same time (Latour, 2005: 52). Actor-networks are constituted of 'intermediators' (actants passively transmitting effects) and 'mediators' (actants actively initiating effects). In order to have any sort of impact on the environment, human and non-human actants must embed their activity into the material world. It is the material realization of the effects, which translates potential influences into actual impact. While this insight may seem obvious, it has widespread consequences, as it redirects the researchers' attention to those material objects, which are invisible in most interactions despite their indispensability (Latour, 2005: 82).

The non-human elements of actor-networks are usually considered to be simple extensions of the autonomous subjects, which is a biased perception rooted deeply in the long history of subject-object dualism. Even if a human actant may have a clear intention about the way and purpose of using a certain tool, that does not imply either the realization of the intention or its exclusivity. Objects also imply directives through their design, which either express the intentions of their creators or emerge as unintended consequences (Latour, 1992). Accordingly, in an actor-network, it is always an open question, whether the human or non-human actors play a decisive role: objects may be used by the subjects and vice versa, subjects may become intermediators that is the extensions of objects. Furthermore, it is also possible that whole networks become represented by single entities in the process of 'translation' (Callon, 1986). From a phenomenological perspective it may be argued, that actor-networks introduce a horizon of meaning, which is not simply constructed in intersubjective interactions, but also based on 'inter-objectivity'. Interpretations of the world motivating and coordinating social action are not exclusively born in individual reflection and communicative action, but also shaped by those effects, which originate from the objects functioning as mediators (Latour, 2005: 195).

The inter-objective lifeworld of actor-networks is capable of integrating the assemblages of subjects and objects, despite them potentially having divergent aims and interpretations of the world. From this perspective, what is understood by immaterial sociology as a social action integrated by universal social forces, can be reinterpreted as a momentary conjunction of the – often conflicting – mediators and intermediators. While this theoretical model was originally developed for the purpose of interpreting micro level social phenomena, it provides tools for interpreting macro level constellations as well. The universality claim of concepts like norms or law are based on the experience of recurring patterns of social relationships. Even though the empirical traces of integration patterns transcending particular settings do not ground a thesis of universality, the recurrences cannot be neglected: actor-network theory explains them by referring to material mediators or translations, which are present in numerous parallel constellations. Even if these highly influential 'plug-ins' enable macro integration, they are not universal at all: instead, they refer to popular, widely used technologies, which influence the inter-objective structure of independent constellations in a similar way. Widespread cultural phenomena and structural constraints can both be explained by referring to those related technologies (as material mediators), which are responsible for similar causal effects in various settings (Latour, 2005: 239).

While Latour's theory sheds light on those social theoretical concepts, which help to describe a constellation, where the boundaries between subject and object become blurred, it is not capable of explaining those substantive tendencies of modernization, which are responsible for the late modern expansion of addiction.[10] For this purpose, further theories need to be introduced, which are capable of highlighting the difficulties of authentic existence; the erosion of phenomenological engagement with the world; and the transformation of temporal structures. For these purposes three examples are overviewed: Honneth's theory of reification, Lash's theory of information society and Rosa's theory of social acceleration. By complementing the actor-network theory with these insights, the social constituents of an addicted being in the world may be elaborated.[11]

The rich conceptual history of reification starts with Marx. According to his diagnosis, as the rise of capitalism reconfigures the balance of use and exchange value by making the latter absolute, the laws of the market organized around the oscillation of demand and supply become deterministic, quasi-natural laws in the eyes of the actors, who are reduced to commodities, while being forced to sell their workforce in exploitative market relations (Markus, 1982). Lukacs complements this diagnosis, by referring to Weber's analyses of instrumental rationalization: as it becomes the principle organizing not only economy, but almost every spheres of life, its consequences are also generally experienced. The whole world is reframed according to the formal logic of utility and profitability: as the individual quality of particular things and subjects is overwritten by a quantitative evaluation, everything – including the actors themselves – is reduced to replaceable things (Arato, 1972). While Marx and Lukacs explained reification by referring mostly to causes related to capitalism, according to Habermas' diagnosis of times, reification is not anymore related to the distortions of the market; rather it becomes a consequence of the 'colonization of lifeworld' by functionalist reason. As the space of speech acts is gradually reduced by the expansion of mediatized interactions, not simply the subjects, but the very structure of intersubjectivity is distorted: instead of enabling the communicative grounding of existence, it contributes to the reproduction of subjects treated as mere things (Habermas, 1986: 318).

While every conceptualization of reification aims at broadening the scope of the notion, most versions still explain it as a consequence of either capitalism, rationalization or system differentiation. Reification as a universal possibility of sociability has been elaborated recently by Honneth. He argues that beside critical theories relying on Marx's initial diagnosis, experiences similar to reification have been analyzed from other perspectives as well (the best example is Heidegger's 'forgetfulness of being' – Honneth, 2006: 111). These analyses also refer to the dangers of a constraint-free, potentially authentic existence. Even if they do not focus on the capitalist market or instrumental rationality, they still highlight the element of misrecognition originating from an objectifying gaze. Whether it is motivated by scientific, administrative or economic reasons, it implies a withdrawal of recognition: the human and non-human elements of the world are perceived schematically, while their individual qualities are ignored. Such lack of recognition is never the initial approach: the moment a phenomenon emerges, it appears as a worthy target of attention, that is an interesting particular object. While this initial perspective implies recognition – which is the precondition of any later processes of cognition – the systematic unfolding of the phenomenon implies a generalizing, classificatory perspective. The application of such perspective reframes the phenomenon in a schematic, reifying way. Accordingly, reification is a universal phenomenological malfunction: the forgetting of the initial recognition (Honneth, 2006: 125).

This interpretation complements the classic ones by highlighting how reification may occur in everyday actor-networks of late modernity. Even if it is more probable in those actor-networks, which include the most influential mediators of the capitalist market or the bureaucratic administrative institutions, it may appear in just about any constellations. If mediators constitute an inter-objective horizon, where the recognition of certain elements of the actor-network is forgotten, then reification emerges. It is not necessarily related to any general tendencies (plug-ins), such as the impact of money or law as translations (even if probably these constellations still remain the most typical occurrences). Instead a configuration preventing recognition may emerge due to the influence of any mediators, which either blocks the perception of individual entities; or transforms the subjects into mere intermediators incapable of initiating and experiencing recognition. In these cases, the actor-network constitutes an environment, where autonomous, active subjectivities are difficult to maintain.

While reification theory indicates the threat of being transformed into a mere object as a result of not being recognized; it does not discuss those technologies, which have the potential of establish actor-networks systematically preventing recognition. At this point, the example of information technology as a widely used, particularly influential mediator needs to be analyzed. According to Lash's approach, action coordination can be understood through the notions of aesthetic reflexivity and the technical-constructed aspect of the social environment. Modernity is characterized by the dialectic of instrumental rationality aiming at classifying and controlling the world and the attempts of evading the consequences of objectification. In late modernity, instrumental rationalization affects not only the normative regulation or the classification of the world; it has become the constitutive element of the technical environment mediating the everyday experiences. These mediators include the technical tools and the built environment structuring the space of everyday actions and representing uncontestable latent norms (Lash, 1999). In this context the information networks play a distinctive role, as they operate on a symbolic level. Unlike meaning constructed either in personal or interpersonal reflection, information being transmitted through networks of mass communication limits interpretation and understanding. Instead of relying on narratives, it is based on the logic of continuous stimulation. As the endless stream of ephemeral information fills the horizon, it also eliminates the time required to process and understand. In this sense the price of real time communication is the elimination of the space of interpretation, that is, the erosion of narratives structuring of experiences (Lash, 2002).

These observations complement the actor-network theory by highlighting a specific late modern technology channelling the logic of instrumental rationalization into everyday actor-networks. The mediators of information technology reconfigure both the horizon of the individuals and the frames of interaction. The data streamed through them is on the one hand a rival of the perceived lifeworld: the attention is divided at every moment between virtual and actual objects. On the other hand, even in those cases, when the non-virtual world stands at the centre of attention, it is accessed through the glass of 'augmented reality', that is information filters provided by the technology: the space is transformed into GPS-coordinates, the things are evaluated according to their online ratings, experiences are constructed from the perspective of their social media representation. Furthermore, the processes of interpersonal and public communication organized by the mediators of information technology are also reduced: as the space for narrative meaning construction is limited, the continuous flow of transmitted and received ephemeral data undermines both mutual understanding and collective deliberation. Consequently, the mediators and translations of information technology, while promising unprecedented control over interpretation, actually normalize the praxes of perceiving and discussing the world according to the oversimplifying and schematic bits of binary codes (e.g. the quantitative logic of 'likes' or ratings replacing qualitative narrations).

The phenomena related to reification and the streaming of information do not leave unaffected the temporal structures of late modernity either. While the acceleration of life has been detected since classic social theories, either as a consequence of rationalization, functional adaptation, profit maximizing or individualization, it has never been analyzed as an independent tendency (Rosa, 2009: 79). Rosa aims at reconstructing the dimensions, causes and consequences of acceleration. Initially the technological (e.g. the transformation of the means of transportation and communication), social (e.g. the unpredictability of production, the insecurity of institutions and the normalization of atypical family and relation forms) and everyday (e.g. the maximization of positive experiences and 'flow' in every possible activity, multi-tasking) aspects can be differentiated as independent sources of acceleration. While these internal dimensions are influencing each other in several ways, still their dynamics differ as the economic (i.e. the speeding of production and consumption as a consequence of market competition), cultural (i.e. the promise of development implying the hastening of change for the sake of change) and structural causes (i.e. the increased complexity of social systems as a consequence of improving adaptation through intensified secondary observation of the environment) of acceleration affect them differently. This explains the emergence of desynchronization as a basic experience of late modern actors (Rosa, 2009: 97). Such experience reconfigures not only the timeframes of institutions (e.g. political subsystem becomes too slow to process information adequately, thus gives up its claim for rationality), but also the fundaments of identity construction. The subject develops only temporary identities, without a prospect of committing to them and starts to live in the present, as the past becomes irrelevant and the future unpredictable (Rosa, 2013: 231).

These observations highlight the specific dynamics of actor-networks in late modernity. Not only do the configurations change at an increased pace, but also the human and non-human elements of the actor-network constitute a desynchronized inter-objective complex. In this constellation, the promise of predictability and stability becomes a scarce resource. Therefore, those actants, which are capable of providing repeatable patterns, become distinguished elements of actor-networks, as they have a good chance of being recognized as reference points. In this competition, human actors characterized by fragmented and temporally disoriented identities are in a disadvantaged position compared to non-human technologies being designed to operate the same way in every constellation. Consequently, they have a better chance of becoming mediators – a bias resulting in the further insecurity of the actors, who do not have other choice but to rely on them in the pursuit of control. As the pace of life becomes attached to the pace of technology, not only acceleration increase, but also the chance of reclaiming an authentic personal time diminishes.

Beyond subjectivity: The phenomenology of addictive actor-networks

After overviewing the phenomenological constituents of addiction along with their late modern structural constituents, an attempt can be made to elaborate a social phenomenology of addiction. Such reconstruction is constituted of three phases: firstly, those burdensome actor-networks are reconstructed, which compel the actors to seek escape-technologies; secondly, those mediator technologies are identified, which provide a way out from the original suffering; thirdly, those normalizing mechanisms are described, which maintain the usage, despite the emerging, new forms of burdensome experiences.

Generally, the passivity and activity of subjects and objects is not predetermined: as both subjects and objects may become mediators and intermediators, the distribution of roles depends on the particular configuration of the actor-network. However, in modernity, several actants and translations emerge, which systematically distort the odds of subjects becoming mediators. Among them, those need to be emphasized in the first place, which are responsible for reification. From an actor-network theoretical perspective, reification refers to mediators and translations, which limit the human actants by preventing any configurations, where they could become mediators themselves.

The example of the capitalist market, or the bureaucratic administrative system exemplify how these configurations operate: subjects entering these actor-networks are immediately subordinated to forces transforming them to a mere workforce or legal entity. Starting from that point, their agency may be expressed solely through the translations of market and the legal system. The mediators involved do not simply frame the action situations, but rather constitute them: they add their own impact to the actor-network by outlining the sphere of possibility (i.e. translating any interactions to the terms of prices or legality); regulating the order of interactions (i.e. differentiating between the roles of worker/employee or legal expert/lay people); and determining the dynamics of activities (i.e. initiating and ending market transactions or administrative procedures). As a consequence, within those actor-networks, where reifying mediators appear – either through translations (e.g. employing or legal authorities), or mediators (e.g. money or contracts) – the subjects are reduced to mere intermediators transmitting other actants' will, while having extremely limited possibility of complementing it with their own intentions. Beside market and legal actor-networks, similar mechanisms may operate in configurations, where the subjects' individual qualities are made to be forgotten, that is being replaced by generalizing schemas preventing recognition. This may occur either as a consequence of interpretations overwriting the perception of the particular other (e.g. stereotypes, prejudices), or circumstances shrouding the sight of the other (e.g. ignorance emerging in over-crowded networks), or liminal conditions, where the mediator-intermediator distinction is blurred (e.g. rites of passage[12]).

Both the field-related and the unspecific actor-networks of reification result in similar experiences, as they lead to an existence, where the subjects are deprived from their agency. They are constrained by relations, which are prescribing specific forms of activity, while excluding any prospect of modifying the frames. Such experience is inauthentic in Heideggerian sense, as the subject is allowed to exist solely as one of the many 'they', who are also exposed to similar constraints. In these actor-networks, the possibility of face experiences in Levinasian sense is also limited, as the dominant mediators veil the individual characteristics. Accordingly, in these actor-networks both the individual and intersubjective paths of becoming autonomous subjects are limited. These human actants do not have other choice but to transform into what they are allowed to be: intermediators transmitting external intentions. These transformations imply the internalization of the mechanic logic of the actor-network that is the logic of instrumentality. Reified subjects become functional elements of a broader complex of human and non-human actants equally following the directives of the dominant mediator. As a consequence, they are not only used by others, but also start relating to themselves instrumentally: that is they manage themselves in a functional way, by controlling their own pain and pleasure through predictable technological mediators.

Besides interiorizing of an instrumental relation to the self (originating from the reifying mediators), these human actants are exposed to experiences varying between distant sense of inappropriateness and explicit suffering. Even if they are not always aware of the lacking potentials, from time to time reified subjects still experience the contrast between the need for agency (that is a mediator position) and the reality of subordination (that is a consequence of an intermediator position). Accordingly, the traces of reification appear on their horizon, as an uncomfortable or unbearable experience motivating the seeking of escape. If the reifying actor-networks do not have alternatives, or disengaging from them is impossible, then the sole direction of overcoming the suffering is seeking mediators, which are capable of absorbing the unbearable experience, even if only temporarily. As a consequence, the reified subjects become susceptible to any technologies capable of making them forget about their prospectless intermediator status.

The reified position may turn into addiction as a consequence of the parallel occurrence of these two impacts: if the subjects relate to themselves the same instrumental way, they are being used in the actor-network; and start relying on technologies temporarily suspending their intermediator status, as a means of escape. The simplest way of escaping the burden of being deprived from agency is to switch off self-awareness by using mood altering technologies. These substances are not only capable of overwriting the suffering related to reified existence, but also providing a sense of control: even if the effect of the technology is temporary, initially the subject is in charge of when it is used. In this sense, they regain a sense of autonomy by becoming a mediator in the actor-network built around the attempt of escaping from the original reifying constellation. Even if these substitutive actor-networks enable a mediator role for the subject (who can choose the activation of the technology providing escape), from the moment the technology starts to operate, the subject is once again reduced into an intermediator. In these actor-networks relating to the world is based mostly on passive synthesis in Husserlian sense. As the subject intentionally activates a technology (for the sake of temporarily becoming free from the reifying constellation), whose main purpose is to disconnect them from the unbearable intermediator role, they also become immersed in the new mediator. This time, however reification is not experienced as a burden, but as a relative salvation: the applied technology creates an alternatively experienced form of reification in place of the burdensome one. Beside the physiological impact of the substances used for alternating mood, the element of becoming mediators for the moments of activating the technology also plays a key role. By actively using the substances, the whole experience of the inevitable reduction to intermediator role is reconfigured: instead of being pure reification, it includes the ambiguity of being on the verge of the mediator and intermediator roles. Even if this is only a cold comfort, yet it may be preferable compared to the original experience.

Beside the use of mediators directly altering the mood, another way of suspending reification is related to the creation of alternative actor-networks, where the actors may not only experience a role of a mediator, but also do that in a predictable manner. Developing actor-networks for the sake of experiencing control is a strategy relying on the replacement (or complementing) of reifying practices instead of switching off the awareness of reification. While such alternative actor-networks provide technologies, which reliably secure a mediator position, they are constructed as artificial bubbles, isolated from the broader social environment threatening with contingencies. The most typical examples of such bubbles are (virtual or live) games, which by providing arbitrary, but feasible challenges place the subject in a mediatory role within a specific setting. Even though these constellations do not affect the subject on a physiological level, as substances do, they follow a similar logic: the translations constituting an artificial actor-network do not address the original problem of reification by altering its configuration, but by creating independent safe terrains. Until the actor may immerse in them, these actor-networks provide a shelter from the burdensome experiences – however, the moment the subjects return to the original ones, their limitations become obvious. Despite the illusion of a mediator role maintained in these actor-networks, the subjects still end up in an intermediator position, because of their dependence on the broader environment (e.g. the cost of their maintenance has to be covered, which requires immersion in reifying market networks). As the artificially isolated actor-network is still embedded in the web of mediators determining its existence, from the perspective of the external mediators every actant within the artificial actor-network proves to be intermediator. Therefore, the artificial shelters are characterized by the same limitations as those substances, which provide escape from reification by altering mood on a physiological level. They are capable of countering the purely reifying actor-networks by creating ambivalent positions belonging to the mediator and intermediator roles at the same time.[13]

Such ambivalence of roles expresses a compromise, which is a fundamental characteristic of addiction: the unbearable experience of reification is replaced by experiences, wherein the reification is not eliminated, but complemented with elements of agency (i.e. the choosing and using of mood-altering substances or the entering of the escapist actor-networks). While this solution does not target the source of the original problem (i.e. it does not aim for changing the reifying actor-network), it creates an opportunity of moving away. The limited agency gained in these constellations inevitably results in paradoxes: as the boundary between mediator and intermediator roles is blurred, the actors have no choice, but to balance between the two. They aim at expanding their sphere of possibilities within an environment constantly limiting them to an intermediator role. The late modern phenomena of information and acceleration society exemplify how subjectivity is transformed within the ambiguous constellations of everyday life into a hybrid actor, who fights reification with technologies partly reifying them as well.

The actor-networks of information society are on the one hand characterized by the promise of interpreting the world according to an unlimited web of data; on the other hand, due to their constant streaming, they eliminate the space of narrative meaning formation. In this sense, they contribute to reification on a fundamental level of preventing the narrative construction of the lifeworld, but at the same time provide tools for inhabiting such constellation by transmitting useful or simply entertaining data in real time, which can be filtered and consumed by actors within a limitedly free framework. The actor-networks of acceleration society are on the one hand characterized by the increase of the density of experiences; on the other hand, create a desynchronized constellation, where both the future and the past become insecure. In this sense, they limit the horizon of time to perpetual present, while providing technologies granting control (e.g. technologies of time saving). As actor-networks following the logic of information and acceleration society constitute large part of the environment of the human actants in late modernity, a hybrid existence is inhabited, which is neither completely reified, nor enabling agency. As these actor-networks dominate the everyday life, the escape from reification resulting in the existential compromise of a hybrid existence is not an individual strategy anymore, but rather the general model of inhabiting the social structures of late modernity. The technologies capable of shifting between mediator and intermediator roles are becoming naturalized constituents of the everyday actor-networks, which means that they are also normatively approved.

The immersion in objects or activities, which provide temporary escape from reification (by creating actor-networks characterized by blurred boundaries between mediators and intermediators), on the one hand results in ecstatic experiences, on the other hand leads to a longing for repetition. The force of these experiences originates from two sources: escaping reification expresses a denial of being reduced to a mere intermediator; also the mediator experiences gathered in hybrid actor-networks refer to meanings, which may seem to be authentic compared to their completely inauthentic counterpart (e.g. being on 'high' every weekend may be perceived as a meaningful activity compared to a daily dull job). These partly negative and positive experiences of escaping an unbearable existence and becoming a hybrid subjectivity become addictive in those cases, if they provide an alternative, which is incomparably more liveable, than the original actor-networks. This means the craving emerges as a consequence of a relative difference between the everyday actor-networks characterized by a burdensome reified horizon and the technologically modified actor-networks characterized by a limited form of mediator roles.

A social phenomenological reconstruction of addiction helps not only to understand more precisely the existential switching taking place in the process, or the specific late modern constituents of these processes, but also highlights the potential ways out from the seemingly endless cycle of 'highs' and 'cravings'. Among the causes of addiction, a distorted social environment – which reduces the subject into a controllable object, while providing means of technological control in order to handle the negative consequences of reification – has central importance. From a health policy perspective, it may be argued, that the whole structure of actor-networks has to be transformed, so they do not threaten with reification in the first place.[14] While such transformations concern the fundamental structures of late modernity (such as capitalist market, bureaucratic systems), any intervention on these levels requires a careful deliberation of the risks and hopes related. This includes the mapping of those alternative ways of organizing actor-networks, which are as free from reification as possible, while maintaining as much functional efficacy as possible. Addiction can be fought by attempting to reconfigure the individual actor-networks: the most burdening, reifying constellations have to be sorted out, if that is not possible, the ones used for escape have to be optimized.

This means that, until the social structural environment of addictive actor-networks is not changed drastically (i.e. general reification is not reduced significantly), therapeutic interventions have to work with those hybrid subjectivities, which are developed by the reified actors for handling their own suffering. In these actor-networks, the specific contribution of those mediators, which are condemned for moral or biomedical reasons, have to be recognized as elements of a constellation providing relative improvement. The simple criminalization or pathologization of these mediators and the consequent banning of them does not provide solution, as it leaves the actor facing the original empty suffering without any countermeasures. Instead, the relative distance between the reifying and hybridizing actor-networks has to be minimized. This means that the dependence on the technologies of escape can be lessened only in parallel with the gradual decrease of the reifying experience of the everyday actor-networks. The existing therapeutic interventions provide several ideas about how this process can be imagined, however these should be complemented and grounded from the above introduced social phenomenological perspective. Actor-networks are needed, which not only provide more differentiated patterns of enjoyment, or less spiritless activities, but also having the potential of reintegrating the fragmented actor-networks of complete reification and of partial agency – that is a prospect of converging towards an existence, which is not authentic, but at least aware of the traps of the primary (reification) and secondary (addiction as a hybrid of agency and reification) challenges of late modern social suffering.

The example of addiction demonstrates not only the complex embeddedness of empty suffering in macro and micro structures, but also the directions of potential responses. In Part III an attempt is made to answer several related questions: what are the difficulties hybrid subjectivities face, while seeking new solutions?; why are new forms of solidarity indispensable in these processes?; and how can a social phenomenology of empty suffering contribute to therapeutic interventions?

Notes

1 Contemporary sociologies of addiction focus on three main topics: meta-theoretical reflection on addiction science; the agency of substances; and the phenomenological analysis of the embodiment of technologies (Fraser et al., 2014: 9). The following analyses belong to the last two subfields.
2 Of course, such attempt of elaborating an idealtypical model is not free from the danger of over-generalization – a problem arising along with the concept of addiction itself, which subsumes various phenomena – ranging from smoking to heroin use – under the same label. In order to avoid the danger of over-simplification, it has to kept in mind that idealtypical models are suitable only for theoretical purposes: when it comes to policy or therapeutic application, a differentiated approach is required (Kaye, 2012). Also it is important to be remembered that the construct of 'addict' itself is inseparable from the social-political-economic complex, which uses the category according to its interest (Fraser et al., 2014: 236). Therefore, the deconstructing of the notion is needed in order to become independent from such biased 'knowledge interest'.
3 It may be argued that addiction is the opposite of an enjoyment, which is paired with responsibility. This means that it emerges in those constellations, where the horizon of lifeworld does not include any references to the face as a source of ethical perspective. A lifeworld lacking the perspective of the other implies the loss of the subject as well, who – as being deprived from intersubjectivity – could relate to the world only through a passive synthesis with objects (Duyndam, 2009).
4 Even if the substances are often considered to have an objective, universal impact on the subject, as they are operating on a strictly bodily level, various research show that not even the most psychoactive drugs have a uniform effect. As the proper way of experiencing the drugs has to be learned, the technologies of altering mind are inevitably embedded in a social and cultural context, which also means that the control they provide has to be experimented with as well (Hartogsohn, 2017).
5 Not surprising that the doubt concerning the strength of such willpower accompanied the history of addiction in modernity, in the form of a 'panic of agency' (Melley, 2002).
6 According to a Deleuzian approach it may be argued that humans are 'desiring machines' by definition. Thus, addiction is not to be understood as a special condition, because of the fixation on certain objects, instead because of the reduction of the dimensions of desire. That is the addicts differ from everyday actors, because of their monomaniac pattern of desiring – thus the treatment also involves the broadening of their horizon, instead of reducing the strength of desire (Oksanen, 2013). In similar spirit, recent analyses relying on Zizek's theory of capitalism argue that addiction arise as commodification and over-intensified consumption distorts the subject's 'economy of desire' (Bjerg, 2008).
7 From a Lacanian perspective it may be argued that unlike pleasures originating from contingent, non-technological sources (e.g. the ones related to intersubjectivity), technological ones are following a rigid order, indifferent to the possibility of satisfaction. As a consequence, they constantly threaten with overdosing (Malone et al., 2015).
8 It may be argued that late capitalism is characterized not only by the exploitation of human labour, but also by the exploitation of desire, which indicates its successful colonizing process (Stiegler, 2013: 81).

9 From this perspective it is not surprising that one of the best known therapeutic method, the '12 steps program' targets these levels simultaneously (Schalow, 2017: 173).
10 Some of the most important criticism of Latour mentions the blindspot of actor-network theory concerning the questions of power and inequalities (Harris, 2005; Hornborg, 2013).
11 This synthesis enables the rephrasing of the problem of addiction as a 'socio-material pathology' (Birk, 2016), that is a complex form of distortion, which is unimaginable solely by either referring to any form of the social or the material.
12 Alcohol is used particularly frequently as a mediator serving such purposes. During adolescence young people find themselves in an ambiguous role between child- and adulthood. In this situation, they have to solve a paradox challenge: in order to become adults, they have to start using an adult habitus; however, this can be practiced only in adult actor-networks, where they could enter only by having an adult habitus. The paradox can be solved by relying on alcohol as a mediator: by letting it act instead of them, they can become mere intermediators not being responsible for the potential failures, while still being able to be present in the situation and practice adult habitus. In these situations the reifying potential of alcohol is used in an instrumental way, for the purpose of overcoming the paradoxes of a liminal condition (Demant, 2009).
13 It is worthy to mention that human actants are never mere intermediators in the actor-networks: even if they are attached or addicted to certain object (such as drugs, games or music), they actively try to use their environment for the purpose of ensuring their 'fix' or if it is needed to prevent themselves to have it (Gomart and Hennion, 1999).
14 Similar claims of a need for social policies grounded on the level of actor-network theory has been phrased by others as well (Fraser et al., 2018: 24). The line of thought elaborated above provides ideas about the execution of such theoretical grounding.

References

Arato, A. (1972) Lukacs' Theory of Reification. *Telos*, 11(1): 25–66.

Birk, R. H. (2016) From Social to Socio-Material Pathologies: on Latour, Subjectivity and Materiality. *Distinktion: Journal of Social Theory*, 17(2): 192–209.

Bjerg, O. (2008). Drug Addiction and Capitalism: Too Close to the Body. *Body & Society*, 14(2): 1–22.

Brodie, J. F. and Redfield, M. (Eds.) (2002) *High Anxieties. Cultural Studies in Addiction*. Berkeley, CA: UCP.

Callon, M. (1986) The Sociology of an Actor-Network. In Callon, M., Law, J. and Rip, A. (Eds.), *Mapping the Dynamics of Science and Technology*. London: Macmillan, 19–34.

Copoeru, I. (2014) Understanding Addiction: A Threefold Phenomenological Approach. *Human Studies*, 37(3): 335–349.

Crocq, M. A. (2007) Historical and Cultural Aspects of Man's Relationship With Addictive Drugs. *Dialogues in Clinical Neuroscience*, 9(4): 355–361.

Demant, J. (2009) When Alcohol Acts: An Actor-Network Approach to Teenagers, Alcohol and Parties. *Body & Society*, 15(1): 25–46.

Di Petta, G. (2018) The World of the Drug Addict. In Stanghellini, G., Broome, M., Raballo, A., Fernandez, A., Fusar-Poli, P. and Rosfort, R. (Eds.): *The Oxford Handbook of Phenomenological Psychopathology*. Oxford: Oxford University Press.

Duyndam, J. (2009) Sincerely Me. Enjoyment and the Truth of Hedonism. In Hofmeyr, B. (Ed.), *Radical Passivity: Rethinking Ethical Agency in Levinas*. Dordrecht: Springer, 55–66.

Fraser, S., Moore, D. and Keane, H. (2014) *Habits: Remaking Addiction*. Basingstoke: Palgrave.

Fraser, S., Valentine, K. and Ekendahl, M. (2018) Drugs, Brains and Other Subalterns: Public Debate and the New Materialist Politics of Addiction. *Body & Society*, 24(4): 58–86.

Golub, A., Bennett, A. S. and Elliott, L. (2015) Beyond America's War on Drugs: Developing Public Policy to Navigate the Prevailing Pharmacological Revolution. *AIMS Public Health*, 2(1): 142–160.

Gomart, E. and Hennion, A. (1999) A Sociology of Attachment: Music Amateurs, Drug Users. *The Sociological Review*, 47(1_suppl): 220–247.

Habermas, J. (1986) *The Theory of Communicative Action Vol.2: Lifeworld and System: A Critique of Functionalist Reason*. Boston, MA: Beacon Press.

Harris, J. (2005) The Ordering of Things: Organization in Bruno Latour. *Sociological Review*, 53(1): 163–177.

Hartogsohn, I. (2017) Constructing Drug Effects: A History of Set and Setting. *Drug Science, Policy and Law*, 3(1): 1–17.

Heidegger, M. (1977) *The Question Concerning Technology*. New York, NY and London: Garland.

Hirschfelder, G. (2014) The Myth of 'Misery Alcoholism' in Early Industrial England: The Example of Manchester. In Schmid, S. and Schmidt-Haberkamp, B. (Eds.), *Drink in the Eighteenth and Nineteenth Centuries*. London: Pickering & Chatto, 91–102.

Honneth, A. (2006) *Reification: A Recognition-Theoretical View*. The Tanner Lectures on Human Values. Online material: http://tannerlectures.utah.edu/_documents/a-to-z/h/Honneth_2006.pdf.

Hornborg, A. (2013) Technology as Fetish: Marx, Latour, and the Cultural Foundations of Capitalism. *Theory, Culture & Society*, 31(4): 119–140.

Kaye, K. (2012) De-Medicalizing Addiction: Toward Biocultural Understandings. In Netherland, J. (Ed.), *Critical Perspectives on Addiction*. Bingley: Emerald Group Publishing Limited, 27–51.

Kemp, R. (2009) The Temporal Dimension of Addiction. *Journal of Phenomenological Psychology*, 40(1):1–18.

Lash, S. (1999) *Another Modernity. A Different Rationality*. London: Blackwell.

Lash, S. (2002) *Critique of Information*. London: Sage.

Latour, B. (1992) Where Are the Missing Masses? The Sociology of a Few Mundane Artifacts. In Bijker, W. E. and Law, J. (Eds.), *Shaping Technology/Building Society*. Cambridge, MA: MIT Press, 225–225.

Latour, B. (2005) *Reassembling the Social: An Introduction to Actor-Network-Theory*. Oxford: Oxford University Press.

Leneghan, S. (2011) *The Varieties of Ecstasy Experience: An Exploration of Person, Mind and Body in Sydney's Club Culture*. Saarbrücken: Lambert Academic Publishing.

Levinas, E. (1969) *Totality and Infinity: An Essay on Exteriority*. London: Kluwer Academic Publishers.

Lynn, M. A. (2009) *Alcohol, Violence, and Disorder in Traditional Europe*. Kirksville, MO: Truman State University Press.

Malone, K. R., Bell, C. R. and Roberts, J. L. (2015) Technology and Addiction: Subjectivity, Scientific Knowledge and the Economy of Jouissance. *Subjectivity*, 8(2): 147–164.

Markus, G. (1982) Alienation and Reification in Marx and Lukacs. *Thesis Eleven*, 5–6(1): 139–161.

Melley, T. (2002) A Terminal Case: William Burroughs and the Logic of Addiction. In Brodie, J. and Redfield, M. (Eds.), *High Anxieties: Cultural Studies in Addiction*. London: University of California Press, 38–60.

Netherland, J. (2012) Introduction: Sociology and the Shifting Landscape of Addiction. In Netherland, J. (Ed.), *Critical Perspectives on Addiction*. Bingley: Emerald Group Publishing Limited, xi–xxv.

Oksanen, A. (2013) Deleuze and the Theory of Addiction. *Journal of Psychoactive Drugs*, 45(1): 57–67.

Peperzak, A. (2009) Sincerely Yours: Towards a Phenomenology of Me. In Hofmeyr, B. (Ed.), *Radical Passivity: Rethinking Ethical Agency in Levinas*. Dordrecht: Springer, 55–66.

Rhodes, T., Stimson, G. V., Moore, D. and Bourgois, P. (2010). Qualitative Social Research in Addictions Publishing: Creating an Enabling Journal Environment. *The International Journal on Drug Policy*, 21(6): 441–444.

Rosa, H. (2009) Social Acceleration: Ethical and Political Consequences of a Desynchronized High-Speed Society. In Rosa, H. and Scheuerman, W. (Eds.), *High-Speed Society: Social Acceleration, Power, and Modernity*. State College, PA: Penn State University.

Rosa, H. (2013) *Social Acceleration – A New Theory of Modernity*. New York, NY: Columbia UP.

Schalow, F. (2017) *Toward a Phenomenology of Addiction: Embodiment, Technology, Transcendence*. Cham: Springer International Publishing.

Shelby, C. L. (2016) The Culture of Addiction. In Shelby, C.L. (Ed.), *Addiction: A Philosophical Perspective*. London: Palgrave Macmillan.

Stiegler, B. (2013) *What Makes Life Worth Living: On Pharmacology*. Cambridge: Polity.

Weinberg, D. (2002). On the Embodiment of Addiction. *Body & Society*, 8(4), 1–19.

West, R. and Brown, J. (2013) *Theory of Addiction*. London: Wiley-Blackwell.

Part III

Beyond suffering

Spontaneous and hybrid strategies dealing with late modern social suffering

By approaching depression, anxiety and addiction from a sociological perspective, not only their increase in late modernity can be explained more precisely, but also our understanding of the potential treatments. Beyond social criticism, the conclusions of Part II may contribute to health policies and therapeutic praxes as well. On the one hand, they may provide new diagnostic possibilities: the identification of distorted networks reveals the depressive, anxious or addictive patterns of social suffering prior to the full development of psychopathologies. On the other hand, the social phenomenology of empty suffering could contribute to the interventions targeting the network of the sufferer instead of the individual cognitive or behavioural patterns: the distorted relation to the world can be deconstructed by increasing the proportion of undistorted micro/macro ties providing resilience on individual and community level. Of course, such approaches are not meant to replace, but to complement psychotherapeutic and psychiatric interventions, which are capable of resolving individual breakdowns, but struggle with treating relapse (related to the social environment). The ambition of Part III is to outline the basis of such critical, diagnostic and therapeutic possibilities.

The exploration of empty suffering would remain one-sided without the analysis of those efforts, which aim at handling suffering. Suffering never stands on its own: it is always embedded in a social context, which evaluates it from the perspective of compassion or ignorance, while providing or withholding support. The most elementary form of treating suffering is the lay praxis. Chapter 7 analyzes narrative attempts of making sense of depressive experiences in widely accessible online public spheres. While these platforms provide opportunity for reinterpreting the objectifying biomedical narratives, they are also burdened with the limitations of the partly also objectifying online communication. Beside these manifest functions, the latent structural components of a secular ritual healing process are also identified: it is argued that online discussions provide a highly contingent, yet capable means of restoring damaged intersubjectivity. Chapter 8 expands the question of empty suffering towards the possibility of solidarity. While in classic modernity, organic solidarity prevailed (exemplified in its most mature form by the ideal of the welfare state), in late modernity, its structural constituents

DOI: 10.4324/9781003197355-10

dissolve, while new types of manageable sufferings also emerge. Based on these premises, the possibility of post-organic solidarity – addressing the challenges of globalization or negative integration in a non-objectifying manner – is explored. Finally, Chapter 9 combines the previous conclusions: an attempt is made to outline the basis of a comprehensive quasi-therapeutic praxis targeting empty suffering. Such intervention does not focus on the individual, rather the distorted social networks themselves. It takes into consideration the genealogical origins and the contemporary specificities of empty suffering, while also reflecting on the possibilities of hybrid subjectivities and post-organic solidarity.

7 From the contingencies of biomedicine to secular ritual healing

An online ethnography of depression forums

The concept of depression as an illness was born in psychopathology discourses. Framing a certain pattern of suffering in biomedical terms implies the affected actor's involvement in the whole biopolitical complex (see Chapter 3). This includes both the objectifying experiences (the sufferer is recognized primarily as 'Körper' instead of 'Leib'), the alienation (the sufferer's access to their own experiences is denied) and the hegemonic authority (alternative discourses are discredited). Even if such constraints may be of secondary importance in case of many illnesses, in case of depression they have a special significance, as depression is inseparable from them. The increase of depressive symptoms is closely linked to reifying and alienating structural transformations emptying suffering. In this sense, the language and praxis provided by modern biomedical institutions are tainted by the same distortions, which are responsible for depression as empty suffering in the first place. This is probably the most evident, when it comes to building adequate 'illness narratives' (Kleinman, 1988). The coherence of the self, which is lost due to depressed mood, can hardly be reconstructed in a reifying framework (Jones and Griffiths, 2015).

The actors have no choice, but to seek ways out from the entangling biomedical framework that is to 'bricolage' (De Certeau, 1984) solutions while using any accessible means. Online forums prove to be exceptionally resourceful, when it comes to search alternative discursive spaces. However, as any mediatized communication, they are also affected by the limitations of the medium itself: the interactions of information society are based on ephemeral impulses constraining narrative meaning construction (Lash, 2002). In this sense, the contemporary subject's quest for escaping empty suffering in the virtual public sphere is destined to remain an ambiguous attempt promising harm reduction instead of a solution.

This chapter aims to explore the ambiguities of lay reinterpretation of empty suffering by analyzing the manifest and latent communicative processes of online depression forums with the tools of online ethnography. These platforms are understood as complex public spheres mediating between expert and lay positions: while their manifest function is information exchange and peer support, they fulfil latent functions as well. These considerations outline

DOI: 10.4324/9781003197355-11

the structure of the following analysis. Firstly, the biomedical interpretation of depressed mood (expressing an objectifying expert perspective) is confronted with a phenomenological one (expressing a lay narrative universe), with a special focus on online forums as potential platforms hosting such debates. Secondly, the main narratives and discursive strategies of depression forums are overviewed based on an online ethnography. Finally, the latent functionality of 'ritual healing' (Csordas, 1983, 1997) is described in a short case study.

Seeking non-reifying depression narratives in the online sphere

Despite its positivist self-understanding, biomedicine is inseparable from the discursive structures ofbiopower (Foucault, 1997). Since biomedical discourse became a dominant language of suffering, its authority was less and less limited to clinical context. Gradually normalizing technologies of the self were elaborated focusing on the right conduct of everyday life from the perspective of healthiness (Rose, 1999: 74). These biomedical frameworks did not simply complement the already existing cultural or moral discourses, but – by claiming to express the 'objective truth' of human nature – marginalized and silenced the alternatives. From their perspective only those aspects of suffering are recognized, which are translatable to the biomedical language games (Kleinman and Kleinman, 1991). This exclusivity is required for grounding an undeniable aura of authority: biomedical discourse implies that most forms of suffering are translatable to medical terms and also solvable with medical technologies (Good, 2007). The biomedical reduction of suffering not only resulted in the elimination of personal narratives responsible for making sense of the suffering, but also an alienated self-understanding making the subject a helpless spectator of their own misery (Kleinman, 1973). As such reductionist approach proves to be inefficient in case of various forms of suffering, it is complemented by technologies of actual objectification. As the overuse of painkillers or anti-depressants prove it, if every attempts of treating the cause of suffering fail, the final solution of biomedical paradigm is the sedating of the sufferer that is depriving them from the chance of reflecting upon their condition (Hardon and Sanabria, 2017).

The silencing of the sufferers, who are turned into passive patients, did not however eliminate the need for personal interpretation. This is reflected in the various criticisms concerning the biomedical framing of mental suffering (e.g. Laing and Esterson, 1964; Scheff, 1999). Being criticized from outside and inside, biomedical psychiatry has lost its aura of unquestionable authority probably more than any other medical fields (Rose, 2018; Rose and Abi-Rached, 2013). In case of mental disorders, the biomedical discourse is not only more contested by alternative ones, but also the importance of lay interpretations is greater. These premises highlight the stakes of online depression forums, which are distinguished platforms of critical and interpretative discussions.

The notion of depression is elaborated in a wide clinical discourse including disciplines such as neurology, psychiatry or the various schools of psychology. Even if these approaches represent a diverse ontological, epistemic and therapeutic universe, they share the basic assumptions of biomedical paradigm by interpreting depression as an objectively describable – physical or mental – pathology (APA, 2013: 160–164; Beck, 1967; Lewinsohn et al., 1979; Seligman, 1975). From such approach comes reductionism: the expert interpretation of depression tends to ignore the phenomenological complexity of the actual experience including distorted intersubjectivity, inter-affectivity, inter-temporality and agency (Fuchs, 2013; Ratcliffe, 2015).[1] These experiences can be contrasted to the biomedical descriptions of depression in order to understand the lay actors' perplexity when applying expert narratives on themselves. The reifying and reductionist descriptions of biomedicine often imply an alienated interpretation of the self – that is an unidentifiable illness narrative.

The representatives of biomedical discourse frame depression as an inherent – either bodily or mental – pathology, which objective condition is treatable according to expert knowledge. In contrast, the lay sufferers experience a burdensome world, a frozen time, an immobilized self and unrelatable others. From these interpretations two contrasting trajectories of treatment follow: while biomedical paradigm is based on bodily intervention or the correction of cognitive, emotive and behavioural habits, phenomenology emphasizes the need for reintegration into an intersubjective being in the world that is the revitalization of the sufferer through intercorporeal interactions re-establishing interaffectivity (Fuchs and Koch, 2014). Such discrepancy has central relevance: in therapeutic interactions the objectifying gaze of the experts becomes a further reinforcement of a world, where the depressed subject could exist only as a helpless object. The very act of biomedical (especially drug based) therapy contributes to the feeling of detachment, instead of being able to reconstruct intersubjectivity. In this sense, independently from the effectivity of the medical or therapeutic treatment, the biomedical framing of the sufferer reinforces a phenomenological horizon similar to the ones being responsible for the emergence of depression in the first place.

Consequently, biomedical framing not only reduces the depressive experience into a pattern of biological and mental symptoms, but more importantly creates an inacceptable narrative for the sufferer, which further reinforces the sense of remoteness. Accordingly, biomedical knowledge inevitably plays an ambiguous role in the process of dealing with depressive experiences, which is expressed in the tension between lay and expert discourses: while providing therapies, because of its reifying gaze, biomedicine further blocks the emergence of an undistorted intersubjectivity. In this constellation a quest for illness narratives begins (Frank, 2013; Kleinman, 1988). Online depression forums play an important role in these processes: they are micro level platforms for the troubled subjectivities seeking answers to personal existential questions.

The lay narratives of depression have been analyzed in various contexts. The experience of any unexpected, uncontrollable illness creates fissure on the actor's identity, which incoherence needs to be eliminated. The primary function of lay self-narratives is to restore coherence by providing a meaningful explanation for a being in the world burdened by illness (Kleinman, 1988: 48). In case of depression, the particular challenge of finding such narratives is related to the ambiguous status of the distorted mood itself: from a first person perspective, mood is considered to be the essential part of the self, which implies moral responsibility (i.e. bad mood is to be corrected by the actors themselves); from the expert perspective, it is considered to be a pathology implying external intervention. In this sense, depression challenges the self on an elementary level: the actors have to choose between not identifying with the distorted mood (thus escape moral responsibility at the cost of losing a constitutive element of the self) or identifying with it (thus keeping the integrity of the self at the cost of a negative self-evaluation). There is no win-win solution to such dilemma, which means that either option implies the giving up on important elements of the self. Thus, the narrative challenge of depression is to minimize such losses (Flynn, 2010). According to several interview based researches, the typical narrative strategies rely on idealtypical dramaturgical steps: the pre-depression past is introduced as golden age compared to the present; a dramatic event is introduced as a starting point of troubles; the inhabiting of a narrow space of agency is described; if there is successful dealing with depression a phase of confession to others is mentioned; along with the lessons learned (Hajela, 2012; Kangas, 2001). It may be argued that these narratives highlight the stakes of the clash between lay and expert discourses that is the expression of the actors' attempt to poise between agency and responsibility.

While these narratives were gathered in offline context, they have relevance for online discourses as well. Firstly, however it has to be clarified in what extent is online communication capable of enabling the construction of complex narratives. Since the antiquity, the public sphere has been a terrain of equals, who form their cooperation without any pre-given hierarchy, purely based on the convincing of each other (Arendt, 1998). The recent rise of information society however has transformed the public sphere as well: while it provided access to previously unseen masses, it also reduced the quality of communication to a level, where rational discussion is barely possible (Davis, 2020). Endangered by the distortive logic of 'anti-public sphere' (e.g. 'trolling'), depression forums have to face not only the challenges of biomedical hegemony, but also the ones originating from the difficulties of online communication. According to the criticism of information society the very logic of information is in contradiction with narratives. The latter requires time, which is limited by the continuously streamed ephemeral bits of information (Lash, 2002).

While such diagnoses certainly highlight a limitation of online communication, several empirical studies show that online communication is capable of reproducing important elements of face to face interactions. Given enough time, the partners may develop codes capable of transmitting emotions and latent meanings similar to non-verbal communication. Of course, not every online platform succeeds in maintaining a confidential, lively discussion. The key factors of success include on the one hand the safeguard of the quality of public sphere: moderation in order to filter offensive and toxic posts; a subtle balancing between anonymity and identification (in order to avoid both recognizability and unreliability at the same time); and the maintaining of boundaries. On the other hand, success depends on the expected positive outcomes, such as the chance of individual catharsis; the support of personal coping strategies; and the experience of being embedded in a supportive community (Murphy et al., 2020).

Even if mediated communication is less intense and its impact is less durable, these contingencies may become advantages in case of sensitive topics, which are harder to be discussed directly. In case of sharing negative feelings, anonymity may be reassuring, thus online platforms may be considered as secure spaces (Derks et al., 2008). Besides the potential of communicating emotions, which is the prerequisite of re-establishing interaffectivity, online communication is also capable of providing community experience (Galegher et al., 1998). Furthermore, participating in online communication has therapeutic potential by providing a safe, low-risk space of self-disclosure (Benzon, 2008). Online public spheres focusing on depression rely on all of these advantages by providing a safe space for experimenting with various lay narratives. These platforms function as 'narrative sandboxes', where an attempt is made to express the experience of depression, to re-enter intersubjectivity in a low threshold interaction and find mutual explanations to the suffering (Kotliar, 2015). In case of online forums, not only the experimenting with various narratives is available in front of a virtual audience, but also support through communication (Prescott et al., 2017): as various participants define their own role differently, such support could equally manifest as a direct attempt (that is telling the other what to do) or an indirect one (i.e. giving advice by telling a similar personal story, while expressing sympathy and understanding). Overall, it seems that despite its limitations, online communication has a potential of elaborating identity-narratives.

Online mental health forums represent an expanding sphere. Previous researches have shown that the main motivation for using them is threefold: they help to overcome social and geographical isolation; enable otherwise missing social relationships; and provide opportunity for gathering practical information and advice (Smith-Merry et al., 2019). While the majority of the users suffer from depressed mood (Powell et al., 2003), the participants of online depression forum should be viewed as a heterogeneous population. According to an online survey, at least four idealtypical groups can be differentiated (Nimrod, 2013): 'concerned about daily living' (mostly female users, higher depression scale scores), 'information seekers' (mostly men, infrequent users), 'interested in all topics' (mostly female frequent users) and 'relatively less involved' (mostly male, frequent users). Due to these variabilities it should be noted that the population of the forums does not cover or represent a clinical population; also the narratives explored cover only the self-expression of those, who choose to express themselves, not the community as a whole. Keeping these limitations in mind, an online ethnography was conducted to reveal those less obvious, latent mechanisms and functionalities, which organise the forum discussions.

As online ethnography is a relatively new subfield, its methodological grounds are yet to be consolidated.[2] Ethnography in general aims at analyzing the social and cultural patterns through observing – and often participating in – social praxes in a systematic way, that is to provide a description of the actors' meanings and way of life, along with the interactions reproducing them. In order to explore a lifeworld from the inside implies the ethnographer's involvement in the social interactions themselves, which epistemological challenge requires reflection on the role of the researcher in a given community (Wolcott, 1999). As online ethnography is conducted in a virtual space, these general features also need to be accommodated to the specific environment. Probably the most important difference concerns the 'façade' of the actors (Goffman, 1959): they are not present in their physical reality, only as 'virtual avatars' existing within the technological framework of the online platforms. While technology is not irrelevant in offline encounters either, it does not necessarily play a decisive role, unlike in case of online interactions, where the subjects appear only as mediatized personas. Accordingly, online ethnography inevitably deals with 'actor-networks' (Latour, 2005) constituted of human and non-human elements playing an equally important role. While the analysis of mediated interactions is characterized by obvious limitations (e.g. the inaccessibility of the offline social and cultural context of the avatars), it also provides unique opportunities, such as the extra-temporal position of the observer. As most interactions are archived, the antecedents and the reactions to any speech acts are accessible, which creates opportunity for reconstructing idealtypical dynamics in their temporal totality.

Based on these premises an online ethnography of several English speaking mental health forums was conducted, which partly or completely focus on depression.[3] Data was systematically gathered and analyzed with the method of 'deep reading' (Lee, 2017; Skageby, 2010). In case of each forum, the new threads were followed for a month in three consecutive waves (in 2018 November, 2019 March and 2019 September). The field work was finished after the third wave, because of saturation (as new narratives and discursive logics did not show up anymore). Posts were categorized according to the substantive topic (e.g. problems with medication, therapy, etc.) and the discursive role they play (e.g. descriptive, argumentative, etc.). Also, the dynamics of the relevant threads were analyzed according to the manifest (e.g. sharing one's personal story) and latent (e.g. supporting the other) components. Based on these initial analyses, various aspects of the online praxes were identified: the substantive topics as they are revealed for a newcomer;

the types of dialogues as they are experienced by adept users forming community ties; the hidden mechanisms, which constitute quasi-ritual patterns.

The quest for meaning: Manifest functionalities of online depression forums

Most visitors of the forums are affected by depression either directly or indirectly. Accordingly, my role as an observant also had to be clarified. The whole rhythm and praxis of the ethnography depends on this: depression forums are used differently by the newcomers having practical questions; shy users wandering around without any concrete purpose; experienced members being involved in one or another type of discursive praxes on a regular basis; and the 'elders' attempting to provide support for those in need. At the beginning, I identified as a shy newcomer, who is indirectly affected by depression: I wanted to know as much about it, as possible with the help of the forum community, without actively taking part in the conversations. I was particularly interested in the reception and the collective reinterpretation of expert discourses. I started to visit the forums as an explorer trying to map the available threads. The technological infrastructure of the forums seemed to shorten this process, as discussions are organized in a complex classificatory system. Although these categories definitively help navigation in the first few times, they become less relevant as one gets familiar with the environment. As one's interest becomes clearer, the key topics and the relevant others become the main reference points. Gradually a 'thematic map' takes shape, indicating the recurring topics and the idealtypical forms of narration.

Such map highlighted how the expert discourses of depression clash with the lay experiences. Biomedical explanations appear in an ambiguous framework: bodily causes are embedded in a broader context of lifestyle, framing the body as an intermediator of external effects instead of being a final *explanans*. Biomedical interventions, while generally approved, are also considered to have limited efficiency: the experts' authority is questioned for several reasons; medications are considered to be highly contingent and potentially dangerous, inefficient on their own; they are rather experimented during the therapeutic process, instead of being applied according to verified protocols.

The sharing of experiences of 'negative automatic thoughts' constitute a significant part of the discussions: attempts are made to distance them from the self; their logic is deconstructed in order to reveal the hidden paralyzing loops. Instead of relying on processes inaccessible to the actors, most narratives of distorted development refer to an environment being responsible for restricting agency. Accordingly, even if psychological explanations are evoked, they are complemented with a social perspective: strategies of control through self-harm, escapism or disconnecting are explained according to an ignorant, intolerant or discriminating social context. Traumas appear as examples of dramatic events turning the subject's being in the world inside out. Unlike in expert discourses however, they do not paralyze the actors, instead provide opportunity to name those, who are responsible for the suffering.

Besides complementing biological and psychological explanations with narratives of a dysfunctional social environment, social distortions also appear on their own right. Burdensome social norms and expectations reveal those symbolic obligations, which set impossible tasks for the individual. Personal failures of succeeding in economic competition or in the struggle for recognition indicate how the experience of losing in the ruthless everyday battles contributes to the emergence of depression. As one's existence is both completely dependent on social worthiness, being proved to be unworthy in various material and symbolic fields threatens with the total dissolving of identity. Finally, the distortions of communities and society are also indicated as a source of suffering: if family and intimate relationships are dysfunctional, they provide space only for burdensome interactions; if the work relations are insecure or exploitative, hopelessness becomes a general experience; if collective action seems to fail on a fundamental level, personal suffering appears as a consequence of universal paradoxes.[4]

Overall, it may be argued that online depression forums host discussions, which are partly relativizing biomedical explanations; partly complementing psy-diagnoses with social ones; partly link the experience of suffering to various dysfunctions or distortions of the social world directly. Accordingly, the forums serve as discursive spaces capable of complementing expert interpretations with lay ones. However, beside such interpretative function they also enable other mechanisms. In order to reveal them, the dynamics of interactions has to be analyzed.

As one is getting familiar with the online platform and the topics, the approach to the forums also transforms. It relies less on the general classificatory categories provided by the interface, instead customized shortcuts are established, which directly lead to the relevant discussions and the significant others. By spending some time with the online community, it becomes clear that most threads have a short life expectancy: in case of targeted questions, concrete answers end the discussion; in case of insecure participants, the first few generic welcoming posts are often not enough to motivate a deeper disclosure. So the more experienced users usually start to move together: they follow each other through various topics and create a subtext of their own within threads dealing with various issues. At this point, the contours of online communities become visible. After getting familiar with the forum, the second step of initiation involves the following one of these quasi-groups. From this perspective, a new dimension of the forum life becomes accessible: beyond the substantive topics, idealtypical discursive strategies appear, which integrate loose networks of experienced users forming virtual communities.

In the process of group formation institutionalized tokens indicating one's status play a central role. Several forums enable not only the customization of avatars, but also their decoration with visual indicators expressing one's rank (which is often based on quantitative factors, such as the length of membership, the number of posts, or 'likes' given by other members). This way a differentiation – and a struggle for recognition – among the participants may occur resulting in the emergence of specific roles and statuses. Such roles include the basic differentiation between the 'newcomer' looking for advice, the 'experienced members' and the 'respected elders', who often act as 'recovering helpers' (Rácz et al., 2015). These various roles enable different discursive strategies: newcomers usually remain in the position of seeking advice; the experienced members may help in the process of narrative reinterpretation; the elders combine personal experience and expertise, which is not based on formal training, but the successful dealing with the suffering.

The first idealtypical role is exemplified by the following discussion:

> NEWCOMER1: Hi, I have recently been prescribed a low dose of antidepressants, these are to try and help me with my low mood. This is the 2nd day of taking them and both days I have been really tired and grouchy in the evening, is this being caused by the tablets do you guys think? I just feel really lazy and that I'm going to be stuck like this forever now :((
>
> EXPERIENCED MEMBER1: What time of day do you take the tablets?
>
> NEWCOMER1: In the morning usually about 10am
>
> EXPERIENCED MEMBER1: In that case it's very likely that the medication is wearing off by the evening, particularly if you're on a low dose.
>
> NEWCOMER1: Thank you:) feel like I'm a track now and just got to keep heading in the right direction:)[5]

In case of pragmatic discussions, concrete questions are raised by the newcomers and answered by the experienced members. These roles outline a hierarchy, which is a constitutive element of these interactions: the newcomer's overuse of emoticons can be interpreted as a sign of embarrassment, while the experienced member maintains a quasi-professional façade focusing strictly on substantive issues. The manifest level of the discussion is about the side effects of a medication. However, on the latent level, a similarly important interaction takes place. By reinterpreting the failure of the medication as an issue of dosage, the overall trust in biomedical treatment can be saved. In this case the experienced member provides a narrative capable of reassuring the newcomer about the rightness of her choice. In this type of discussion, the participants do not step out from the hegemonic biomedical paradigm, instead support is provided for inhabiting its framework by relying on narratives enabling adjustment to its limitations.[6]

The second idealtypical dynamics is exemplified by the following discussion:

NEWCOMER2: Looking back on my 24 years on this planet I can see a long pattern of fear and avoidance. I have let fear and insecurities rule my life for as long as I can remember. I'm just a coward. Whenever a challenge arises I immediately look for ways to avoid it, I think to myself 'How can I get out of doing this scary thing I don't want to do?' How can I summon the courage to take risk and change my life for the better?

EXPERIENCED MEMBER2: I don't believe you are a coward. Just living in this dangerous world of ours requires unbelievable courage. It is as though most [?] people have become addicted to negative framing and criticism and unable to appreciate any more.

EXPERIENCED MEMBER3: Courage is having confidence in yourself and just not caring enough about the consequences. It's something that can be improved upon. You are not a coward, just pushing yourself outside of your comfort zone takes practice.

EXPERIENCED MEMBER4: Labelling yourself is hurtful and that particular label deserves to be challenged. You're not getting a fair trial in your own head, my friend. Let's try another plausible explanation for your behaviour that doesn't come pre-loaded with a judgment. Maybe your amygdala is hyperactive? Try a little compassion for yourself

NEWCOMER2: You're right, I have shamed myself for years lol. It's weird but it's so much easier to have compassion for others than for myself. I'll definitely try to be easier on myself. Thanks for your reply!

This excerpt shows how the depressive self-narrative is reframed according to various interpretative frames. While in case of pragmatic discussion, the boundaries of the initial framing were maintained, in this case the participants challenge the sufferer's self-interpretation in several ways. Experienced member2 provides a contrasting narrative based on a diagnosis of the society: as it is considered to be dangerous and overly-critical, what is described as cowardice can be reinterpreted as a logical reaction. From this point of view, the lack of agency introduced by newcomer2 is relativized by highlighting the impossibility of acting in contemporary world. Due to this strategy a narrative becomes available, which takes away the guilt of the actor by relieving her from the charge of being coward. Experienced member3 relies on a narrative, which also reinterprets cowardice as a shortcoming, which can be improved by proper training. From this perspective, the helplessness is not an essential condition of newcomer2, but a consequence of lacking practice. Experienced member4 highlights a biological narrative. In this case the aim of reframing is similar to the previous ones, however the substantive argument differs: instead of relativizing agency by social or psychological terms, in this case the biological determinedness is evoked. Newcomer2 is grateful for all of these suggestions, independently from their content, which means that the access to alternative perspectives themselves is more important than the substantive explanation. From a phenomenological point of view, it may be argued that these discussions provided opportunity for re-entering a long missing intersubjectivity capable of moving them away from a stuck position. The significance of these engagements is not necessarily the substantive content of the posts, but rather the creation of a multidimensional narrative space enabling the reinterpretation of one's self-narrative.[7]

The third idealtypical dynamics is exemplified by the following excerpt:

NEWCOMER3: I always had a problem verbalizing my feelings, so I never did. Actually, this is my first time trying to describe what I'm feeling. I have to reach out to somebody even if that someone is a total stranger on the internet. I'm 25-year-old female and I think I've been suffering from depression and anxiety for a very long time. However, I never experienced any big trauma, I grew up with both parents, had a normal childhood, I was never molested or anything like that. That's why I feel like I'm making this all up, or that my problems are not as serious when compared to other people, so I feel guilty for even thinking I need help.

ELDER1: Welcome to the forum. Glad you have posted. You are obviously struggling. It is not too late to seek help. Am just wondering if your uni has a counselling service. If so you can contact them. Please don't ever think your problems are not as serious as anyone else's. Also mental illness doesn't always need an obvious cause. Please keep posting here too.

ELDER2: Hey obviously you are having problems and no one's life is really more or less 'deserving' we are all quite messed up humanity that is. And anyway that is the hallmark of depression having low self-esteem. And no you are not a waste of time and please start to talk positive in your life otherwise you become what you fill your head with. Just some friendly advice.

NEWCOMER4: Your story sounds very similar to mine. How do you go about first going to counselling? It is something I have looked at but am terrified of verbalizing how I feel. It's bad enough typing this. I would love to talk through how I feel just online. Does this exist? Would this also help you? Any advice from anyone feeing similar things would be greatly appreciated

ELDER3: Hi and welcome. We're happy to have you in our ranks and as each of us is struggling with some mental health issue, we get how you feel about yourself. Regarding what you wrote about your reaction to seeking professional help, I think you've made a step forward by sharing your struggle here. I want to encourage you to continue contributing to this conversation and see if it at all helps to get it out of your head and know others understand.

This discussion highlights a third, latent function of online depression forums beside the reinterpreting of uncertain biomedical explanations and treatments, or the attempts of reframing self-narratives. In this case, newcomer3 and 4 refer to personal experiences inexplicable by common psychological knowledge. This experience is disturbing enough, as the sufferers feel to be lost in the discursive space: they have the impression to be depressed, but cannot justify the self-diagnosis, because they lack the assumed criteria (e.g. trauma). In this situation the elders apply double strategy: on the manifest level, they try to shepherd the newcomers towards biomedical help, on the latent level they conduct a communication based on the principles of 'unconditional positive regard'.[8] This purpose expressed by the recurring topoi like 'Glad you have posted', 'you are not a waste of time', 'and know others understand'. Similar phrases are used in most of the posts of the most experienced members playing the role of 'recovering helper'. More importantly, they are almost exclusively used by the elders, which indicate their specific functionality.[9] These speech acts are evoked almost automatically, whenever a new participant attempts to share their experiences in a reluctant way. These ritual elements of interaction are responsible for reinforcing the newcomers that their suffering is recognized and understood not only in an objectifying, but in a hermeneutic way. In this sense their purpose is to create the initial commitment, which is often missing from new members feeling insecure and unsure about their first steps of initiating intersubjectivity in a virtual platform.

Such communicative pattern can be considered to be ritualistic due to its repetitive, collective and transformative function. Collective rituals have transformative power due to the experience of 'collective effervescence', which enables the restructuring of the self, according to the social frames (Durkheim, 1995: 218). Of course, their online version lacks several important components of the original ones, thus having only a contingent transformative power. Nevertheless, online forums still hold the potential of hosting rituals by combining pragmatic, interpretative and approving communicative panels into coherent mechanisms.

Latent dynamics: Ritual healing in online depression forums

In sum, the topics dominating online forums indicate how the hegemonic biomedical discourse is interpreted by the actors themselves. Furthermore, their dynamics reveal those latent mechanisms, which impact the depressed being in the world itself: beside pragmatic advises, online communities also provide experiences of cognitive restructuring of automatic thoughts and interactions having the potential of re-establishing interaffectivity. In order to explain a latent functionality of these mechanisms, the concept of 'ritual healing' is called upon.

From a phenomenological perspective, healing is a transcendental experience, inseparable from the impression of wonder: as illness transforms the whole world into a burdensome horizon, the reconfiguration is always contingent until its occurrence. Thus, it always happens unexpectedly – when one is healed, the element of transcendental intervention is present, as the unsure hope becomes reality (Csordas, 2002: 24). As phenomenologically the process of healing is a reconfiguration of the being in the world, it traditionally includes both the influencing of bodily symptoms and the reinterpretation of narratives. In every cultural setting certain authorities have the right of managing such process, which means that healing relies on power relationships constituting a discursive hegemony capable of effectively influencing the narrative structures (Csordas, 2002: 25). While such authority is usually personified by a healer, who is in charge of the process, it is actually the rite itself, which is responsible for the healing. As every power relationship has a subjectificating aspect (Foucault, 1982), one's being in the world can also be changed by relying on a depersonalized power: for this purpose, the subject needs to be subordinated to a discourse capable of reinterpreting the suffering. Accordingly, healing rituals may occur in constellations, where the technologies of power are not connected to concrete persons, but institutions or structures (Prince, 1980). The key elements of the rite include three steps: securing mutual predispositions, empowerment of the sufferer and transformation of the being in the world (Csordas, 2002: 27).

The latent function of online depression forums can be understood from this description of ritual healing. Even if the religious element and the clearly recognizable healing authorities are missing on structural level, a constellation is constituted, which includes analogies to all three steps identified above. In case of depression, the nature of suffering undermines the horizon of mutual dispositions as depressed subjects lack the ability of entering intersubjective relationships. This challenge is handled by latent forum dynamics securing unconditional positive regard. They are capable of evoking a very limited, but easily accessible interaffectivity, which could serve as a basis of further steps leading out from isolation. The functional equivalent of the second step of ritual healing, the summoning of the transcendental is secured by the pragmatic forum dynamics, which evokes an authority in the form of the scientifically justified biomedical discourse. This is not transcendental at all, but fulfils the function of an unquestionable knowledge. By referring to scientific truths, the universal laws of nature are applied to concrete problems: the depression experienced by the subject appears as the expression of a universal phenomenon. The functional equivalent of transformation is the discursive reframing of the depressed subject's narratives. In this phase alternative frameworks are offered to the subject, who has the chance of reflecting on her life from this perspective, re-evaluate the original attributions of the causes of depression and the potential outcomes as well.

From this perspective, online depression forums can be reinterpreted as spaces holding the potential of hosting secular quasi-healing rituals. In these rituals both the newcomers, experienced members and elders play a particular role. In order to be able to picture the details of the process, a short case study is introduced summarizing the various forum dynamics.[10]

> Paul is in his late twenties, he has been dropped out from college, likes to play video games, online streaming and suffers from depression for almost a decade. He has been active in online depression forums since 2013.

At the beginning, he only reacted to other's posts, with the intention of expressing and relating to his own misery: 'Yea this happens to me sometimes as well. Some people ask why do you want to be alone, wouldn't you rather be with people? But what many people don't understand is that it is entirely possible to be far lonelier with a group of people than you ever could be by yourself'. As he does not get too much feedback, after a few months, he decides to start his own thread about the crisis he went through at that time, the suspension of his studies: 'Hello, been lurking on this forum for some months now, and I never started a post because I never felt like what I had to say was important enough to start a whole new topic. I guess until now. So I'm a young college student dealing with some serious depression. Because of this I was thinking of taking the next semester off'. The initial answers to the topic frame the problem as a practical issue, so advices are given about the length and details of suspending the studies, while Paul's depression is not thematised. Consequently, the topic is ended in a few weeks, as Paul finally decides to leave college.

After this first attempt, Paul experiments with various new threads including his difficulties of interacting with others, practicalities of finding the right therapist, difficulties of friendship and love, medicines. While these topics receive various feedback, it is clear that Paul seeks not simply practical advices, but something more. In those rare moments, when he gets approval and understanding (e.g. feedbacks like: 'I can relate' or 'I hear you'), he seems to be overjoyed. Gradually he gets to know his way around, which transition is expressed most visibly by the shifting structure of his speech acts: initially he is strictly centred on his own problems, expecting support from the others; later he learns that the key to receive reinforcements is the turning to the others and providing care. The communicative pattern of his last thread clearly exemplifies this transformation.

At this time, he plans to join a training program – the problem is once again helplessness, which is framed this time as 'cowardice': 'Looking back on my 24 years on this planet I can see a long pattern of fear and avoidance. I have let fear and insecurities rule my life for as long as I can remember. I'm just a coward'. Reinforcing messages start to arrive almost instantaneously: 'So sorry that you are feeling stuck! Courage is not the absence of fear. Start with one small step and go from there. It will get easier with practice. Good luck!' or 'I think you are a very noble person. Hopefully you will get lots of responses to your post'. At this time Paul has already mastered how to keep the flow of reinforcing messages going, so he reacts to the supportive messages not simply by thanking them, but also returning the compassion, which is exemplified by his reaction to a depressed post claiming that courage can be gained after 'everything has been lost'. Paul reacts by reversing the roles and providing comfort himself: 'I'm sorry to hear that you've lost everything. I can't imagine what that might mean'.

This role reversal indicates a turning point in Paul's story as well: while previously he shared mostly concerns and insecurities, at this point his perspective is reconfigured due to the support received. He expresses himself more and more confidentially, opens up to the others, while interiorizing the role of the recovery helper: 'It's been about a month since my program started so I guess its time for an update. Waking up in the morning everyday is absolutely the worst part of the day. Everyone in the class is fairly nice and I get along with everyone. The only thing that's weird is that sometimes I find myself not knowing what to say in conversation. Also, if you're reading this I hope your depression is improving! :)'. What needs to be emphasized at this point is the interrelatedness of supporter and supported roles expressed by the extended participation in ritual speech acts. In order to overcome the mood of helplessness, one needs to become a helper. The ritualised communicative patterns of the forums provide an easily accessible way to do just that: as Paul's example shows, even someone who does not have the competences initially can acquire them by following the conversation and gradually apply its language games. As Paul becomes a 'recovering helper' himself, he also opens up for the support provided to him – by repairing the damaged intersubjectivity, the depressed being in the world also transforms.

Of course, rituals require continuous practice to maintain their reinforcing impact: when Paul's condition improves, he loosens the strings, when his negative thoughts return, he reinforces them. As he states, few months after starting the program: 'Hey guys, sorry it's been so long since I've provided an update on my situation. My supervisor and all my coworkers are pretty nice people. But, let's talk a little bit about my depression. I wake up pretty much everyday in a horrible mood. Aside from the mornings I do find myself thinking about death a lot more. I know in the past few months I have made a lot of changes in my life to help improve myself, but I can't help but think how pointless everything I'm doing is'. Such relapse – occurring despite the fortunate turn of events in his life – does not find Paul unprepared. At this point, he knows that he could count on the others, all he has to do is joining the ritual communication: 'No thank you for continuing to follow my journey and being an active member of this thread. I wouldn't keep posting to this thread if it wasn't for people like you who provide me with amazing feedback and support'. These closing thoughts express the hardly found security related to the ritual discursive mechanism enabling coping with depression.

Just as living with depression is not a distinct condition, which has a clear start and end, this story also includes various dynamics: Paul introduces his problems; the community establishes a safe and inclusive environment; practical advices are given; successes are celebrated; relapse is experienced; ritual healing is restarted. What needs to be emphasized is that during these discussions the biomedical framing appears only in the background: depression is not discussed as an illness, but rather as an element of being in the world. The 'elder' supporters work on this mood by being ready to form intersubjectivities, where Paul may reconfigure his being in the world. As he is reinforced continually about acceptance and understanding, he can share his worries and start reflecting about ways out. Gradually, he also starts to engage in the ritual speech acts, while trying to support those peers, who helped him, but need reinforcement themselves. It is known from the discussion that Paul relies on medical therapy as well, but it remains clear that the online community becomes an essential reference point, which is capable of providing comfort even at the times of relapse.

Cases like this can be interpreted as healing rituals in a sense that they include every key functional components. However, they are not organized into an actual coherent ritual being practised by authorities nominated to the task. Instead they are practised by various independent discursive dynamics. They have the chance of appearing in the same discussion, but this occurrence remains highly contingent, as there are no institutionalized roles being responsible for organizing them. The coexistence of the preconditions of ritual healing in online forums is only a structural potential at this moment. However, reflecting on them provides opportunity to improve the chance of actualizing: by re-establishing intersubjectivity and providing alternative framings, the depressed experience can be reconfigured on a level biomedical intervention is incapable of operating. Overall, depression forums are not only spaces for discussing the consequences of objectification – they also hold the potential of narrative transformations. In this process the biomedical narrative plays an equally important role as the complementary ones: it may provide the secular substitutive authority needed for ritual healing. Accordingly, late modern illness narratives are not constituted against biomedical ones, but in a hybrid way, by combining and reconfiguring lay and expert knowledge.

This general conclusion concerns not only depression forums, but also highlights a possibility for treating empty suffering. Lay attempts of providing alternative narratives of depression, which are capable of grounding a self-identity beyond the reifying 'ill' or 'patient' roles are born in hybrid public spheres equally giving space for biomedical discourse and first-hand experiences. In these online platforms, despite the limitation of online communication, the narrative experimenting seems to succeed in many cases. Besides the critical engagement with biomedicine, latent healing rituals emerge at the fissures of the hegemonic discourses and technologies. The dysfunctions of biomedicine are not endured passively by the actors, who attempt to complement the available narratives with alternative ones. Their efforts may be fragmented, but certainly have the potential of compensating the missing functional elements. By reflecting on these lay praxes, medical anthropology may just provide the missing link for them to become efficient: it may highlight those structural components, which are already present in a fragmented way, but require further integration.[11] For this purpose, both the general frames of solidarity and the details of therapeutic praxes adequately addressing empty suffering need to be highlighted. Chapters 8 and 9 explore these directions.

Notes

1 While the universalist descriptions of depression reveal the general, existential dimensions of a distorted phenomenological pattern, it should also be emphasized that any particular 'being in the world' is also culturally contextualized. The affordances of embodiment, time consciousness, agency and intersubjectivity equally depend on the tools provided by the social actors and institutions. Therefore, a phenomenology of depression implies an 'ecosocial approach' (Kirmayer et al., 2017).

2 Online ethnography also raises ethical questions of its own. Although there are several ethical guidelines about doing such research (e.g. AoIR et al., 2012; BPS, 2017), as each field has unique features, decisions fitting the specific context have to be made. In our case, it was decided that solely those materials are to be accessed, which were anonymously posted, do not require subscription, login, or password. As these posts are intended to be publicly viewed (a consent is given by accepting the 'terms of use'), there is wide ethical consensus that their access does not require a specific approval from the participants, the administrators of the forum, or a specific approval from an IRB (Kotliar, 2015: 4; O'Brien and Clark, 2012: 279; Salzmann-Erikson and Eriksson, 2012: 11). In order to further secure anonymity, the nicknames of the avatars are also changed and the forum links are not published.

3 The observation covered several depression forums, which can be considered to be the largest ones based on the Google search results (for reasons of concealment no links are provided – in case of database related questions, please contact the author).

4 Similar narrative clusters and asymmetries were identified by a quantitative discourse analysis (Németh et al., 2020).

5 For the protection of anonymity, the citations are slightly modified and no links are provided (in case of database related questions, please contact the author).

6 Several previous researches provide a detailed picture about the implicit reproduction of biomedical discourse in online forums. According to a quantitative study, questions related to medication and therapy constitute a significant and robust segment (approximately 10%) of the overall discussion (Feldhege et al., 2020). In various ways these posts are responsible for reiterating and reinterpreting the biomedical discourse.

7 The multidimensionality of mental health recovery narratives is an extensively mapped topic (Llewellyn-Beardsley et al., 2019): the major dimensions include the genre of 'escape' (based on the experience of distress and trauma), 'enlightenment' (based on the topoi of an epistemic turning point), 'endeavour' (based on the narrative of recovery) and 'endurance' (based on a survival identity).

8 This term was originally introduced as a specific therapeutic tool (Rogers, 1956), but became widely used in psychotherapy. Accordingly, it is amongst the commonplaces of psy-discourses, and as such, imitated by better informed lay actors – such as recovering helpers – as well.

9 Previous research on online mental health peer support emphasize the potential of challenging stigmas together, while strengthening hope through recovery stories and learning from others' stories and experiences (Naslund et al., 2016). While these findings are strengthened by our experiences, we argue for complementing them. Peer support does not remain merely information exchange, it also has a ritual element that is the collective reframing of the world, as it is explored in the last section.

10 The case study is based on the overviewing of the online activity of a particular user. As the forums provide opportunity for specifically searching the posts and threads written by any user, long-term discursive dynamics become analyzable. In Paul's case this included systematically reading and annotating (according to the previously introduced thematic and discursive categories) the first posts belonging to his 'newcomer' era and the ones being written by him as an 'experienced member'. Also, in both cases the related reactions were overviewed in a similar fashion.

11 While others have been advocating the importance of the medical staff getting familiar with lay illness narratives (Heilferty, 2009), my argument goes further. Online forums do not have the sole potential of informing medical experts about the first person accounts of the illness – they may be viewed as platforms, where peer support may be facilitated, given that the latent potentials are appropriately revealed.

References

AoIR (Association of Internet Researchers) Ethics Working Committee, Markham, A. N., and Buchanan, E. (2012) *Ethical Decision-Making and Internet Research 2.0: Recommendations from the AoIR Ethics Working Committee.* http://www.aoir.org/reports/ethics2.pdf.

APA (American Psychiatric Association) (2013) *Diagnostic and Statistical Manual of Mental Disorders* (5th edition). Washington, DC: American Psychiatric Publishing.

Arendt, H. (1998) *The Human Condition.* Chicago, IL: UCP.

Beck, A. T. (1967) *Depression: Clinical, Experimental and Theoretical Aspects.* New York, NY: Harper & Row.

Benzon, K. (2008) A Dark Web: Depression, Writing, and the Internet. In Clark, H. A. (Ed.), *Depression and Narrative: Telling the Dark.* Albany, NY: State University of New York Press, 145–156.

BPS (British Psychological Society) (2017) *Ethics Guidelines for Internet-mediated Research.* INF206/04.2017. www.bps.org.uk/publications/policy-and-guidelines/research-guidelines-policy-documents/research-guidelines-poli.

Csordas, T. (1983) The Rhetoric of Transformation in Ritual Healing. *Culture, Medicine, and Psychiatry,* 7(4): 333–375.

Csordas, T. (2002) *Body, Meaning, Healing.* New York, NY: Palgrave Macmillan US.

Csordas, T. (1997) *The Sacred Self: A Cultural Phenomenology of Charismatic Healing.* Berkeley, CA: University of California Press.

Davis, M. (2020) The Online Anti-Public Sphere. *European Journal of Cultural Studies.* https://doi.org/10.1177/1367549420902799.

De Certeau, M. (1984) *The Practice of Everyday Life.* Berkeley, CA: University of California Press.

Derks, D., Fischer, A. H. and Bos, A. E. (2008) The Role of Emotion in Computer-Mediated Communication: A Review. *Computers in Human Behavior,* 24(3): 766–785.

Durkheim, É. (1995) *The Elementary Forms of Religious Life.* New York, NY: The Free Press.

Feldhege, J., Moessner, M. and Bauer, S. (2020) Who Says What? Content and Participation Characteristics in an Online Depression Community, *Journal of Affective Disorders,* 263: 521–527.

Flynn, D. (2010) Narratives of Melancholy: A Humanities Approach to Depression. *Medical Humanities,* 36(1): 36–39.

Foucault, M. (1982) The Subject and Power. *Critical Inquiry,* 8(4): 777–795.

Foucault, M. (1997) *Society Must Be Defended: Lectures at the Collège De France. 1975–1976*. New York, NY: St. Martin's Press.

Frank, A. W. (2013) *The Wounded Storyteller: Body, Illness, and Ethics*. Chicago, IL: University of Chicago Press.

Fuchs, T. (2013) Depression, Intercorporeality and Interaffectivity. *Journal of Consciousness Studies*, 20(7–8): 219–238.

Fuchs, T. and Koch, S. C. (2014) Embodied Affectivity: On Moving and Being Moved. *Frontiers in Psychology*, 5(1): 1–12.

Galegher, J., Sproull, L. and Kiesler, S. (1998) Legitimacy, Authority, and Community in Electronic Support Groups. *Written Communication*, 15(4): 493–530.

Goffman, E. (1959) *The Presentation of Self in Everyday Life*. New York, NY: Doubleday.

Good, M. J. D. V. (2007) The Medical Imaginary and the Biotechnical Embrace: Subjective Experiences of Clinical Scientists and Patients. In Biehl, J., Good, B. and Kleinman, A. (Eds.), *Subjectivity: Ethnographic Investigations*. Berkeley, CA: University of California Press, 362–381.

Hajela, S. (2012) The Monster Within: Understanding the Narratives of Depression. *Psychological Studies*, 58(1): 10–19.

Hardon, A. and Sanabria, E. (2017) Fluid Drugs: Revisiting the Anthropology of Pharmaceuticals. *Annual Review of Anthropology*, 46: 117–132.

Heilferty, C. M. (2009) Toward a Theory of Online Communication in Illness: Concept Analysis of Illness Blogs. *Journal of Advanced Nursing*, 65(7): 1539–1547.

Jones, B. A. and Griffiths, K. M. (2015) Self-Objectification and Depression: An Integrative Systematic Review. *Journal of Affective Disorders*, 171: 22–32.

Kangas, I. (2001) Making Sense of Depression: Perceptions of Melancholia in Lay Narratives. *Health: An Interdisciplinary Journal for the Social Study of Health, Illness and Medicine*, 5(1): 76–92.

Kirmayer, L. J., Gomez-Carrillo, A. and Veissière, S. (2017) Culture and Depression in Global Mental Health: An Ecosocial Approach to the Phenomenology of Psychiatric Disorders. *Social Science and Medicine*, 183: 163–168.

Kleinman, A. M. (1973) Medicine's Symbolic Reality: On a Central Problem in the Philosophy of Medicine. *Inquiry*, 16(1–4): 206–213.

Kleinman, A. M. (1988) *The Illness Narratives: Suffering, Healing, and the Human Condition*. New York, NY: Basic Books.

Kleinman, A. M. and Kleinman, J.(1991) Suffering and Its Professional Transformation: Toward an Ethnography of Interpersonal Experience. *Culture, Medicine and Psychiatry*, 15(3): 275–301.

Kotliar, D. M. (2015) Depression Narratives in Blogs. *Qualitative Health Research*, 26(9): 1203–1215.

Laing, R. D. and Esterson, A. (1964) *Sanity, Madness and the Family*. London: Penguin Books.

Lash, S. (2002) *The Critique of Information*. London: Sage.

Latour, B. (2005) *Reassembling the Social*. Oxford: Oxford University Press.

Lee, M. (2017) Don't Give Up! A Cyber-Ethnography and Discourse Analysis of an Online Infertility Patient Forum. *Culture, Medicine, and Psychiatry*, 41(3): 341–367.

Lewinsohn, P. M., Youngren, M. A. and Grosscup, S. J. (1979) Reinforcement and Depression. In Depue, R. A. (Ed.), *The Psychobiology of the Depressive Disorders*, New York, NY: Academic Press, 291–316.

Llewellyn-Beardsley, J. et al. (2019) Characteristics of Mental Health Recovery Narratives: Systematic Review and Narrative Synthesis. *PLoS One*, 14(3). https://doi.org/10.1371/journal.pone.0214678.

Murphy, E., Donohue, G. and McCann, E. (2020) Exploring Mental Health Issues Through the Use of Blogs: A Scoping Review of the Research Evidence. *Issues in Mental Health Nursing*, 41(4): 296–305.

Naslund, J., Aschbrenner, K., Marsch, L. and Bartels, S. (2016) The Future of Mental Health Care: Peer-to-Peer Support and Social media. *Epidemiology and Psychiatric Sciences*, 25(2): 113–122.

Németh, R., Sik, D. and Máté, F. (2020) Machine Learning of Concepts Hard Even for Humans: The Case of Online Depression Forums. *International Journal of Qualitative Methods*. https://doi.org/10.1177/1609406920949338.

Nimrod, G. (2013) Online Depression Communities: Members' Interests and Perceived Benefits, *Health Communication*, 28(5): 425–434.

O'Brien, M. R. and Clark, D. (2012) Unsolicited Written Narratives as a Methodological Genre in Terminal Illness: Challenges and Limitations. *Qualitative Health Research*, 22(2): 274–284.

Powell, J., McCarthy, N. and Eysenbach, G. (2003) Cross-Sectional Survey of Users of Internet Depression Communities. *BMC Psychiatry*, 3(19). https://doi.org/10.1186/1471-244X-3-19.

Prescott, J., Hanley, T. and Ujhelyi, K. (2017) Peer Communication in Online Mental Health Forums for Young People: Directional and Nondirectional Support. *JMIR Mental Health*, 4(3): e29. https://doi.org/10.2196/mental.6921.

Prince, R. (1980) Variations in Psychotherapeutic Procedures. In Trianclis, H. C. and Draguns, J. C. (Eds.), *Handbook of Cross-Cultural Psychology*. Boston, MA: Allyn and Bacon, 291–349.

Rácz, J. et al. (2015) The Therapeutic Journeys of Recovering Helpers – An Interpretative Phenomenological Analysis. *International Journal of Mental Health and Addiction*, 13(6): 751–757.

Ratcliffe, M. (2015) *Experiences of Depression*. Oxford: Oxford University Press.

Rogers, C. (1956) *Client-Centered Therapy*. Boston, MA: Houghton-Mifflin.

Rose, N. (1999) *Governing the Soul: The Shaping of the Private Self.* London: Free Association Books.

Rose, N. (2018) *Our Psychiatric Future: the Politics of Mental Health*. London: Polity Press.

Rose, N. and Abi-Rached, J. M. (2013) *Neuro: The New Brain Sciences and the Management of the Mind*. Princeton, NJ/Oxford: Princeton University Press.

Salzmann-Erikson, M. and Eriksson, H. (2012) LiLEDDA: A Six-Step Forum-Based Netnographic Research Method for Nursing Science. *Aporia*, 4(4): 6–18.

Smith-Merry, J. et al. (2019) Social Connection and Online Engagement: Insights From Interviews With Users of a Mental Health Online Forum. *JMIR Mental Health*, 6(3): e11084. https://doi.org/10.2196/11084.

Scheff, T. J. (1999) *Being Mentally Ill: A Sociological Theory*. New York, NY: Aldine de Gruyter.

Seligman, M. E. P. (1975) *Helplessness*. San Francisco, CA: Freeman.

Skageby, J. (2010) Online Ethnographic Methods: Towards a Qualitative Understanding of Virtual Community Practices. In Ben Kei, D. (Ed.), *Handbook of Research on Methods and Techniques for Studying Virtual Communities: Paradigms and Phenomena*. Hershey, PA: Idea Group, 410–428.

Wolcott, H. F. (1999) *Ethnography: A Way of Seeing*. Walnut Creek, CA: AltaMira Press.

8 Beyond organic solidarity

From the paradoxes of late modern welfare state to the moral challenges of crisis management

Suffering is not a discrete notion: it is complemented by those supportive relationships, which have the potential of reducing it. The pattern of – actual, lacking and distorted – social support expresses solidarity, which is the collective reaction to suffering. Solidarity is not only a key concept of sociology, but also a central notion of moral and political philosophy. Accordingly, it has multiple stakes: both the social integration, the dignity of the subject and the democratic quality of the political sphere depends on it. Furthermore, solidarity is a complex phenomenon: it affects the practical level of everyday interactions (supporting the other with material or symbolic resources); the phenomenological level of norms and values (institutionalized discourses of deservingness and responsibility); and the structural level of integration (mechanisms of inclusion and exclusion). As the emergence of empty suffering is related to all of these stakes and levels, in this chapter a comprehensive concept of solidarity is outlined. In order to avoid reductionism, a multilayered model is elaborated, which addresses the historical paradoxes of modernization (elaborated in Part I) and also the distortions of social interactions and broader networks (according to Part II).

The various transformations of late modernity challenge solidarity in many ways. On structural level, the emergence of global capitalism is responsible for new dimensions of inequality and new forms of social integration reacting to the increased contingency. In the preceding era of 'organized capitalism' (Lash and Urry, 1987) the administrative system of the nation state was responsible for handling the risks of the labour market. The mature form of this constellation is manifested in the emerging 'welfare state' taking responsibility for social challenges through legally coordinated expert systems (Castel, 2002). This welfare paradigm became challenged in the 'information age' (Castells, 1996), as the nation states gradually lost their capability of countering the swings of the globalizing market. However, beside these negative consequences, also new integration mechanisms emerged, which enabled adaptation to the increased uncertainties and contingencies. While these new forms of integration can either be characterized as 'disorganised' (Lash and Urry, 1987) or 'liquid' (Bauman, 2000), they also establish new

DOI: 10.4324/9781003197355-12

frames for solidarity through the provided reflexivity (Beck, 1992) and network flexibility (Castells, 1996).

On phenomenological level, both the values grounding solidarity and the related praxes are reshaped. The moral narratives of justification change: the previous substantive claims (or 'cités'), such as efficiency, expertise, merit based on fair contest and hard work (Boltanski and Thévenot, 2006) are gradually replaced by principles based on the exclusive praise of flexibility, real-time availability, self-branding and network embeddedness as adaptive skills in 'project capitalism' (Boltanski and Chiapello, 2005). These transformations of the public moral sentiments reframe those principles of justice, which previously served as the basis of attributing deservingness and responsibility. Beside of the principles themselves, the scope of those who are included in the moral community also changed: as a consequence of globalization, the extent of transnational and global responsibility becomes a fundamental question (Brunkhorst, 2008). On the level of social praxes and technologies, solidarity also becomes ambiguous. The contingencies and controversies of operating the expert systems of the national welfare state increased, as they were not only burdened with the competitiveness of the global market, but also with inner pressures originating from the increasing number of precarious denizens (Standing, 2011) and the consequences of recurring economic and ecological crises (Giddens, 1990). Beside the nation state, new actors of solidarity appeared (such as international organizations and global NGOs), which are supposed to provide more flexible answers in a globalized world by experimenting with emergency mechanisms of crisis management (Castells, 2015).

All in all, solidarity in late modernity becomes contingent both on structural level (as the welfare state is weakened due to the rise of global capitalism), phenomenological level (as the normative frames of deservingness and responsibility are blurred) and practical level (as the communities and welfare institutions of solidarity become fragmented). These tendencies threaten with the disintegration of social units and the distortion of supportive relations at the same time. Even if these grim prospects have recently become more probable, it would be premature to conclude that solidarity is completely hopeless in late modernity (e.g. Crouch, 2004). Not only because of the various attempts of finding new solutions on the level of the nation state, the international organizations or the global civil society – but also because of the undeniable remnants of solidarity, which still have integrative and supportive potential, even if only to a limited extent. This chapter aims at exploring the ambiguous late modern solidarity, which is not based anymore on the proud and optimistic enthusiasm of the Enlightenment, but rather on compromises and hybrid forms aiming at treating certain forms of suffering without promising to find long-term solutions to the overwhelming challenges and paradoxes.

These considerations indicate the line of thought of the chapter. In order to avoid reductionism, an attempt is made to analyze both the structural, phenomenological and practical levels of solidarity, while also reflecting on their interrelatedness. Firstly, classic and contemporary social theories are overviewed in order to describe the structural transformations resulting in the emergence of 'post-organic solidarity'. These analyses introduce historical processes resulting in the fragmentation of 'organic solidarity'. Durkheim's model is used as a reference not only because of its substantive conclusions, but also because of its exceptional theoretical comprehensiveness. Durkheim explains how the premodern paradigm of mechanic solidarity was gradually giving place to a new, organic form: the latter did not completely replace the former one, instead complemented and transformed it. The model of post-organic solidarity is introduced in a similar fashion: its emergence is explained as a consequence of the functional inadequacy of the mature expression of organic solidarity (that is the national welfare state facing global challenges)[1]; its main features ('Sisyphean' efforts of harm reduction without the promise of long-term solutions) are explained as an adaptation to the late modern structural constraints (the uncertainties and inequalities of globalized informational capitalism); also its impact on the prevailing elements of mechanic (negative collective consciousness) and organic solidarity (deconstruction of welfare state) is elaborated into a comprehensive model.

The social theoretical elaboration of the structural background of a post-organic solidarity is followed by the analysis of the parallel transformation of the norms of responsibility and the criteria of deservingness. While in case of the first section, the analyses of modernization played the main role, in the second section, mostly moral and political theories are reinterpreted in order to clarify the normative claims capable of grounding the model of post-organic solidarity. Even though these philosophical argumentations are not necessarily adopted by the everyday actors or the institutions, they are considered to be essential sources, when it comes to reconstructing the discursive space of justifications, which ground the transforming contemporary solidarity. This overview enables the outlining of a negative normative basis, which can be used to refine the model of post-organic solidarity: those networks of crisis management are considered to have a solidarity function, which are in accordance with these principles.

The clarification of the structural and normative elements of late modern solidarity is followed by an analysis of contemporary interventions. In the third section, anthropological analyses of humanitarian actions are overviewed in order to highlight the practical ambiguities of post-organic solidarity. It is argued that the hybrid networks of solidarity relying on the 'logic of emergency' threaten with the suspension of any sort of morality – including those principles, which are summarized in the minimalistic negative model. Accordingly, the logic of emergency turns out to be a factor undermining the very possibility of post-organic solidarity. These conclusions are summarized in the final section: based on the theoretical and empirical insights, an attempt is made to outline a comprehensive model of solidarity, which is not only sociologically grounded, normatively clarified and empirically refined, but also capable of addressing the challenges of empty suffering.

The paradoxes of organic solidarity – The emergence of crisis management networks

Even if various theories of late modernity differ in many ways, they share one general diagnosis: they claim that the former stability of the social world is replaced by overwhelming uncertainty. Although contingency is an inherent characteristics of modernity since the beginning, expert knowledge and the related institutions maintained a predictable horizon of expectations in its classic phase (Giddens, 1994). Since the Enlightenment, a scientific logic of risk management replaced the concept of Providence, while establishing a non-religious sense of security (Beck, 1992). Experts calculating the probability of various risks enabled the emergence of a system based on the logic of assurance: vulnerabilities and responsibilities were discursively constructed in the biopolitical complex. This classic modern paradigm of solidarity was manifested in the institutions of the welfare state, which not only took over the responsibilities of the family and community, but also started to elaborate strategies of managing the wide circle of social risks through the legally coordinated, tax-financed system of social security. As social integration became linked to the capitalist market and the division of labour, the most important risks became also related to them: the right for secure work conditions, fair salaries, benefits and the prevention of unemployment constituted the central welfare demands (Castel, 2002).[2]

While this constellation has provided a functionally differentiated alternative to the traditional paradigm of solidarity, recently it became undermined by the emergence of new structural inequalities and risks related to globalization and the industrial exploitation of the environment. Inequalities in the global era are irreducible to any single dimension, such as the violation of the principles of justice (Sandel, 1998); the limitation of capabilities (Sen, 1999); or the deprivation from recognition (Fraser, 1997). Instead, inequalities represent a complex problem: class, ethnicity, race, gender, religion, nation, linguistic community, able-bodiedness, sexual orientation and age are considered to be the most significant axes of the space of inequalities, which is also characterized by the intersectionality of various dimensions (Walby, 2009: 60). Furthermore, these inequalities are not constituted anymore within the frames of the nation state, instead they are shaped by global economic, cultural and political dynamics. Global scale accumulation, dispossession and environmental harms affect the elementary level of the everyday life of local communities; while authoritarian state practices and technologies of surveillance embedded in hierarchical global networks determine the space of local political action (Koch, 2018). As the inequalities become more complex and embedded in global structures, the institutions of the welfare state cannot handle them anymore within the frames of the existing rigid expert systems. The increased complexity of inequalities was not followed by a similar functional differentiation of the social security system, which became incapable of addressing intersectional disadvantages. Especially, as it also lacks the fiscal tools required for countering the negative impact of global market swings.

Even if these dysfunctionalities are not responsible on their own for the discrediting of expert systems in general (and a paradigm of solidarity based on it), they certainly contribute to the intensification of such tendency. Scientific knowledge and related expert systems equally lost their – formerly taken for granted – legitimacy due to the emergence of new 'irreversible' risks, such as recurring economic crises, nuclear catastrophes or pollution (Beck, 1992). Even if the discursive power relations based on the authority of expertise were not eliminated completely, new power structures emerged, such as the 'post-panoptic' one originating from the inequality of the inevitably rigid local and the infinitely flexible global (Bauman, 2000). In this new constellation, the flexibility requirements of the globalized world became a fundamental constraint of solidarity aiming at decreasing inequalities. As any forms of institutional rigidity proves to be powerless in a competition based on flexibility, attempts of building stable expert systems of solidarity become difficult. In this constellation, the chance of an overall defeatist solidarity increases, as the new paradigm tends to give up on the systematic treatment of the causes of social suffering (related to various inequalities), while contenting itself with the harm reduction of the most visible, extreme cases. This defeatism becomes tangible, if the instruments of the 'old' (classic modern) and 'new' (late modern) social policies are contrasted: while the former operated with direct transfers (e.g. child allowances), employment protection interventions and income replacements (e.g. benefits); the latter relies mostly on indirect tools, such as re-commodified child and elderly services, pension insurances and reintegration projects (Häusermann, 2012).

These structural transformations highlight the key contemporary challenges of the solidarity paradigm designed in classic modernity as a system of social security. Even if the classic institutions of the welfare state become more adaptive, they are still burdened with paradoxes due to the incompatible demands of predictability and flexibility. Solidarity is one of the key binding forces of any particular social units in a sense that it outlines the moral economy of deservingness, community responsibilities and supportive obligations. It relies on a minimal level of trust, which grounds long-term collective expectations (Putnam, 2000). If such minimal trust is missing, then the basis of solidarity – that is a projection of mutuality – is undermined. As the increased insecurity (caused by extreme need of flexibility) erodes the mechanisms of solidarity (thriving on trust), a paradox is being born: one of the most decisive vulnerability of late modernity originates from instability; therefore, a need for a solidarity mechanisms capable of strengthening stability arises; however, solidarity itself is paralyzed as the basis of trust is corroded.

All in all, it seems that the distortive tendencies of late modernity are untreatable by praxes invented in classical modernity not simply because of their inefficiency, but because of fundamental incompatibilities. From this perspective, it seems that late modernity is characterized by imminent crises of disintegration. In contemporary societies the regression to previous forms of solidarity is a realistic scenario, which is indicated by the recent rise of neo-nationalist populism according to many analyses (Muis and Immerzeel, 2017). However, regression and disintegration are not the only potential consequences: new paradigms of solidarity arise as well, holding the potential of grounding yet unexplored forms of integration (Castells, 2015; Olesen, 2004). While the available sociological reflections – focusing on either regressive or progressive ways out from the solidarity crisis – highlight ideal-typical tendencies, they also tend to end up in one-sided diagnoses. In order to avoid such one-sidedness, an attempt has to be made not only to incorporate both distortions and emancipatory tendencies, but also to theorize about their interaction. Luckily, such a complex theoretical enterprise is not unprecedented in the history of sociology: the closer examination of a similar liminal condition, that is the paradigm shift between mechanic and organic solidarity may provide hints for clarifying the challenges and paradoxes of late modern solidarity.

There are several reasons, why Durkheim's classic analysis still inspires attempts of reinterpretation – among its many merits, the extreme theoretical carefulness is certainly a central one. He reflected on several aspects of a paradigm of solidarity related to the 'division of labour' (Durkheim, 2013): the historical antecedents (that is the 'solidarity by similarities'); the causes of the dissolving of mechanic solidarity (that is individualization induced by functional differentiation); the distortions of the transformation (that is the anomic or forced division of labour); and also the critique of one-sided theories (such as the Spencerian contract theory). All of these components are present in the construct of organic solidarity, which is not an ahistorical form, but a result of complex transformations. While it reconfigures the basis of social integration, it still bears the reminiscences of the previous form of solidarity: as contractual relations are inevitably grounded on the level of collective consciousness (no contract can ensure the keeping of a contract, only a moral commitment), a certain level of mechanic solidarity is indispensable in modern societies as well (Durkheim, 2013: 178). On the other hand, the collective element in modern solidarity is not simply a reduced version of the premodern mechanic solidarity, but also its altered version: it is not reproduced anymore directly in collective rituals enabling the experience of 'collective effervescence' (Durkheim, 1995: 218), but lived through indirectly as the individualized actors realize their own dependence on each other's outputs.

The collective consciousness of organic solidarity lacks any shared substantive traditions; instead it is based on the general exposedness to the system of the division of labour and the consequent experience of being a functional element of a social totality. In this constellation, the individual interests partly overlap with the collective ones, thus the challenge of establishing a collective consciousness of individualized actors is resolved indirectly: instead of participating in the same rituals, the actors taking part in the division of labour are subordinated to the same functional constraints, which results in a collective experience (Durkheim, 2013: 102). The same analysis also reveals the fragility of such form of integration, compared to the robustness of ritually reproduced collective consciousness of tribal societies. Anomic division of labour is the proof of the instability of a moral order based on such contingent experiences: the weakening of the norms is a possibility in the first place, because they are not renewed anymore in collective rites, but become dependent on distinct, individual interpretations (Durkheim, 2013: 288).

From a meta-theoretical perspective, these analyses are exemplary, because they succeed in conceptualizing a major structural transformation while avoiding one-sidedness. This meta-theoretical guideline can be used for conceptualizing the contemporary crisis of organic solidarity itself and the space of possibilities of a 'post-organic solidarity'. Such pattern should be understood as a historical entity, which emerges on the reminiscences of the institutions of the welfare state. It does not simply reduce these institutions, but also twists them by creating a new constellation characterized by the modification of the original (biopolitical) goals of the nation state: those adaptive tendencies become dominant, which fit the new negatively integrated global environment (see Chapter 2). From the specific late modern structural constraints, new formative experiences emerge, while grounding a new form of collective consciousness. It is not anymore based on a functional co-dependence, but rather on a global risk community (Ottmann, 2010) and the tensions originating from global inequalities (Talani and Roccu, 2019). In this sense, the post-organic solidarity is inevitably embedded in the 'transnational space', which means that it is not solely dependent on any particular nation state, but also on factors originating from their interrelatedness.[3]

If organic solidarity expressed the thinning of the substantive core of solidarity by relying on a contingent individual experience instead of actual collective rites, it may be argued that a post-organic solidarity takes this transformation to the next level. The collective consciousness based on the experience of global risks is not simply an abstract one, but – expressing negative integration – also a suspicious one: unlike in case of organic solidarity, where the other's contribution to one's well-being provided a positive element of sociability, in the latter case, the experience of the mutual benefits from the division of labour is overshadowed by the perception of the other as a rival or a threat, which needs to be contained. Accordingly, the post-organic solidarity is inevitably a mixture of these two aspects: it is based on the balancing between the dependency on the local and global chains of the divisions of labour and the climate of mutual suspicion, fear and harm reduction related to the other. Such ambivalent relation to the other is built in the basic level of post-organic solidarity: the other is never simply perceived as the member of the virtual or actual community implying both moral obligations and expectations, but rather as a potentially dangerous, but at the same time indispensable actor. In this moral framework solidarity itself becomes interwoven with hostility, which expresses the incorporation of the paradoxes of late modernity into its core structure.

If organic solidarity was endangered by the over-thinning of the underlying normative basis of integration (that is anomie), then a post-organic solidarity is burdened with even more severe crisis potentials: the oscillation between solidarity and hostility threatens not only with the extreme contingency of support (if suddenly suspicion becomes dominant), but also the tainting of supportive interactions with the potential of abuse (as the actors can never be sure, if the seemingly helpful attempts are not based on hidden malevolent intentions). Late modern solidarity operating in such structural environment has to give up many moral features, which were previously considered to be indispensable. At the same time new institutions and mechanisms are developed in order to secure its functioning.

All in all, this ambiguous transformation is similar to the previous transition between mechanic and organic solidarity. In the historical case, the sense of community and the actors' similarity was given up, which was counterbalanced by the emergence of functional systems securing solidarity in an abstract and general framework. In case of the transition to post-organic solidarity, the *modus operandi* of the welfare state is transformed: as it is not capable anymore of providing a stable system of social security, it starts to rely on improvised attempts of crisis management. Consequently, crisis becomes an element of the horizon of expectations, as stability seems to be impossible. The permanent crisis management implies a 'Sisyphean solidarity', which is based on the continuous efforts of harm reduction without the claim or hope for providing a sense of security.

While such compromising form of solidarity is based on less commitment, it also implies alternative mechanisms, which counterbalance its flaws. In order to make a system based on permanent crisis management work, the further increase of functional differentiation is needed. According to contemporary system theory, the evolutionary dynamics of any systems, including social ones, is based on the development of information processing subsystems capable of monitoring the environment in a more detailed and precise way. In this sense, the key to reduce the unlimited complexity of the environment is the increase of the inner complexity, that is the functional differentiation of second-order observation subsystems (Luhmann, 1995). In late modernity, with the emergence of information society, such capacities are extensively expanded (Castells, 1996). A technological and institutional infrastructure becomes available, which is capable of processing massive amounts of data in real-time. Furthermore, these data are not anymore limited to collected statistics, but being produced in hybrid 'actor-networks' (Latour, 2005) constituted of human and non-human elements (i.e. big data). Such techno-social infrastructure may provide tools for a post-organic solidarity: until the signs of crises threatening with quick escalation are adequately monitored, the lack of actual insecurity may be veiled by the efficiency of real-time intervention. One of the most obvious advantages of such flexible structure is the expandability: as the technological infrastructure is just partly limited by social and cultural constraints, it may be applied on international or global scale. Accordingly, it holds the potential of addressing those challenges of late modernity, which are related to global risks.

Such hybrid post-organic solidarity also creates social challenges and distortions of its own. In case of organic solidarity, the distortions were related to the shrinking of the collective moral ground; in case of post-organic solidarity, the loss of the securities of the welfare state play a central role. Most importantly, while the welfare state is legally bound, that is based on the political control of the members of the political community, the technologies of crisis management are not necessarily – a difference having severe consequences. Despite its many flaws, the welfare state defines its legal obligations by referring to forms of suffering deserving social intervention. In this sense, it is based on the moral recognition of subjects, who rightfully expect support from the institutions of the system of social security. In contrast, the logic of crisis management is based on the exclusive logic of preventing the escalation of threats, which results in the ignorance of abstract moral claims. In post-organic solidarity, the subjects lose their distinguished role: they do not have unalienable rights based on citizenship or universal human dignity anymore. The logic of crisis management suspends any stable legal framework in the name of the ultimate claim of preventing hazards. Consequently, the moral economy of deservingness is reconfigured: instead of relying on universal rights, only those forms of suffering matter, which are relevant from the perspective of crisis management, that is the ones threatening with quick and widespread escalation. Those forms of suffering, which are containable and do not threaten with spreading, become invisible. This increases the ignorance towards classic forms of suffering, such as poverty, unemployment, health hazards of deprived and segregated populations – even if these were treated by the welfare state in an ambiguous manner, at least they appeared on the horizon, unlike in case of technologies of crisis prevention.

Further potential distortions of the hybrid networks of solidarity are related to the inequalities of the access to the harm reducing technologies. As the moral claims of solidarity shrink to an almost invisible level, the only criteria of having access to the complementary technologies promising to monitor and prevent imminent crises is the material resources. Those actors will be granted the chance of predicting and potentially avoiding the dangers, who are connected to specific actor-networks of information processing. This tendency – further increasing the impact of 'futile ownership' (see Chapter 1) – creates a new type of inequality both on local and global scale: a segment of national and global population is connected to the crisis management networks only as a potential source of threat to be monitored, while others are able to profit from the alerting system as well. These inequalities are further augmented by the increased pressure of reification related to the embedding in the emerging hybrid actor-networks of crisis management – a potential, whose significance can be understood from the perspective of the self-objectifying medical power (see Chapter 3). In order to make these systems functional, masses of the local and global population have to be connected: this implies not only the giving up of privacy and autonomy, but also the subordination to the logic of surveillance technologies, which is justified by the dominant, undisputable discourse of – often biomedically justified – crisis management.

Of course, the emergence of post-organic solidarity should not be viewed as the complete replacement of the organic patterns (similarly, the emergence of organic solidarity did not mean the disappearance of mechanic). Instead, these transformations refer to the addition of a complementary layer to the contemporary paradigm of solidarity, which reconfigures the already existing ones as well. As the logic of post-organic solidarity expands, the preventive securities provided by the welfare state are replaced by the reactive interventions of crisis management. The expansion of 'managerialism' and the neoliberal transformation of social services exemplifies the consequences of such shift, as they lead to a professional, but ignorant institutional praxis, incapable of taking into consideration the individual needs of the clients (Harlow et al., 2013). The alienating reconfiguration of the expert institutions affects the reminiscent of mechanic solidarity as well. It is not based anymore on a narrowed and individualized collective consciousness, but rather on a disillusioned one organized around negative collective identity and suspicion (as it is elaborated in Chapter 2).[4] Table 8.1 summarizes these conclusions, by comparing the classic and late modern model of solidarity.

All in all, from a social theoretical perspective, the space of possibility of late modern solidarity is characterized by the reducing and twisting of organic solidarity institutions and the consequent emergence of a hybrid techno-social complex of crisis management legitimized by the experiences of being exposed to global risks. While this paradigm of solidarity – similarly to the organic one at its time – enables the expansion of integration (even beyond the nation state), it is capable to do so at the cost of further thinning the moral basis of solidarity and the threat of increasing ignorance for actual forms of suffering, new types of inequalities and intensified reification. In this sense, the cost of expanding the circle of those who are included (from the nation state to the global) is the further increase of contingency of the

Table 8.1 The comparison of organic and post-organic solidarity

	The model of organic solidarity	*The model of post-organic solidarity*
Historical antecedent	Mechanic solidarity (i.e. solidarity by similarity)	Welfare state as the mature version of organic solidarity
Key structural transformation	Individualization induced by functional differentiation	Emergence of global risks and inequalities (including economic and health related components)
Emerging new layer of solidarity	Organic solidarity (i.e. solidarity by functional co-dependence) rooted in a narrowed version of collective consciousness	Post-organic solidarity (i.e. global networks of 'Sisyphean' crisis management)
Reconfiguration of the old constellation	Individual experience of depending on the others' outputs and being subordinated to the same functional constraints	Negative collective consciousness (i.e. mixture of co-dependence and suspicion, hostility towards the other) deconstructed welfare state (i.e. no prospect of real solutions, only harm reduction; temporal solutions, instead of rights)
New possibilities	Integrating virtual communities (i.e. nation states) through the system of the division of labour and the welfare state	Integrating global risk communities through flexible networks of crisis management
Distortions and pathologies	Anomic or forced division of labour	Reified management of suffering; inequalities of access to technologies of crisis management

moral basis of solidarity. While this prospect may seem to be a grim one at first sight, the clarification of the possible moral grounds helps to ground a normative basis fitting post-organic solidarity.

The limitations of justice – The emergence of transnational solidarity

The notion of solidarity has been viewed with suspicion by most moral philosophers being preoccupied with the universalist principle of justice. Since Kant's critique, the 'moral law' was primarily elaborated in a negative way: as one's originally unlimited freedom is limited by the respect of other's similarly unalienable freedom, those maxims are considered to be justifiable, which stand the test of universalizing. In this broad framework, the primary concern of moral philosophy has been to identify the further implications, either within the frames of a hypothetical contract made behind the 'veil of ignorance' (Rawls, 1971) or democratic institutions controlled by actual public debates (Habermas, 1996). Inserting the question of solidarity in the framework of post-Kantian moral philosophy was never an unambiguous task: as solidarity implies substantive obligations and affective responsibilities targeting particular others, it seems to be incompatible with the negative concept of freedom, universalism and a purely rational grounding. Despite these difficulties, the various communitarian criticisms – blaming theories of justice for narrowing the scope of moral philosophy to the issues of universal principles – often found notions related to solidarity inspirational. As a result of these engagements, in contemporary moral philosophy several attempts were made to highlight the contours of a complex solution implementing elements from both the universalizing principles and the particular obligations, while viewing the two sides as complementary (Bayertz, 1999). As these attempts embrace and incorporate the tensions and paradoxes of contrasting approaches, they could ground a normative basis fitting an ambiguous phenomenon, such as the late modern networks of post-organic solidarity.

The first type of arguments focuses on the various ways solidarity may contribute or enable the emergence of justice. In modernity, the individualized actors follow their own interest – thus, solidarity does not emerge anymore as a general social norm. However, that does not render it dispensable: in order to achieve individual goals, the actors may still require social support beyond the ones granted by the imperfect state, which means that any expressions of solidarity are valuable. Despite the impossibility of generalizing solidarity through the legal system built on the principles of universal justice, its complementary mechanisms are universally beneficial. The experiences of being helped by legally unbound others has a 'socializing' function: it unintentionally promotes a virtue of supporting the ones in need, even beyond the legal obligations (Baurmann, 1999). Such virtue is a public good in two senses: it strengthens the commitment to the moral law, while complementing the expert system of social security characterized by inevitable flaws, inefficiencies and dysfunctions.

In accordance with these conclusions, several theories synthesize the liberal and communitarian accounts (e.g. Forst, 2002). Their goal is to find a middle ground, which is capable of connecting the liberal and communitarian accounts. One of the most influential sources for such synthesis can be found in the recognition theories expanding the scope of justice. They argue that not only material goods and negative freedom, but also the possibility of recognition needs to be redistributed in a fair way. In other words, the intersubjective space of solidarity has to be included among the principles of justice (Juul, 2010). Other approaches focus on the frontier zones of justice by asking, what a theory of justice has to offer for entities being excluded from a social contract (e.g. people living with disabilities, deprived of citizenship or sentient animals – Nussbaum, 2006). As these examples reveal the limitations of any contract theories of justice, they point to the 'capabilities of the sentient beings',[5] instead of freedom having the potential of universalizability. A just political order could be grounded on the level of these capabilities: only they ensure human dignity, that is the ultimate goal of any social contracts based on universal justice. According to this framework, the possibility of justice (as a system of universal rights securing the moral law) is intertwined with solidarity (as a collective responsibility for these substantive claims).

Among the various analyses dealing with the intertwining of justice and solidarity, those play a distinguished role, which focus on a problem becoming central in late modernity, that is the question of transnational and global solidarity. The criterion of inclusion has provoked ongoing philosophical debates as the extent and content of international solidarity is far from being unambiguous (Stjerno, 2005: 327). Most theories of solidarity latently rely on the background assumption of the nation state: a commitment of actively supporting the other implies an ethical community, which has been historically built around national-ethnic lines. However, despite the seemingly impassable, solid dividing lines, cosmopolitan solidarity is not a mere theoretical hope, but also an institutional reality (e.g. UN, WHO, UNICEF) complemented with civic activities trying to represent and enhance global responsibility, which was unprecedented prior to our times (Wilde, 2013). As there is no basis for *a priori* denying the possibility of global solidarity, the task of reflecting upon its extent remains relevant. At the heart of the problem lies a phenomenological question concerning the preconditions of transcending the affective and conventional bases of intersubjectivity: the key element of such transition is reflectivity. By relying on the maxim of treating the others as an 'end-in-itself', reflective solidarity has the inherent potential of aiming at continuously expanding the horizon of inclusion, which is the key of transcending particularizing frameworks (Dean, 1995).

The challenge of transcending the national framework is similar to the one related to the birth of modern nation states: they also depended on the invention of institutions enabling the inclusion of actors outside of actual communities. In late modernity, it is not the boundaries of actual local communities, but the virtual communities of the nation, which need to be overcome. Despite this difference, the solution may be similar: nation states secured the extension of solidarity by improving constitutional democracy, as these institutions could ensure trust in the general other. Of course, this process was not without conflicts in the past either: the history of solidarity is inseparable from the history of transcending various forms of exclusion. In a globalized world exclusion does not simply target certain religious or ethnic groups – although these conflicts do not pass away either (Brunkhorst, 2008) – rather the 'surplus population' (Brunkhorst, 2005: 123). These people represent the paradox of a one-sided globalization: while the expanding global markets rely on them as cheap, replaceable workforce, the institutions, which could handle the negative consequences of the reifying and exploitative market relations are missing. The main obstacle in the way of transcending the exclusion of the global precariat is the lack of constitutional democratic institutions operating on global scale. In order to establish them, a global public sphere – capable of influencing political decision – would be needed in the first place. In order to enable constitutional democracy to transcend those forms of exclusion, which segregate the global surplus population, a strong, global version of 'communicative power' is needed (Brunkhorst, 2005: 153; Pedersen, 2006).[6]

Transnational solidarity affects core elements of universal justice and the very possibility of particular solidarities as well, which are both relying on it in various ways. However, it should not be forgotten either that such relation is not one-directional, as the global solidarity also relies on the principles and sentiments of the national. Nation states are the best available examples of solidarity ties transcending local intersubjective communities. Accordingly, it is plausible to envisage the birth of global solidarity as the stretching of the scope of national solidarity – even if nationalism implies the logic of exclusion. Building a global solidarity is a paradox process: it requires the strengthening of national solidarity and its transcendence at the same time. In order to theorize this ambivalence, it should be viewed as a dialectic process, instead of a linear one, which is based on the oscillation between the particular and the universal (Schwartz, 2007). A set of restrictions for nationalistic solidarity may be listed originating from the principles of justice in order to highlight the frames of a justifiable middle ground. These include the criteria of efficiency (protecting more refugees than its feasible alternatives); consensus (it should be approved by the supporters and supported); anti-prejudice policy (affinities cannot be based on essentializing concepts, such as race); egalitarianism (the support of one group cannot imply the worsening of the conditions of another); emancipation (transcending the nationalistic framework as a result of the affinity based support – Hobbs and Souter, 2019).

Besides the purely rational claims, in case of global solidarity the affective elements also play an important role. The intertwined relation of sentiments and rationality has been a resurging topic since the Enlightenment, which becomes particularly relevant in case of moral questions dealing with suffering (Rorty, 1989). In case of global solidarity, sentiments may help to solve the 'motivational gap' often preventing commitment: the shared experience of vulnerability that is the – actual or symbolic – identification with the others' suffering may create bridges even in those circumstances, where national, cultural or other differences create distances (Woods, 2012). At this point, the question of mediation becomes crucial: suffering is never a self-evident phenomenon, but rather a construction both on the level of the percipient and the transmitting mediums (Boltanski, 1999). Therefore, the inequalities of representation and the susceptibility to manipulation always needs to be taken into consideration. Even if sentiments can ground the motivation for – the otherwise improbable – global solidarity, their public usage should be viewed critically: evoking and mediatizing sympathies might maintain latent power structures as well (Woods, 2012: 46). In order to minimize such dangers, in the mediatized public sphere, grounding (post-organic) solidarity should not rely on 'grand narratives'. Instead it may be imagined as an 'agnostic solidarity' relying on the voices of vulnerability without either giving up principles of justice or simply reducing them to any grand narrative of justice (Chouliaraki, 2013: 24).

Sentiments capable of reinforcing solidarity are not only endangered by the limitations of the contemporary political public sphere, but also by the broader neoliberal constellation: individualization, anti-egalitarianism and anti-democratic practices contribute to the emergence of 'responsibilized individualism' and 'weak forms of calculative solidarity' (Lynch and Kalaitzake, 2020). As such meritocratic attributions become the mainstream framework of deservingness and responsibility, the political horizon does not include anymore the emotional motivation or the rational justification of a global solidarity, instead it relies on narratives 'blaming the victim'. Within this ambiguous setting, solidarity becomes a contingent, constantly changing possibility. The boundaries between its various forms (such as mechanic/organic, rational/emotive, or national/global) are blurred (Thijssen, 2012). Such amorphous solidarity incorporates contradictory concepts – this way it navigates around the paradoxes of late modernity. In order to clarify how a constantly changing concept of solidarity may be institutionalized, the metaphor of networks once again becomes useful. Transnational solidarities can be envisaged as overlapping networks mediating between the abstract principles of justice and the empirical level of intersubjectivity, while being burdened with the task of translating the logic of the universal to the language of the particular (Gould, 2007).

All in all, solidarity is viewed by many as part of a broader set of moral principles. It complements the concept of justice by emphasizing non-universalistic social support; recognition; basic capabilities; and transnational inclusion. However, these supplementary principles also imply paradoxes for moral theory: transcending certain forms of exclusion (in a constitutional way) creates new distinctions; national and transnational solidarities mutually presuppose and oppose each other; the universal and particular or the rational and affective components constitute a dialectic relation. In sum, solidarity is needed for justice, and also transnational justice is needed for national solidarities to prevail – however, the synthesis of these components has its own challenges, which can be managed only by continuous reflective balancing between emancipatory and distortive potentials. Post-organic solidarity is inseparable from such balancing: its key moral tension concerns the contradiction between the efficiency of crisis management and the distortions of the applied technologies.

Accordingly, it is impossible to provide a substantive list of normative criteria for post-organic solidarity – the appropriate principles are rather dialectic. The normative basis of post-organic solidarity focuses on the transformative and self-correcting potentials. Networks of crisis management are in accordance with the moral principles, if the space of recognition is not suspended; the human capabilities are not blocked; if feedback mechanisms are enabled (providing two-way interaction between the supporters and the supported); if mutually approved constitutional securities are developed;

neither national nor global interests become exclusively dominant; dialectical network dynamics are not eliminated. Even though, these negative principles may not provide a secure horizon, yet they may be the only option to introduce morality in constellations lacking any basis for positive integration, while being held together by the logic of a global risk community. In order to evaluate the relevance of this model, some empirical results are overviewed, which analyze the transnational networks of crisis management.

The controversies of emergency – The empirical patterns of transnational crisis management networks

The rise of transnational solidarity initiatives in the post-colonial era is inseparable from the dynamics of globalization: in parallel with the intensifying economic relationship between the global south and north, the inequalities and the sufferance related to global capitalism also became more visible. As a consequence, nation states, economic and civic actors equally started various humanitarian projects targeting the most obvious, bodily forms of suffering, such as hunger or illnesses, while avoiding the sensitive questions related to the structural causes of their emergence (Agamben, 1998). As a consequence, most of these humanitarian interventions became the unreflective intermediators of biopolitics, either in a form of a 'politics of life' (Fassin, 2009) or 'necropolitics' (Mbembe, 2003).

One of the key aspects of international solidarity interventions is the lack of democratic communicative processes. Most initiatives have predefined goals and technologies based on expert knowledge, which not only predetermine their space of possibilities, but also do it in an unquestionable way. Due to the inherent unbridgeable material inequality characterising transnational interventions, the latent instrumental logic remains unchallenged, which *status quo* is further reinforced by the claim of 'anti-politics'. In order to maintain its expert legitimacy (based on scientific 'neutrality' and 'objectivity'), the interventions prevent the articulation of any explicitly political element for being inevitably biased. However, by trying to depoliticize a process involving social issues (irreducible to value-free scientific questions), the political dimension is never eliminated. Rather, the outcome of depoliticizing is the ignoring of the perspective of the subordinated local communities in the name of expertise (Ferguson, 1990). Beside natural scientific claims, discourses of rule of law and development may also be abused: by becoming hegemonic, those who talk in their name, take uncriticizable positions. Consequently, any alternative ideas phrased outside of their discursive frames is discredited, which may contribute to the silencing of local voices in the long-run (Mattei, 2010). Global solidarity interventions are burdened with a hidden power disproportion: the goals and instruments are not defined in mutual deliberation, but in a one-sided, latent fashion.

Of course, such bias is not universal: there are examples, where the local context is taken into consideration, even if not as a consequence of the benevolence of the actors, rather out of necessity. The example of the global handling of AIDS provides important conclusions in this sense.[7] The dynamics of the intervention can be divided into three phases: acute crisis management; the public declaration of the defeat of the threat; its transformation into a contained, marginal problem. In the first phase, until a biomedical solution was not available, the space for taking into consideration the social and political aspects of the risk was relatively wide. Without an effective cure, the sole direction of managing the crisis was the governance of behaviour, which was unfeasible without taking into consideration the perspective of the targeted population. Accordingly, in this phase civil actors were allowed to play a key role in the deliberation of crisis management; they were capable of influencing the policies themselves (Seckinelgin, 2017: 63). However, in the second phase, the discovering of a medical treatment reconfigured the whole power structure of intervention: triumphant biomedical authority started to dominate the AIDS discourse, which resulted in the decrease of global solidarity and the general exclusion of the civil society, now considered to be dispensable (Seckinelgin, 2017: 101). As a direct consequence, the issue of AIDS has been getting off the agenda: the less global attention meant that the countries lacking material resources were simply forgotten and left without proper medicine. As an indirect consequence, in the developing countries the overall efficiency of fighting AIDS has been weakened: the limitedness or unavailability of treatment combined with the general decrease of civil society influence in policy making (related to the declared biomedical triumph over the disease) left these countries fall between two stools. Accordingly, in the third phase, what used to be a global concern, now has become a dimension of global inequality: as the threat proved to be containable, it was not treated anymore on global level, only locally, inasmuch the material resources enabled it (Seckinelgin, 2017: 159).

The example of global solidarity emerging (and wearing away) around AIDS reveals that there is space for integrating the voice of the local communities, inasmuch the biopolitical logic of governance needs it: if there are no medical technologies of containment available, the social perspectives become relevant; however, if the landscape changes, they quickly become dispensable. In this sense, the instrumental, depoliticizing logic of humanitarian intervention is suspended only in the absence of better solutions; while it is enforced from the moment, effective technologies become available. Accordingly, the relation between the potential of democratization and the efficiency of the biomedical intervention is characterized by a latent conflict of interest: on the one hand, the local actors are forced to adapt to the biopolitical logic, inasmuch it proves to be efficient; on the other hand, their autonomy and voice increases in proportion to the inefficiency of the same technologies. These ambiguities reveal that global solidarity interventions always induce paradox dynamics, uncontrollable by both sides: the local actors are dependent on the efficiency of the intervention, at the cost of their autonomy; while the success of the intervention decreases the local actors' autonomy, which could undermine the whole project in the absence of resources.[8]

This paradox of efficiency versus autonomy is complemented by other mechanisms originating from the intertwining of latent global power structures and manifest local ones. Despite its declared neutrality, no intervention is unaffected by the inequalities, prejudices and conflicts of the local society. These local features also become part of the complex impact of the humanitarian actions: they influence not only the circle of the beneficiaries, but the mechanisms of support as well. A case study of the battle against AIDS in the Republic of South Africa reveals how the local historical background reconfigured a program seemingly serving an evident public interest (Fassin, 2007). The spreading of AIDS occurred at times, which were defined by the long-waited end of the apartheid era. However, the racial and economic tensions did not pass without a trace; they reappeared on a latent level, which affected the struggle against the virus in many ways. The mutual suspicions and prejudices fuelled by decades of repressed tensions resulted in distrust in the competence and truthfulness of the government (blamed for various forms of corruption and the faking of mortality statistics); criticism of unfair policies of the international pharmaceutical industries (originating from negative historical experiences with the exploitative West). As a consequence, the historically embedded local conflicts transformed the space of possibility: what was supposed to be a public health intervention became a highly sensitive political battle revolving around long-silenced, unresolved collective traumas (Fassin, 2007: xvii). Unsurprisingly, in this climate the biopolitical interventions failed, which not only lead to the sharpening of racial and economic tensions, but also to the increase of distrust concerning the technologies available. Overall, the crisis originating from the unlucky intertwining of unresolved local power struggles and the so called apolitical attempts of intervention lead to the normalization of death caused by AIDS, as most of the families have members affected by the disease (Fassin, 2007: xx).

The RSA story of AIDS-prevention complements the global one: it is not only the biopolitics, which could become an external, hegemonic, reifying element of the power structure (eliminating autonomy in the name of efficiency), but the opposite is also possible. Biopolitical efficiency could be ruined, if the implementing power is burdened with devastating tensions. These two idealtypical cases represent the cornerstones of the space of possibility of global solidarity interventions: not only autonomy may be eliminated by efficiency, but elementary instrumental rationality may also be undermined by the distortions of the local power structures. As it is exemplified by other case studies, there are several other varieties of similar abuses of local or global power structures, while the way out of these traps often depends on preventing the exclusive dominance of either of them. The unchecked exclusivity of any sources of dominance is against the basic principles of modern rule of law based on the logic of the division power. The only exception is the 'state of emergency', which is used as a claim for justifying the suspension of moral and legal principles. A worrisome possibility, if we take into consideration its overly frequent use in contemporary solidarity actions, especially in transnational context.

Despite its seeming evidence, emergency is a social construct having its own genealogy and implications. It refers to shocking, extraordinary situations requiring immediate intervention beyond the scope and frames of ordinary institutions. Emergency is part of the public discourses since the earthquake of Lisbon: the first religious, theodicy based explanations were gradually replaced by the development and progress based narratives of the Enlightenment. However, in the age of globalization, the horizon of emergency is reconfiguring: humanitarian intervention becomes the dominant framework of reacting to catastrophes, which events are constructed by the global press. As these constructions are born under the pressure of providing a constant flow of ephemeral, yet thrilling news, the catastrophes themselves are also reduced to such format. Indirectly they not only prevent deeper causal explanations, but also the establishing of institutions aiming at systematic solutions (Calhoun, 2010). In this sense, the framing of emergency (implying visible, but temporal solutions) is in a structural contradiction with the institutional logic of solidarity (based on less spectacular, long-term planning).

The importance of emergency lies in its expansive potential. Although it was born to describe extraordinary situations, gradually it has taken over the whole logic of solidarity, as 'humanitarian reason' – governing both national and transnational interventions – recently became the dominant framing of social challenges (Fassin, 2011). The paradigm of humanitarian governance reconfigures the morality of compassion by introducing a new language of problematization: 'inequality' gives its place to 'exclusion'; instead of 'injustice' 'suffering' is discussed; while the rawness of 'violence' is reintroduced in the language of 'trauma'. These semantic shifts of emphasis indicate the reconfiguration of solidarity as a tool of handling exceptional malfunctions, instead of a countermeasure aiming at the systematic social distortions. The translation of social hardships to the language of mental disorders; the implementation of the biological criteria of illness as a principle of inclusion; the over-used framing of trauma (in case of armed conflicts, oppressive regimes or natural disasters) veiling violence and (global) inequalities (Fassin, 2011: 15–16) – these are just a few unintended consequences of the humanitarian discourse, which overshadows the recurring, thus expectable general social dysfunctions, while focusing on individual tragedies framed as extraordinary emergency. In this sense, humanitarian reason transforms post-organic solidarity into 'emergency solidarity': those principles of deservingness and responsibility, which were related to organic solidarity (such as justice and equality) are reframed in the temporal schema of emergency. Extraordinary crises do not cease to motivate solidarity, but do it in a limited way: they imply immediate, but temporary solutions, and only to the most extreme or visible particular sufferings.

The notion of emergency is complemented by other concepts, such as 'catastrophization' or 'securitization' highlighting additional aspects. The classification of an event as catastrophe is not only an interpretation, but also a political act itself. Stronger political entities may use it as an instrument of reconfiguring their apparatus (intensifying security-related branches, while collaborating with humanitarian agents); NGOs may use it in order to strengthen their own position against weaker governmental institutions characterized by a collapsing apparatus. Even if differently, but in both cases the catastrophe is instrumentalized: it is either used as a terrifying possibility or as an actual crisis to be overcome (Ophir, 2010). Securitization refers to the discursive transformation of a particular issue into a security threat that is a reason for extraordinary measures. Securitization does not simply constitute a new normative order, but also does it in a way, which prevents any further debates: by transforming a question into a security issue, the democratic control mechanisms are automatically suspended and replaced by the authority of chains of command (Balzacq, 2005).

While the framework of emergency creates a horizon justifying extraordinary measures (beyond institutional and legal frames), the logics of catastrophization enables the prolonging of such constellation for an undetermined period. A 'temptation of emergency' is born, that is a motivation for transforming not only unexpected crises into emergency, but also those events, which are not unexpected but wanted to be handled within extra-legal framework. There are plenty of examples for situations, where either national (Lezama, 2010) or international (Makaremi, 2010) crises are managed this way, not only because of the extraordinary nature of the problem, but rather because of the possibility of abusing the emergency framing. In this sense, the temptation of emergency is a fundamental distortion of contemporary solidarity, which threatens not only with the suspension of institutional frames, but also with the rise of absolutist power structures (either local or global).

Post-organic solidarity and empty suffering

Based on these conclusions, a comprehensive theory of late modern solidarity may be outlined taking into consideration both the sociological, moral and political challenges related to empty suffering. As the structural constituents of organic solidarity weaken, a new constellation emerges, while adapting to the constraints of a global risk society. The idealtype of post-organic solidarity is constituted through networks of crisis management, which are characterized by the weakening of the integrative force of both 'collective consciousness' and the 'division of labour'; the logic of negative integration based on the pressure of a collective risk community, instead of the mutual benefits of functional differentiation; the dialectical handling of paradox tendencies; temporary solutions instead of institutional answers. Even if these networks hold the potential of the expansion of solidarity ties beyond the nation state, they also threaten with the neglecting of suffering, along with new inequalities and reification. Therefore, a normative basis needs to be highlighted indicating the dividing line between these possibilities. According to contemporary moral theories, only those networks of (global) crisis management should qualify as expressions of solidarity, which are in accordance with several, mostly negative principles: they do not prevent either the autonomous attempts of reducing suffering, or the channels of recognition, or human capabilities; also they include feedback mechanisms; do not disturb the spaces for democratization; prevent the hegemony of either global or local interests by securing their continuous dialectical dynamics.

These negative principles enable the acknowledgment (instead of the ignoring) of the inevitable moral paradoxes characterizing late modern solidarity: not every hybrid networks of crisis management are morally approved, only those, which counter the reifying consequences of the intervention itself. Although, these moral claims outline a minimalistic set of principles for a post-organic solidarity, still they help to clarify a social theoretically realistic and morally sustainable position. However, even these minimalistic claims have latent presuppositions: the possibility of a seemingly legitimate way of suspending any moral and legal principles remains in their blindspot. As the various empirical field studies of global solidarity reveal it, this possibility is not at all a marginal one: the temptation of emergency (complemented by catastrophization and securitization) seems to be a fundamental challenge for any forms of global solidarity.

When global solidarity is expressed through emergency interventions, not only the impossibility of institutions providing long-term solutions is implied, but more importantly, the warranties provided by morality and legality disappear. As the state of emergency is independent from the binding force of any sort of predefined regulations, its declaration – usually justified by the urgency of the crisis – implies the suspension of normative concerns. Therefore, in constellations framed as emergency, the very possibility of normativity is undermined: the moral criteria of solidarity networks become unaccountable and nothing stands in the way of transforming even the best-intentioned interventions into reifying, ignorant ones. Therefore, in order to elaborate the possibility of late modern solidarity, beside the moral principles, a clause of resisting the temptation of emergency also needs to be included. This step should not be understood as an additional normative claim, among the others, rather as a fundamental claim aiming at securing the very possibility of normativity: without the resisting of emergency, potential networks of solidarity are exposed to the distorting effect of unaccountability (a possibility abused by either local or global agents).

All in all, at this point the inherent paradox of late modern solidarity becomes tangible: on the one hand, it can be imagined as being constituted of temporary networks of crisis management constrained by negative moral principles; on the other hand, the framing of emergency threatens with the suspending of those moral principles, which are supposed to prevent the reifying tendencies of crisis managing networks. The possibility of late modern global solidarity depends on solving this paradox not only in theory, but also in practice. Only those networks of crisis management may become platforms of solidarity, which are functioning outside of the frames of emergency, securitization and catastrophization. This requires the re-normalization of crisis: by accepting the inevitable recurrence of phenomena representing global risks, the framing of emergency loses its potential of justifying the suspension of morality and legality. Crises should be treated as unexpected only in their concrete form, but expectable as a general possibility; also as not trivially avertable, but – with the development of appropriate technologies and networks of solidarity – presumably manageable.

This way, the totalizing potential of the semantics of emergency can be overcome: instead of being a claim for completely suspending normalcy, crises are transformed into a controlled condition of losing control. Late modern solidarity may emerge as a 'stoic' network of crisis management: it is not based on the shock caused by the unexpected, rather on the principles of accepting the inevitable and operating within the field of the transformable. Such stoic way of crisis management promises to resolve the paradoxes of late modern solidarity: instead of reacting to the unexpectedness by evoking the overwhelming atmosphere of emergency (overwriting the possibility of normalcy), it ensures the social basis of support within the frames of (a minimalistic) moral accountability.

The potential countermeasures of empty suffering are accessible from this complex perspective. The biomedical concepts of depression, anxiety and addiction imply the framing of emergency on an individual level: by treating expressions of empty suffering as unexpected individual 'crises', the horizon of treatment is also put on a limited track. The agency of the sufferer is suspended and subordinated to the biomedical complex. This implies that various forms of empty suffering are categorized according to expert (medical-legal) discourses, which define not only the form of treatment, but also the whole solidarity-network surrounding the sufferer. The quality and form of support depends on the logic of (global) collective risks: those forms of suffering, which threaten with expanding crises (either on individual or in collective level) are taken care of, while the isolable ones remain ignored. The form of intervention is also independent from the actual suffering: the countermeasures aim at averting wider risks not personal hardships. In this sense, various forms of empty suffering are burdened with a secondary distortion: the mechanisms, which supposed to treat them are also tainted by the same dysfunctions, as the ones being responsible for their emergence. Futile ownership, negative integration and self-objectifying power threatens not only with depression, anxiety and addictions, but also emptied solidarity ties.

However, this conclusion does not imply the impossibility of overcoming empty suffering. Rather it helps to identify the realistic points of intervention. The collective countermeasures and health policies targeting depression, anxiety and addiction have to be freed from the framework of emergency. Viewed from the perspective of their historical and social constituents, they do not appear anymore as individual crises, but as the existential consequences of late modern structural distortions. Based on such framing, potential countermeasures also appear in a new light: as no one is free from the dangers of empty suffering, the related threats constitute a global risk community, requiring global intervention. Any sort of solution, which ignores such global exposedness mistreats empty suffering, as it cannot be handled without addressing the interrelated questions of futile ownership, negative integration and self-objectifying technologies of pain. This global hazard could provide a minimalistic basis for post-organic solidarity. The space of effective collective strategies is rather slim – however, within the frames of the above defined negative moral principles and the (stoic) resistance of the overwhelming logic of emergency, countering empty suffering at least does not seem to be impossible. The final chapter explores therapeutic praxes, which could translate these conclusions to the individual level.

Notes

1 Of course, the Durkheimian concept of organic solidarity and the notion of welfare state cannot be equated, as the latter includes elements of mechanic solidarity as well (e.g. the 'invented traditions' of the nation state). However, according to Durkheim, even if a minimal level of mechanic solidarity is indispensable for the organic to prevail, in modernity collective consciousness plays a secondary role compared to the functional constraints. This applies to the welfare state as well, which is primarily organized as a system.

2 Of course, neither the division of labour, nor the collective risks are entirely new in modernity: the social history of both capitalist market economy and the technologies of handling the related risks goes back to the late medieval era. The two co-evolved: the challenges originating from the markets motivated the experimenting with new solidarity praxes, which stabilized the market economy (Castel, 2002).

3 Despite this parallelism, post-organic solidarity is not identical with the notion of 'transnational solidarity' (e.g. Gould, 2007; Nowicka et al., 2019): while the former concept is rooted in a social theoretical tradition (approaching solidarity from the perspective of the functional constraints of integration), the latter is embedded in moral and political philosophy (approaching solidarity from the perspective of moral obligations and legal regulations – Krunke et al., 2020). Accordingly, while transnational solidarity is an important reference for normatively grounding post-organic solidarity, it does not cover all of its essential aspects.

4 Despite its fundamentally negative character, the reconfiguration of mechanic solidarity by the emergence of post-organic solidarity also opens up new potentials for reflexive communities and identities. These are not based on similarities anymore, instead the acceptance of the inevitable plurality (Bauman, 2000: 176).

5 Such list includes living the full lifespan, sustaining bodily health, authority over one's body, the ability of using senses, imagination, thought, the freedom of experiencing emotions, the development of practical reason, the establishing of affiliations, the engagement with other species, the ability to play and the control over political and material environment (Nussbaum, 2006: 392).

6 While it may seem that the transnational expansion of solidarity is a value choice, there are several arguments emphasizing the moral necessity of the global expansion of solidarity. Even in case of those immigrants, who leave the economic hardships of their countries in a hope of a better future (not due to war or humanitarian

reason), a claim for the 'right to equal access to natural resources' applies (Steinvorth, 1999: 36). Furthermore, as every human being is entitled to have a chance of becoming a member of social units, in case of those subjects, who lost their social ties by becoming refugees, the granting of membership in our own society is a moral duty (Straehle, 2020).

7 An example, which is instructive, when it comes to reflecting on the trajectories of the long-term, global management of the COVID-19 pandemics.

8 Of course, it should also be emphasized that the actor networks of the global expert interventions and the locally embedded actors is never one-sided: in many cases the hard-won mutual ground is the key to establishing functional solidarity ties (Good et al., 2014).

References

Agamben, G. (1998) *Homo Sacer: Sovereign Power and Bare Life*. Stanford, CA: Stanford University Press.

Balzacq, T. (2005). The Three Faces of Securitization: Political Agency, Audience and Context. *European Journal of International Relations*, 11(2): 171–201.

Bauman, Z. (2000) *Liquid Modernity*. Cambridge: Polity.

Baurmann, M. (1999) Solidarity as a Social Norm and as a Constitutional Norm. In Bayertz K. (Ed.), *Solidarity. Philosophical Studies in Contemporary Culture* (Vol. 5). Dordrecht: Springer, 243–272.

Bayertz, K. (1999) Four Uses of "Solidarity". In Bayertz K. (Ed.), *Solidarity. Philosophical Studies in Contemporary Culture* (Vol. 5). Dordrecht: Springer, 3–28.

Beck, U. (1992) *Risk Society: Towards a New Modernity*. London: Sage.

Boltanski, L. (1999) *Distant Suffering: Morality, Media and Politics*. Cambridge, UK: Cambridge University Press.

Boltanski, L. and Chiapello, É (2005) *The New Spirit of Capitalism*. London and New York, NY: Verso.

Boltanski, L. and Thévenot, L. (2006) *On Justification. The Economies of Worth*. Princeton, NJ: Princeton University Press.

Brunkhorst, H. (2005) *Solidarity. From Civic Friendship to a Global Legal Community*. Cambridge: MIT Press.

Brunkhorst, H. (2008) Democratic Solidarity Under Pressure of Global Forces: Religion, Capitalism and Public Power. *Distinktion: Journal of Social Theory*, 9(2): 167–188.

Calhoun, C. (2010) The Idea of Emergency: Humanitarian Action and Global (Dis) order. In Fassin, D. and Pandolfi, M. (Eds.), *Contemporary States of Emergency: The Politics of Military and Humanitarian Interventions*. New York, NY: Zone Books, 20–53.

Castel, R. (2002) *From Manual Workers to Wage Laborers: Transformation of the Social Question*. New Brunswick, NJ: Transaction Publishers.

Castells, M. (1996). *The Rise of the Network Society, The Information Age: Economy, Society and Culture* (Vol. I). Cambridge, MA/Oxford, UK: Blackwell.

Castells, M. (2015) *Networks of Outrage and Hope: Social Movements in the Inter-Net Age*. Cambridge: Polity.

Chouliaraki, L. (2013) *The Ironic Spectator: Solidarity in the Age of Post-Humanitarianism*. London: Polity.

Crouch, C. (2004) *Post-Democracy*. London: Polity.

Dean, J. (1995). Reflective Solidarity. *Constellations*, 2(1): 114–140.

Durkheim, É (2013) *The Division of Labour in Society*. London: Palgrave Macmillan.

Durkheim, É (1995) *The Elementary Forms of Religious Life*. New York, NY: The Free Press.

Fassin, D. (2007) *When Bodies Remember. Experience and Politics of AIDS in South Africa.* Berkeley, CA: University of California Press.

Fassin, D. (2009) Another Politics of Life Is Possible. *Theory, Culture & Society*, 26(5): 44–60.

Fassin, D. (2011) *Humanitarian Reason. A Moral History of the Present.* Berkeley, CA: University of California Press.

Ferguson, J. (1990) *The Anti-Politics Machine: "Development," Depoliticization and Bureaucratic Power in Lesotho.* Cambridge: Cambridge University Press.

Forst, R. (2002) *Contexts of Justice.* Berkeley, CA and Los Angeles, CA: University of California Press.

Fraser, N. (1997) *Justice Interruptus.* London: Routledge.

Giddens, A. (1990) *The Consequences of Modernity.* Cambridge: Polity.

Giddens, A. (1994) Living in a Post-Traditional Society. In Beck, U., Giddens, A. and Lash, S. (Eds.), *Reflexive Modernization. Politics, Tradition and Aesthetics in the Modern Social Order.* Cambridge: Polity.

Good, B. J., Good, M. J., Abramowitz, S., Kleinman, A. and Panter-Brick, C. (2014) Medical Humanitarianism: Research Insights in a Changing Field of Practice. *Social Science and Medicine*, 120: 311–316.

Gould, C. C. (2007) Transnational Solidarities. *Journal of Social Philosophy*, 38(1): 148–164.

Habermas, J. (1996) *Between Facts and Norms: Contributions to a Discourse Theory of Law and Democracy.* Cambridge: MIT Press.

Harlow, E., Berg, E., Barry, J. and Chandler, J. (2013) Neoliberalism, Managerialism and the Reconfiguring of Social Work in Sweden and the United Kingdom. *Organization*, 20(4): 534–550.

Häusermann, S. (2012) The Politics of Old and New Social Policies. In Bonoli, G. and Natali, D. (Eds.), *The Politics of the New Welfare State.* Oxford: Oxford University Press, 111–132.

Hobbs, J. and Souter, J. (2019) Asylum, Affinity, and Cosmopolitan Solidarity With Refugees. *Journal of Social Philosophy*, 51(4): 543–563.

Honneth, A. (1996) *The Struggle for Recognition: The Moral Grammar of Social Conflicts.* Cambridge: Polity.

Juul, S. (2010) Solidarity and Social Cohesion in Late Modernity: A Question of Recognition, Justice and Judgement in Situation. *European Journal of Social Theory*, 13(2): 253–269.

Koch, I. (2018) Towards an Anthropology of Global Inequalities and Their Local Manifestations: Social Anthropology. *Social Anthropology*, 26(2): 253–268.

Krunke, H., Petersen, H. and Manners, I. (Eds.) (2020) *Transnational Solidarity: Concept, Challenges and Opportunities.* Cambridge: Cambridge University Press.

Lash, S. and Urry, J. (1987) *The End of Organized Capitalism.* Cambridge: Polity.

Latour, B. (2005) *Reassembling the Social: An Introduction to Actor-Network-Theory.* Oxford: Oxford University Press.

Lezama, P. V. (2010) Compassionate Militarization: The Management of a Natural Disaster in Venezuela. In Fassin, D. and Pandolfi, M. (Eds.), *Contemporary States of Emergency: The Politics of Military and Humanitarian Interventions.* New York, NY: Zone Books, 197–216.

Luhmann, N. (1995) *Social Systems.* Stanford, CA: Stanford University Press.

Lynch, K. and Kalaitzake, M. (2020) Affective and Calculative Solidarity: The Impact of Individualism and Neoliberal Capitalism. *European Journal of Social Theory*, 23(2): 238–257.

Makaremi, C. (2010) Utopias of Power: From Human Security to the Responsibility to Protect. In Fassin, D. and Pandolfi, M. (Eds.), *Contemporary States of Emergency: The Politics of Military and Humanitarian Interventions*. New York, NY: Zone Books, 107–128.

Mattei, U. (2010) Emergency-Based Predatory Capitalism: The Rule of Law, Alternative Dispute Resolution, and Development. In Fassin, D. and Pandolfi, M. (Eds.), *Contemporary States of Emergency: The Politics of Military and Humanitarian Interventions*. New York, NY: Zone Books, 89–105.

Mbembe, A. (2003). Necropolitics. *Public Culture*, 15(1): 11–40.

Muis, J. and Immerzeel, T. (2017). Causes and Consequences of the Rise of Populist Radical Right Parties and Movements in Europe. *Current Sociology*, 65(6): 909–930.

Nowicka, M., Krzyżowski, Ł and Ohm, D. (2019) Transnational Solidarity, the Refugees and Open Societies in Europe. *Current Sociology*. 67(3): 383–400.

Nussbaum, M. (2006) *Frontiers of Justice: Disability, Nationality, Species Membership*. Cambridge, MA: The Belknap Press of Harvard University Press.

Olesen, T. (2004) The Struggle Inside Democracy: Modernity, Social Movements and Global Solidarity. *Distinktion: Journal of Social Theory*, 5(1): 19–35.

Ophir, A. (2010) The Politics of Catastrophization: Emergency and Exception. In Fassin, D. and Pandolfi, M. (Eds.), *Contemporary states of Emergency: the Politics of Military and Humanitarian Interventions*. New York, NY: Zone Books, 59–89.

Ottmann, J. (2010) Social Exclusion in the Welfare State: The Implications of Welfare Reforms for Social Solidarity and Social Citizenship. *Distinktion: Journal of Social Theory*, 11(1): 23–37.

Pedersen, F. T. (2006) Global Solidarity as Global Constitutionalism. *Distinktion: Journal of Social Theory*, 7(1): 117–126.

Putnam, R. D. (2000) *Bowling Alone: The Collapse and Revival of American Community*. New York, NY: Simon & Schuster.

Rawls, J. (1971) *A Theory of Justice*. Cambridge, MA: Belknap Press of Harvard University Press.

Rorty, R. (1989) *Contingency, Irony, and Solidarity*. Cambridge: Cambridge University Press.

Sandel, M. (1998) *Liberalism and the Limits of Justice*. Cambridge: Cambridge University Press.

Schwartz, J. M. (2007). From Domestic to Global Solidarity: The Dialectic of the Particular and Universal in the Building of Social Solidarity. *Journal of Social Philosophy*, 38(1): 131–147.

Seckinelgin, H. (2017) *The Politics of Global AIDS: Institutionalization of Solidarity, Exclusion of Context. Social Aspects of HIV.* Dordrecht: Springer International Publishing.

Sen, A. (1999) *Development as Freedom*. Oxford: Oxford University Press.

Standing, G. (2011) *The Precariat*. London: Bloomsbury Academic.

Steinvorth, U. (1999) The Concept and Possibilities of Solidarity. In Bayertz K. (Eds.), *Solidarity. Philosophical Studies in Contemporary Culture* (Vol. 5). Dordrecht: Springer, 29–37.

Stjerno, S. (2005) *Solidarity in Europe: The History of an Idea*. Cambridge, NY: Cambridge University Press.

Straehle, C. (2020) Associative Solidarity, Relational Goods, and Autonomy for Refugees: What Does It Mean to Stand in Solidarity With Refugees? *Journal of Social Philosophy*, 51(1): 526–542.

Talani, L. S. and Roccu, R. (2019) *The Dark Side of Globalisation*. London: Palgrave Macmillan.

Thijssen, P. (2012) From Mechanical to Organic Solidarity, and Back. *European Journal of Social Theory*, 15(4): 454–470.

Walby, S. (2009) *Globalization and Inequalities: Complexity and Contested Modernities*. Los Angeles, CA: Sage.

Wilde, L. (2013) *Global Solidarity*. Edinburgh: Edinburgh University Press.

Woods, K. (2012) Whither Sentiment? Compassion, Solidarity, and Disgust in Cosmopolitan Thought. *Journal of Social Philosophy*, 43(1): 33–49.

9 Ways out from suffering

On quasi-therapeutic networks

Suffering is an ambiguous experience: due to the difficulties of expression, it implies solitude; due to the related compassion, it constitutes intersubjectivity. Furthermore, it is a self-explanatory 'datum'; also an 'unassumable' experience demanding interpretation (Levinas, 1998). Despite its phenomenological complexity, most expert praxes dealing with suffering rely on over-simplifying approaches: either reduce it to physical pain, or frame it as a mental distress (or mix the two approaches). The paradigmatic positivist model of suffering refers to a 'subject' enduring 'objective' hardships (of physical, mental or social origin). Throughout the previous chapters, this model has been challenged based on various social phenomenological models. Now these attempts are concluded: those specific interventions are outlined, which could address the historical and social complexity of empty suffering.

In the last chapter, the shortcomings of a positivist account are contested on two levels: both the objectivity of the causes and the subjectivity of the experiences are reconsidered. It is argued that the interpretation of pain or distress plays a fundamental role: narratives may equally increase or decrease their severity. This premise highlights the existential aspect of suffering: in order to handle its various forms (related to physical, mental or social causes), narratives are required, which are capable of replacing meaninglessness and helplessness with a new horizon. For this purpose, the overly individualistic account of suffering is also contested: in order to highlight ways out from meaninglessness, the concept of a solitary lifeworld is replaced by a fundamentally intersubjective one. By relating to the suffering of the other, ethical meanings of responsibility and care may be born – these forms of intersubjectivity hold the potential of overcoming meaninglessness.

In the first section various phenomenological conceptualizations of suffering are overviewed. It is argued that the collapse of the sufferer's lifeworld can be overcome if the solitary experiences are shared. In the second section, the socio-historical forms of empty suffering elaborated in the previous chapters are revisited from this perspective. It is argued that empty suffering is *per se* an intersubjective experience: depression, anxiety or addiction is inseparable from the distortions of intersubjectivity. They do not exist as distinct,

DOI: 10.4324/9781003197355-13

individual phenomenological patterns, rather as extensions of dysfunctional networks preventing the sharing of suffering. Consequently, treating them requires intervention on the level of those social constraints, which prevent the emergence of meaningful interactions, providing reassuring narratives. In the third section, several widely used interventions are overviewed from the perspective of their potential of treating the emptiness of suffering. It is argued that the most common psychotherapeutic technologies (dealing with traumatic forms of damaged intersubjectivity) and interventions of social work (dealing with social dysfunctions) need to be complemented: as they cannot target those historically shaped, yet naturalized distortive networks and structures, which are responsible for the emptiness of suffering, new therapeutic praxes are also needed. Without such complementary praxes, even the best intended psychotherapies and social work interventions may fail, as the danger of transforming hardships into existential suffering – due to the persisting patterns of futile ownership, negative integration and power from indirect pain – remains significant. In the final section, the basis of such complementary praxis is outlined.

Beyond pain and distress – An intersubjective phenomenology of suffering

In the long conceptual history of suffering phenomenology opened a new chapter. Instead of focusing solely on its natural or transcendental causes and the moral or political consequences, phenomenology approaches suffering as an 'existential experience'.[1] Such analysis is made uneasy due to several contradictions: on the one hand, suffering emerges as a meaningful experience; on the other hand, it is revolving around negativity, as it expresses a world deprived from meaningfulness. Accordingly, while suffering seems to emerge as any other phenomena, actually it refers to a 'backward consciousness' struggling with the impossibility of any reassuring meanings. Suffering is characterized by fundamental uncertainty and perplexity: it is not a substantive experience, instead bears the traces of the denial of meaning (Levinas, 1998: 91). The experience of suffering is inherently burdened with a paradox – although not an intellectual, but a phenomenological one, originating from the failure of constituting meanings. The impressions related to suffering express the dissolving of the world as an inhabitable horizon. Therefore, they turn the subjects into passive observers of their own life instead of active contributors. The sufferers lack an explanation to the hardships lived through, which disorientation is added to the initial physical pain or mental torment. It leads to the experience of being deprived from agency and those capacities, which would normally give sense to the world: if one is stuck in passivity, the openness to the world is transformed into vulnerability (Levinas, 1998: 92). These elementary sensations contribute to the experience of an evil inseparable from the negative experience of the useless and purposeless suffering. Such evil presence is not necessarily personified.

Instead, it appears as an undefined and uncontrollable source of uncomfortable sensations – a lingering shadow haunting the subject (Levinas, 1998: 93).

This existential description of suffering can be refined according to those specific analyses, which focus on its more specific aspects, such as pain (Kleinman, 1973) or mental distress (Aho, 2019). According to medical phenomenological approaches, suffering emerges in case of those bodily illnesses and mental disorders, wherein the existence as a whole is affected by the hardships. It is never simply the physical pain, which induces suffering: even the most severe ones (such as the agony caused by chemo-therapy) can be endured, if meaningful narratives secure the sense of control (Cassell, 2004: 32). The interpretative context plays a central role: if the source and the length of pain are undefined, then the subject becomes helpless, thus pain starts to colonize the totality of lifeworld. In this sense, the transformation of pain into suffering depends on a phenomenological momentum: it occurs only if no such interpretative frameworks – in other words, no such intersubjectivities – are available, which could provide a reassuring narrative of pain by highlighting its causes and explaining its outcomes (Cassell, 2004: 35). Accordingly, healing praxes depend not only on the treatment of the physical causes of the illness, but also on the construction of meaningful narratives of the agony. Only the appropriate interpretative frameworks and interactions can re-establish the lost sense of control: with their help, the painful sensation may be prevented from taking over the totality of lifeworld, so the transformation of pain into suffering could be stopped (Cassell, 2004: 287).

Suffering not only causes a rupture in the life narrative, but it also disrupts agency. Of course, not any minor hindrances imply suffering, only those, which concern the core values of the subject. If those activities are blocked, which ground one's identity, then suffering may emerge independently from any medical conditions (Svenaeus, 2014). The blocking of identity-defining activities is similar to the experience of illness: instead of being betrayed by a living-body (*Leib*) turning into an obstacle (*Körper*), in this case the subjects are alienated from their own foundations as a consequence of external constraints (Svenaeus, 2014: 413). The possibility of disembodiment and self-alienation expresses two different sources of suffering: these examples highlight how the world may lose its meaningful foundations and turn into an inexplicable, hostile horizon.[2]

Being an alienating experience, suffering creates a distance, not only from the self, but also from the others: what is inexplicable for the self is also uncommunicable to the others. Yet, that does not mean the suffering of the other necessarily remains unnoticed. Unlike the suffering of the self, which is characterized by the impossibility of meaning, the suffering of the other has a substantive meaning. The signs of the other's agony induce an ethical imperative: an urge to support emerges. The perceived suffering creates an intersubjective unity: the hardships of the other are lived through, without the paralysing consequences. In this shared experience the sufferer and the observer mutually open their lifeworld. An intersubjective space is emerging, where suffering is transformed into an ethical call. As it is in the power of the other to ease one's suffering (at least by providing an emphatic, comforting presence), an elementary bound is born: the suffering is transformed into moral responsibility for the observer, while the care represents a glimpse of hope for the sufferer (Levinas, 1998: 94). Therefore, in the context of intersubjectivity, the helplessness and denial of meaning, which dominates the solitary sufferer's lifeworld is replaced by newly found meanings being born in the interaction. These meanings are not about a subject exposed to hardships or a constraining world, but fundamentally moral ones originating from the sharing of suffering.

Accordingly, intersubjectivity fundamentally reframes the phenomenology of suffering: while subjects on their own are trapped by the perplexity of useless suffering; in intersubjective relations, the horizon of responsibility and care emerge. This feature highlights the stakes of the social in the phenomenology of suffering: the others represent a possibility of redeeming those meanings, which seem to be ultimately lost in sufferance. From a phenomenological perspective, suffering is characterized by the collapse of lifeworld, which can be overcome only through the other, who could choose to open up, thus provide an elementary sense of belonging and meaningfulness. Suffering is socially contextualized *per se*; it does not simply emerge due to a medical condition, mental distress or blocking of activities related to core values (which are all events threatening with self-alienation). The lifeworld collapses only if intersubjectivity is distorted in a way that no one else is there to take up the responsibility for the self in agony. In this sense, the phenomenological question of suffering is inseparable from the way social relations are organized: independently from the facticity of hardships, the experience of a burdensome existence is transformed into suffering if the others who could provide comfort are missing. It needs to be emphasized that the others' responsibility is not simply the treatment of the objective causes of the hardships (as most medical or psychotherapies and social interventions view it), but also the turning to the others: the meaninglessness characterizing suffering may only be overcome, if the lifeworld is shared.

Social theories outline various processes of sharing the lifeworld in actual interactions, latent structural or system mechanisms. Among these theories, those play a distinguished role, which are capable of grasping the various forms of sociability in a unified manner. Similarly to Chapters 5 and 6, once again network theories are called upon. While relying on minimalistic conceptual tools, they view the subject as being embedded in the constantly changing flux of connecting and disconnecting ties (White, 2008). From this perspective, suffering ceases to be a discrete, individual experience: it is viewed as a specific network constellation, where the intersubjective sharing of the lifeworld is made impossible by reifying or atomizing dynamics. In these constellations the other may not appear as a 'face' implying responsibility (Levinas, 1969) – the horizon of care is lost, thus suffering emerges.

While suffering as an existential experience originates from various distortions of intersubjectivity, it does not mean it is shaped solely by the present network constellation. Besides their temporary effect, social networks also have a socializing function, which is based on the incorporation of the socially provided interpretations by participating in the communicative reconstruction of lifeworld (Habermas, 1987). Accordingly, ignorant networks from the past might imply suffering in the future as well. They socialize the subjects in a distorted way by incorporating an unhandled, solitary suffering. These experiences are 'traumatic' in a sense that they may resurge uncontrollably at any given time.[3] Traumas do not operate as distinct phenomenological patterns, rather they reconfigure the perception of otherwise banal network distortions, thus amplifying a negative impact (McDonald, 2019). Due to their latency, they become intertwined with present social distortions, which leads to a special challenge for praxes attempting to deal with existential suffering.[4] It is not enough to simply transform the network constellation in a way that intersubjectivities of care may emerge; dealing with the traces of past distortions is also indispensable.

These tasks outline the space of possibility of quasi-therapeutic praxes, which aim at dealing with the intersubjective phenomenological complex of suffering. In order to succeed, they should constitute a social environment, where not only attempts are made to eliminate the objective elements of the hardships, but also networks of intersubjective care may emerge. Such networks hold the potential of overcoming the collapse of the sufferer's lifeworld by embedding the subject in a web of relations promising to replace the meaninglessness with a new horizon. Besides treating the suffering of the present, these networks also need to address the traces of past social distortions incorporated by the subject in the form of a trauma.

Emptied sociability – The social phenomenology of late modern existence

In order to elaborate the details of emancipatory networks, those specific forms of hardship need to be identified, which undermine the construction of meaningful narratives and identities: quasi-therapeutic praxes may become effective only by targeting these constellations. In late modernity several factors contribute to the elimination of social relationships, where reassuring narratives could be born – in other words, where the unresolved hardships are transformed into existential suffering. The lack of reliable intersubjectivities not only puts an enormous pressure on the institutions responsible for eliminating the causes of hardships, but also renders the subjects particularly vulnerable. In this section, the three previously elaborated idealtypical patterns of empty suffering are overviewed: the depressive pattern of communication and redistribution originating from the emergence of an exclusive concept of ownership; the anxious distortion of tradition and recognition related to negative integration; and the addictive distortion of hybrid actor-networks responsible for managing pain and desire in a reifying biopolitical setting. The aim is to synthesize these various distortions of modernization into a coherent diagnosis of times.

The pre-modern history of suffering reveals a religious naturalization and even the praise of suffering; the lacking instrumental worldly time (complemented by the horizon of unworldly redemption); also an oppressive but omnipresent intersubjectivity. In contrast, early modernity was characterized by the significant transformation of these parameters: suffering ceased to be religiously justified; instrumental horizon of time emerged (beside the eschatological); intersubjectivity remained dense, while becoming competitive. This ambiguous pattern prevailed until the paradoxes were resolved by the birth of ownership as absolute dominion. Since then, the social framing of hardships became inseparable from property: the religious framing of suffering was replaced by an exclusively instrumental one (implying that hardships are meaningless, thus eliminable, as much as one's resources allow it); time consciousness was completely secularized (eschatological time is eliminated, while instrumental goals of accumulation is dominant); intersubjectivity was reduced to social competition for the resources (implying alienation from the other). Consequently, hardships were framed in a completely new fashion: while pre-modernity reinterpreted them according to religious meanings, thus treated suffering narratively; in modernity technological solutions were sought, while the meaningfulness of hardships (besides the ones contributing to accumulation) were neglected. This is the first dimension of emptying: in the name of finding technological solutions to suffering, modernity gave up on comforting narratives, while labelling them as mythological or metaphysical non-sense.

The most important dimensions of social integration adapted to these constraints: fields of competition emerged along material and symbolic goods; systems of mediatized communication expanded perfecting the exclusive logic of efficiency, profitability and functionality. Even if these social structures do not necessarily result in suffering (they provide more and more efficient ways of detecting and eliminating its objective causes), as they neglect the narrative aspect of hardships, the failure of their technological solutions threatens with a new, overwhelming form of hopelessness. This possibility is exemplified by the birth and generalization of depression. In those fields, which are characterized by unconvertable capitals, biased challenges, arrogant illusions, segregation and terror (in sum, by the exclusive logic of market competition), the chance of experiencing insecurity, deprivation from recognition, negativistic collective identities and helplessness grows high. Also, in those forms of cooperation, which rely on either overly complex, discredited mediums, or incompetent, fragmented, exclusive speech acts (driven by the logic of functional efficiency), depressive mood also have a higher chance to emerge. In these social networks existence is deprived of meaningful narratives, therefore hardships are more likely to be transformed into sufferance.

Among late modern tendencies, the most important ones concern the gradual dissolving of positive motivations for cooperation. The integration mechanisms of classic modernity, such as the functionally differentiated division of labour, legal-bureaucratic legitimacy, rationalized lifeworld or systems outlined a promising horizon of expectation: they justified the giving up of pre-modern worldviews and structures by referring to more effective, fair and overall advantageous forms of sociability. However, the same cannot be said about those integration mechanisms, which emerged in late modernity, while gradually overshadowing the classic ones. Even though global networks based on information processing and reflective forms of risk management provide technics supporting adaptation to the extremely unpredictable and contingent globalized world, they are not promising stable solutions or a predictable horizon of expectations. Without such hopes, the sole source of motivation for cooperation remains fear, which expresses the second dimension of the emptying of sociability: in late modernity not only the transcendental narratives of comfort are missing, but also the belief in those expert discourses, which could replace them by promising solutions to suffering.

From this perspective, instead of fields or systems (based on the integration logics of redistribution and communication), networks of routines and reflectivity, love, solidarity and legal recognition become the central platforms of narratively framing hardships. In those cases, where such networks are organized in a tabooing, unpredictable, unsupportive way, while relying on a hedonist, nihilist, moralizing or stigmatizing culture, the fear originating from negative integration becomes a general experience: routines based on dogmas, reflections lost in relativism, uncertain love, unsupportive communities, unpredictable legal institutions are just a few examples of a social environment characterized by a crisis of trust. In these settings, the others do not appear anymore as a reliable support: they either appear as risks themselves or ignorant observers at best. Accordingly, in these constellations fear is detached from particular events and reframes the whole world in an anxious manner. While the structures and interactive patterns emerging from the idea of absolute property emptied the supply of reassuring narratives by denying everything outside of meanings being born in social competition (expressing the 'final truth' of the social world) and scientific discourses (expressing the 'final truth' of nature), the networks of negative integration erase the possibility of believing in a sociability providing security. The horizon of expectation is emptied of trustworthy intersubjectivities and certainty originating from the other.

The third dimension of emptying sociability is related to the transformation of pain management and the grounding of power. Pre-modern authority is based on the act of causing pain to the other, while pain from illnesses is considered to be untreatable, thus irrelevant experience. The process of civilization gradually reshaped both of these dimensions: direct violence has been expelled from both the public and the private life, while pain became a manageable hardship. However, these transformations resulted in an ambiguous constellation: authority still relies on the potential of causing pain, while biomedical technologies are far from completely controlling pain. Therefore, a constellation emerged, which is shadowed by the threat of persisting, untreatable pain (not caused by any authorities, but existing despite the biomedical promise of its elimination). Such pain grounds power in an indirect way: a formal authority emerges, lacking any concrete representatives. It does not hurt the subjects willingly, instead leaves them to suffer indirectly. As a consequence, a paradox experience of subordination is born expressing the third dimension of the emptying the narrative universe of suffering. The wielders of power position themselves as neutral experts making decisions solely on the basis of objective, rational reasons. Their authority is incontestable, as it is based on the hegemony of scientific discourses grounding the biomedical paradigm. Consequently, those who are enduring pain in this constellation find themselves in a perplexing situation: the experts claiming to control pain leave them on their own (if biomedical technologies fail, there is no alternative forms of care within the positivist framework), while eliminating any other discourses (which are considered to threaten the biomedical paradigm). Due to the emptied narrative space of caring, pain management implies a self-objectifying horizon: the subject has no choice but to experiment with the optimal combination of sedatives and mood enhancers.

In this constellation, actor-networks of reification, information and acceleration play a decisive role. The biomedical paradigm approves solely technological ways of managing pain; also as it becomes a hegemonic discursive authority, any forms of suffering are reinterpreted according to its frames. Consequently, technological answers of pain management become the general model of treating suffering – a paradigm becoming paradoxical in case of hardships, which are unmanageable in a technical way. When existentialist dilemmas or the difficulties of identity construction are addressed in an objectifying way, their complexity is reduced to the binary semantics of joy and pain. As such reifying networks become a dominant factor of one's social environment, the actors have no choice, but to adapt to their logic by developing an instrumental relation to the self, based on the technological stimulus of moods. Consequently, an addictive behaviour pattern is born, which is based on the illusion of controlling joy and pain by the subjects themselves. The goal of gaining control in a reifying environment results in self-objectifying hybrid subjectivities constituted of human and non-human components of technologically mediated actor-networks. In these constellations, the subjects partially interiorize the role of an automaton, while trying to expand their agency within the given framework. Various impacts, such as the nivellating logic of information, or the continuous pressure of acceleration also contribute to these constellations, as they eliminate the space required for narrative meaning construction. As a consequence of these effects, the very possibility of a self, which is grounded in narratives is lost: what is left is the optimizing of the technologies of joy and pain, with the available technological tools.

In case of this third dimension, the emptying of late modern existence occurs on the level of the subject. As the culturally shaped narrative tools of giving sense to hardships and the reliable others as partners of narration are missing, the individuals incorporate these constraints and compromise: they seek solutions by relying on the available technological tools. These three dimensions express the various structural constraints contributing to the increasing probability of suffering as an existential crisis in late modernity. In sum, late modernity is burdened with a special source of hardship, which is related to the dissolving of those intersubjectivities, where comforting narratives may be born and – more importantly – applied for grounding relations of care. Accordingly, those praxes, which aim at treating suffering in late modernity need to address these structural constraints: without this step, the efforts of constructing networks treating the objective hardships remain futile due to those impacts, which empty the cultural, social and subjective levels of establishing reassuring intersubjectivity. In the next section, the possibilities and limitations of existing therapeutic praxes are overviewed from this perspective.

From individual traumas to social dysfunctions – Making sense of psycho- and social therapies

The technologies handling various forms of suffering have a long history. Premodern communities relied mainly on religious or mystical collective rites, which were responsible of grounding a meaningful universe (Durkheim, 1995). In modernity, functionally differentiated institutions take on the task of re-establishing a lifeworld, which collapses due to various hardships. These therapeutic praxes vary according to their target, which could be solely the subject (psychotherapy) or their social environment as well (social work). In this section, some of the most influential psychotherapeutic schools are overviewed from the perspective of their potential contribution to treat empty suffering.

Probably the most influential form of psychotherapy is Freud's psychoanalysis. According to its principles, the subject is shaped by processes of development affected by both biological drives, normative regulations and most importantly the tension between these two sources. The structures of personality are formed within these frames: the id (subconscious self), the ego (conscious self) and the superego (internalized social self) are differentiated, while the stage is set for their potential conflicts. If the intentions and motivations originating from these different sources prove to be incompatible, anxiety or 'neurosis' may develop, along with the emerging self-defensive mechanisms such as repression, denial, projection, sublimation or rationalization (Freud, 1952). Within this framework, the experience of suffering is the result of unresolved inner tensions between the id, the ego and the superego. Therefore, the treatment requires the mapping of their roots in the biographical complex and the correction of distorted paths of ego-development.

In this process the therapist relies on interpersonal communication: linguistic mistakes, discrepancies of acting and speaking and the intersubjective dynamics of transference and countertransference reveal the conscious and subconscious dimensions of the self, thus enable intervention on these levels (Corsini and Wedding, 2008: 15–59; Sharf, 2012: 28–82).

Most traditions of psychotherapy developed in the 20th century complemented these basic ideas. Probably the two most influential contemporary schools, cognitive and person-centred therapies can be understood according to their alternative conceptualizations of key inner conflicts. Cognitive therapy argues that the perception of the world is shaped by a learning process based on continuous interaction with the things and the others. As a result, patterns of 'automatic thoughts' emerge, while providing unreflected schemas for relating to the world and the self as well. Within this framework, the experience of suffering is born as a consequence of a maladaptive learning process: over-dramatizing negative events, over-generalizing their probability or over-emphasizing negative feedback are just a few examples of how an overall pessimistic interpretative framework may emerge, which is unnoticed by the subjects (Beck, 1967). The related treatment aims at identifying and reflectively reworking the automatic thoughts. The therapist teaches strategies of noticing their functioning and technics of neutralizing their effect, so a corrected cognitive relearning of the world may occur (Corsini and Wedding, 2008: 263–291; Sharf, 2012: 373–389).

According to the approach of person centred therapies, personality and mental disorders are rooted in hidden conflicts between self-perception and social evaluations. While a well-functioning self is capable of handling critical opinions by accepting or refusing them (based on a judgment call), insecure subjects perceive them as an absolute danger threatening the totality of the self. Consequently, these subjects lose the ability of maintaining a dynamic relation with their environment: they either lock themselves up in an isolated world, or completely subordinate themselves to the others. Suffering in this context originates from a developmental process resulting in emotional insecurity due to the lack of trusting relationships providing supportive understanding in the past and the present. The related treatment focuses on supplementing these missing relations, thus enabling the emotional growing up of the subject. The key elements of the intervention include the unconditional recognition and the supportive understanding of the subject (Rogers, 1959). If such an accepting and trustworthy intersubjectivity is established, an opportunity for personality development arises. The previous overly-defensive or overly-submissive relation to the world may be replaced by an autonomous being in the world (Corsini and Wedding, 2008: 141–181; Sharf, 2012: 211–221).

Beside the psychoanalytic, cognitive and person-centred therapies, alternative approaches could also be mentioned. However, as the overviewed basic ideas cover some of the most widely used elements of contemporary therapeutic praxes, the idealtypical limitations and possibilities of psychotherapy may be outlined with their help. The basic intention of these interventions is to correct those phenomenological distortions, which originate from earlier developmental, learning or socializing processes. It is presumed that the various forms of suffering in the present are rooted in unresolved inner difficulties or distortions from past: in case of psychoanalysis, the tension between the id and superego; in case of cognitive therapy, the exclusive focus on negative aspects; in case of client centred therapy, the insecurity of the self is considered to be responsible for suffering. While it is not completely neglected, the intersubjective component remains latent: despite the superego is the expression of norms; despite the worries are inseparable from social interpretations; and despite insecurity of the self depends on the lack of recognition and understanding, the structure of intersubjectivity and the broader social environment remains in the blindspot for psychotherapies. Consequently, an essentialist model prevails: psychotherapeutic interventions aim at correcting the incorporated social distortions within the subject, while leaving the formative social environment unchanged. It is presumed that not only technics of self-reflectivity may be taught and subconscious conflicts may be resolved, but also the missing experiences of emotional support may be supplemented in the therapeutic interactions. Also, it is presumed that the reconfiguration of the self in the particular therapeutic interactions has an impact, which lasts outside of the therapeutic relation as well.

In order to overcome these limitations and paradoxes underlying psychotherapy, the essentialist concept of subject needs to be replaced with a socially contextualized one: what seems to be an inner conflict for psychotherapy may be reformulated as an incorporated distortion of intersubjectivity. From this perspective, the structure of the formative social relationships ceases to be of secondary importance, instead it becomes a key constituent of personality and mental disorders. The norms expressed in the superego, the collective patterns of automatic thoughts and the patterns of interaffectivity and recognition are not unchangeable quasi-natural conditions; instead, they are related to particular social settings, which need to be addressed in the therapeutic process. This means first of all, that not only the early nurturing relationships, intimacy or childhood experiences matter, but the totality of the social world including various fields of redistribution, mediatized systems, traditional and expert institutions, solidarity and legal frames and technological context. As the distortions, which are internalized originally appear simultaneously on all of these levels, so should the corrective mechanisms operate on them as well.

Obviously, this claim is incompatible with the very idea of a face to face therapeutic interaction, which strictly operates on the level of the individual. If the essentialist model of the subject is replaced by a socially contextualized one, the possibility of correcting distortions originating from – and maintained by – the totality of the social world, a singular relationship seems to be inadequate. Instead, the need for a praxis arises, which targets the totality of the social environment. Such praxis aims at reconfiguring the subject not by transforming them on their own, but by transforming their surrounding networks: if the repressive, fearful or untrustworthy ties of the past and the present are replaced with open, secure and trustworthy ones, the new environment may reshape the subject in a less- or undistorted manner.

However, besides their limitations, therapeutic praxes provide many insight, which could orient emancipatory network interventions. Based on psychoanalysis, the importance of subconscious intersubjective tensions may be emphasized. Psychoanalysis invites the subject to a quest of discovering hidden conflicts within themselves – similarly, a social mechanism may be developed to monitor and discuss past and present intersubjective conflicts. Such reflections provide opportunity for immersing in the past of ourselves and our social relationships, in order to reveal those repressed structural tensions, which distort the interactions. Related reflective networks should provide opportunity for mutual and collective self-criticism aiming at identifying the contradictions and paradoxes of the personal and social identity rooted in the past. Based on cognitive therapy, the limitations of the collective interpretative schemas may be emphasized. This therapy detects the maladaptive elements in our thought patterns – similarly, a social network may be developed to monitor the social process of adapting to a particular setting. These functionalist self-reflections reveal not only how the external challenges are constructed, but also the cost and consequences of the applied countermeasures. Accordingly, they provide opportunity for detecting the blindspots and dysfunctionalities of the collective routines and interpretative frameworks. Based on person-centred therapy, the importance of a secure and understanding environment may be emphasized. These therapies aim at supplementing the missing experiences of trust and approval – similarly, predictable social ties may be developed in order to provide an environment, where the subject may experiment safely with their boundaries. The purpose of these networks is not to reflect on hidden tensions or dysfunctions, rather to incorporate a less- or undistorted social framework. In their case, the process of enabling autonomy – by not limiting the experimenting subject – plays a key role.

Emancipatory networks should be viewed as opportunities for these tasks. They may function as platforms of reflecting on past and present constellations; and also chances of living through distorted formative experiences in a safe intersubjectivity. Alternative social constellations may serve as new reference points: both the distortions of the past and the present may be compared to them. Furthermore, the new networks may host a process of resocialization, if supplementary social ties are established, which could replace or at least complement the distorted ones. For this purpose, those variants of communicative and competitive networks need to be identified, which are not only free from the structural distortions of late modernity, but rather serve as contrasts to them. Being attached to networks of suffering, they hold the potential of a quasi-therapeutic impact. Table 9.1 collects some examples of these transformations.

Table 9.1 Examples of emancipatory networks

	Distorted social environment	*Networks of conflict reflectivity (the logic of psychoanalysis)*	*Networks of functional reflectivity (the logic of cognitive therapy)*	*Networks of supplementary experiences (the logic of person-centred therapy)*
Depressive forms of integration (see Table 4.1)	Unconvertable, resourceless, biased fields/traumatized, unworldly, ignorant illusions/segregated, authoritarian habitus	Revolutionary illusion	Cooperative illusion	Pacified field/hospitable habitus
	Overly complex, discredited systems/stigmatized, incompetent, fragmented, incoherent communicative action/unsuccessful, moralizing lifeworld	Mediating, self-disclosing communication	Mentoring, pedagogical, communication	Self-limiting systems/open lifeworld
Networks of anxiety (see Table 5.1)	Limitations of reflectivity: rigid patterns of connecting and disconnecting/overly busy network dynamics lacking vertical ties/reciprocity of ties is low	Pragmatic, reforming reflectivity	Strategic, instrumental, calculative reflectivity	Trustworthy reflective institutions/relaxing routines
	Deprivation from recognition: lacking ties between members of cliques/formation of cliques only between far ties/low network heterogeneity/fragmented structure of ties/frequent change of control regimes/low density of vertical ties	Inclusive, creative solidarity	Utilitarian solidarity	Fair and transparent legal system, welfare rights/lasting, caring love
Actor networks of addiction (see Chapter 6)	Reifying socio-technological environment	Deconstructionist platforms	Environmentalist, techno-critical information	Information filtering technologies/virtual intimacy

According to Chapter 4, depressive social environments are constituted of insecure, unrewarding, pessimistic, self-blaming, uncontrollable and rigid forms of competitive and communicative integration patterns. If depressive competitive networks are connected to ones, which are based on revolutionary ideas of renewing the *status quo*, then the unbearable hidden power structures become visible and their overcoming becomes an accessible goal; if they are connected to networks characterized by a cooperative illusion, then the very logic of a cruel competition is questioned, and the path is opened for re-evaluating existing practices; if they are connected to a network characterized by pacified redistributive struggles, a generous, hospitable habitus may replace the frightened one. If depressive cooperative networks are connected to ones, which enable the mediation of views and the disclosure of the self at the same time, then the hierarchies biasing communicative action may be suspended; if they are connected to educational ones, then the adaptive competence may be improved; if they are connected to self-limiting systems stopping their own colonizing tendencies, then an open lifeworld may be internalized, which is neither suspicious towards mediatized communication, nor being enclosed in various forms of dogmatism.

According to Chapter 5, networks of anxiety are constituted of tabooing, unpredictable, unsupportive, culturally one-sided (hedonist, nihilist, moralizing, stigmatizing) patterns of ontological security and recognition. If the anxious networks are connected to pragmatic actors, then the over-burdened dynamics may be reformed by focusing on the mutual goals instead of the long kept hurts; if they are connected to strategic ones, then the rigid frames of cooperation may be optimized by improving flexibility; if they are connected to trustworthy institutions, then reassuring and relaxing routines may be developed providing ontological security. If the anxious networks of recognition are connected to solidarity ties innovating new forms of inclusion, then the formerly unresolvable conflicts expressed in cliques may be renegotiated; if they are connected to utilitarian ties, then the adaptive improvement of the community may establish a new sense of order; if they are connected to a fair and lasting legal system promoting welfare rights, then intimate relationships are not overburdened by structural pressure, thus they may freely be stabilized.

According to Chapter 6, actor-networks of addiction are constituted of a reifying socio-technological complex, enabling agency only within the frames of self-reifying compromises. If these actor-networks are connected to deconstructionist platforms of communication and information, then the ruptures of the technologically mediated constraints may be intentionally widened enabling the confrontation with the hidden subordination; if they are connected to information streams focusing on the broader consequences of technology, then the functionality of the constellation may be re-evaluated from these perspectives; if they are connected to technologies enabling the filtering of information and the blocking of noise, then intimacies promising mutual understanding may emerge within the frames of a virtual space (for further details see Chapter 7).

Of course, these are just a few theoretical examples of emancipatory networks, which seem to be capable of reproducing quasi-therapeutic effect outside of therapeutic interactions. In order to test these hypotheses further empirical evidence and experimenting is needed. Still, based on the conclusions of the previous chapters, it may be argued that being attached to networks of empty suffering, similar emancipatory networks may counter meaninglessness by establishing reassuring, caring intersubjectivities providing new meaning. If such emancipatory networks are refined according to the logic of conflict reflectivity, functional reflectivity and the enabling of supplementary experiences, then suffering may be challenged on the level of everyday interactions.

Treating empty suffering – Overcoming the structural constraints of late modernity

Psychotherapies are not the sole sources of inspiration for the potential countermeasures of empty suffering. In the last section, those schools of social work are overviewed, which also have the potential of incorporating the establishment of emancipatory networks. While mainstream psychotherapies do not aim at transcending the boundaries of therapeutic interaction and essentialist models of the self, there are several schools, which focus on these possibilities.[5] Even if these approaches express a distancing from essentialist accounts, they still remain reluctant, as they focus on a single form of sociability, while neglecting the broader social world. In order to find treatments wholly embracing the model of a socially embedded subject, one must turn to the contemporary theories of social work.

The classic theories of social work relied extensively on psychotherapeutic literature: psychodynamic and psychosocial models focus on the clients' personality and mental disorders, along with the dynamics between the social possibilities and personality structures; humanistic and existentialist models focus on the lack of autonomy and meaninglessness; behaviourist and cognitive models focus on the difficulties of adaptation to social constraints. Because these approaches define suffering similarly to psychotherapies (as a subjective experience), they are burdened with the same limitations. Alternative schools of social work however break with these background assumptions and conceptualize the social environment in detail: role theories explain suffering as a consequence of burdening or stigmatizing expectations and social labels; relational theories explain suffering from the perspective of lacking or inadequate social relationships; system theory explains suffering as the lacking or inadequate integration in the functionally differentiated social realm; crisis intervention denies specific theoretical grounding, instead explains suffering as a general probability of the life course. These theories move beyond the horizon of psychotherapies, as they ground their interventions on social theoretical level: they aim at reworking roles; supporting community ties;

promoting social integration; or provide acute support in emergency (Payne, 1991; Teater, 2010).

Despite these efforts, the scope of even these social work praxes remain limited for several reasons. On the one hand, they take into consideration only particular aspects of sociability, therefore they miss to address the social issues in a comprehensive manner. On the other hand, they fail, where psychotherapies fail as well: by not reflecting on the structural consequences of their interventions, they risk to become the instruments of disciplinary biopower (Rose, 1999). Even though social work may apply the chosen scientific discourses out of pure expert devotion, if it forgets about reflecting on the structural context, it reinforces the related power inequalities (Epstein, 1999). This potential is particularly important, when it comes to dealing with forms of suffering, which are related to the late modern structural constraints, such as depression, anxiety or addiction (originating from a pattern of futile ownership, negative integration and indirect pain management). Those psychotherapeutic and also social work interventions, which neglect the related constraints – while operating within their framework – risk to become ineffective, as they contribute to the reproduction of the suffering they intend to eliminate.

Of course, these dangers are not completely unknown for contemporary theories of social work either. Critical theories unveiling power inequalities related to class, race or gender have appeared on the horizon of various critical social works. If social suffering is related to the dominant structural inequalities, a social work, which aims at treating suffering cannot avoid to approach them critically. This is expressed in the continuous attempts of deconstructing explicit and latent mechanisms of oppression within and outside the interventions (Dominelli, 2002). These attempts involve the continuous critical reflection on the institutional frames of social work itself: no expert knowledge should be applied blindly, instead the latent structural consequences should be analyzed on the practical and the social policy level as well. At this point social work becomes social criticism in action, ceaselessly contesting linguistic and institutional expressions of unjustified power relations and confronting inequalities in the public sphere (Adams et al., 2002).

While these theories of critical social work address the issues of hidden structural distortions, they still remain limited in two sense: on the one hand, they usually pick a particular normative basis targeting certain social groups (e.g. class, gender or race)[6]; on the other hand, they miss the chance of reflecting upon the genealogical dimension of the constraints being criticized and contested. This latter limitation is not a marginal one: without taking into consideration the broad social historical processes resulting in a specific set of structural distortions characterizing late modernity, fundamental challenges remain inaccessible. As a final point of our analyses, the contours of those praxes are highlighted, which are capable of dealing with the historical-structural complex of empty suffering in a comprehensive manner.

Futile ownership, negative integration and indirect pain management regimes equally contribute to the emptying of the reserve of interactions and narratives capable of framing hardships in a meaningful manner, thus preventing the emergence of an experience of useless suffering. While the quasi-therapeutic networks described in the previous section seem to be capable of handling those acute situations, where these effects dominate one's lifeworld, on their own they do not provide answer to the structural challenge of empty suffering. The emancipatory networks mentioned in Table 9.1 may represent various ways out from extreme cases of suffering caused by a hegemony of distorted relationships. Also they may indicate substantive goals for a praxis informed by both psychotherapy and social work. Yet, they need to be complemented with an additional dimension in order to prepare them to effectively counter the structural constraints responsible for empty suffering.

The way out from the suffering of the self leads through the caring for the suffering of the other. Any therapeutic praxis could profit from this insight, especially those, which are social theoretically reflected: in their case, the target of the intervention is not the subject anymore, but the totality of intersubjectivity surrounding them. Genealogical reflection further expands this horizon by situating the constraints of intersubjectivity historically: at this point it is not simply the distortions of the intersubjectivity itself (that is the social networks), but also the latent structural constraints outlining the space of possibility of intersubjectivity, which needs to be worked on. Struggling the emptiness arising as a consequence of futile ownership, negative integration and indirect pain management implies the reinvention of substantive meanings capable of filling the narrative void. New motivational bases need to be found, which are capable of motivating the suffering subjects to turn to the other's suffering. In other words, the negative frames of post-organic solidarity (as explained in Chapter 8) need to be filled with substantive content.

At this point, the temptation of leaving the realms of social theory appears: those substantive principles and believes, which used to have the force of grounding the motivational basis of solidarity and care were usually grounded in religious, ethical or political ideas. Certainly, there are still many actors, who identify with similar vocations, thus become motivated to enthusiastic, selfless acts of solidarity. However, relying on this possibility as a general phenomenon in late modernity, which is being emptied on so many levels, seems to be insufficient. Therefore, it is more realistic to approach the question from the perspective of post-organic theory of solidarity, which takes into consideration the same constraints of late modernity that resulted in empty suffering.

In late modernity, solidarity may be born inasmuch as a global risk community justifies its need. It could operate within the dialectical dynamics of support and self-reification. Empty suffering can be understood as a latent global risk: it prevails as a consequence of futile ownership, negative integration and indirect pain management, which eliminate the narrative space of handling hardships. From this perspective the global hazard of empty suffering has a mobilizing force: it may motivate actors to confront actively their own constraints by turning to others. However, this does not happen out of pure altruism. Rather it may occur within hybrid solidarity networks mixing care and personal interest. In accordance with the logic of post-organic solidarity, it is one's self-interest to provide support – even if only in a minimalistic way, that is by helping only particular groups, and only as much as it is convenient. Becoming actors of a post-organic solidarity for self-therapeutic reasons means, that the subject helps the other not because they care, but because they want to escape their own suffering (see Chapter 7).

Such instrumentalized, hybrid, semi-altruistic expressions of solidarity are indispensable elements of late modern emancipatory praxes.[7] When it comes to outlining the contours of the praxes treating empty suffering, it is not enough to highlight those networks, which require reconfiguration; it should also be emphasized, who could become the actors. They are the same subjects, who endure the empty suffering of late modernity – that is the growing masses of people burdened with depression, anxiety or addictions. A chance must be provided for them to contribute to the networks of solidarity, even if only for their own selfish reasons: by becoming active mediators in the solidarity networks (transforming distorted ties into quasi-therapeutic ones) may they find the meaning, which is missing so much from the emptied existence. At the same time, the negative, reifying consequences of such instrumental selfishness also needs to be addressed: this is the very dialectical dynamism of hybrid late modern existence and post-organic solidarity. In sum, the therapy of empty suffering is the turning away from the suffering of the self, while caring for the suffering of the other – a possibility enabled by networks of post-organic solidarity. This may not seem to be a promising prospect at the moment[8] – yet, it may be a starting point for the changes dynamizing an otherwise prospectless era, stuck in its own paradoxes.

Notes

1 A similar term, 'existential feeling' has been elaborated as a twofold sensation: on the one hand a bodily feeling, on the other hand an experience of the space of possibilities (Ratcliffe, 2012).

2 At this point the link between suffering and depression can be highlighted: being exposed to experiences distorting the relation to the self threatens with the naturalization of a meaningless, helpless world (Ratcliffe, 2015).

3 Trauma is a past hardship, which was failed to be transformed into a meaningful experience (with the help of the available narrative tools), thus became incorporated by the subject and resurges uncontrollably (Bernet, 2000; Gusich, 2012). Traumatic impressions are independent from the social framings: they follow their own inherent logic anchored in the biographical complex of the subject. Accordingly, traumas provide an additional phenomenological dimension of suffering: not only the present social distortions may be responsible for failing to find comforting narratives, but also past experiences of unresolved hardships may prevent the elaboration of adequate interpretations. Therefore, the present social distortions

and the traces of past sufferance constitute an inextricable compound. Suffering as an inexplicable loss of meaningfulness is never solely the result of the failing intersubjective narratives or the resurgence of previous untreated sufferings, rather the mixture of the two.

4 Even though not every socially induced suffering becomes trauma, there is always a chance for traumatization, if a hardship is silenced and becomes incorporated by the individual. Furthermore, not every trauma is the direct consequence of social distortions (e.g. serious illness may equally induce inexplicable suffering), yet it is hard to imagine one, which is completely unrelated to the social environment: at least indirectly (e.g. due to the previous ignorance of suffering), most of them are socially contextualized.

5 The best examples are the various family system therapies. According to these approaches, as mental disorders are inseparable from the intersubjective space of the nuclear family, the therapeutic intervention cannot avoid the targeting of the whole family system instead of particular subjects (Corsini and Wedding, 2008: 402–432; Sharf, 2012: 534–558).

6 Even though the challenge of intersectionality (Collins, 2000) is not unknown for social work practitioners (Murphy-Erby et al., 2009), their theorizing usually remains one-dimensional.

7 However, that does not mean they do not represent risks of their own. As it is widely discussed in anthropological research, amateur voluntarism is full of controversies due to its potential of reification (Zakariás, 2019). Accordingly, the self-interested, instrumental care for the suffering of the other can be viewed as another element in the dialectical dynamics of post-organic solidarity.

8 Although, there are many empirical researches supporting this position: as it is documented in wide analyses based on various methodology and scale, voluntarism is one of the most important protective factor of depression and anxiety issues (Jenkinson et al., 2013).

References

Adams, R., Dominelli, L. and Payne, M. (Eds.) (2002) *Critical Practice in Social Work*. New York, NY: Palgrave.

Aho, K. (2019) *Contexts of Suffering: A Heideggerian Approach to Psychopathology*. New York, NY: Rowman & Littlefield International.

Beck, A. T. (1967) *Depression: Clinical, Experimental and Theoretical Aspects*. New York, NY: Harper & Row.

Bernet, R. (2000) The Traumatized Subject. *Research in Phenomenology*, 30(1): 160–179.

Cassell, E. J. (2004) *The Nature of Suffering and the Goals of Medicine*. Oxford: Oxford University Press.

Collins, P. H. (2000) Gender, Black Feminism, and Black Political Economy. *Annals of the American Academy of Political and Social Science*, 568(1): 41–53.

Corsini, R. and Wedding, D. (Eds.) (2008) *Current Psychotherapies* (8th edition). Belmont: Thomson Brooks/Cole.

Dominelli, L. (2002) *Anti-Oppressive Social Work Theory and Practice*. New York, NY: Palgrave.

Durkheim, É (1995) *The Elementary Forms of Religious Life*. New York, NY: The Free Press.

Epstein, L. (1999) The Culture of Social Work. In Chambon, S. A., Irving, A. and Epstein, L. (Eds.), *Reading Foucault for Social Work*. New York, NY: Columbia University Press, 3–27.

Freud, S. (1952) *A General Introduction to Psychoanalysis*. New York, NY: Garden City.

Gusich, G. (2012) A Phenomenology of Emotional Trauma: Around and About the Things Themselves. *Human Studies*, 35(4): 505–518.

Habermas, J. (1987) *The Theory of Communicative Action* (Vol. 2). Boston, MA: Beacon.

Jenkinson, C. E. et al. (2013) Is Volunteering a Public Health Intervention? A Systematic Review and Meta-Analysis of the Health and Survival of Volunteers. *BMC Public Health*, 13: 773. https://doi.org/10.1186/1471-2458-13-773.

Kleinman, A. M. (1973) Medicine's Symbolic Reality: On a Central Problem in the Philosophy of Medicine. *Inquiry*, 16(1–4): 206–213.

Levinas, E. (1969) *Totality and Infinity: An Essay on Exteriority*. London: Kluwer Academic Publishers.

Levinas, E. (1998) Useless Suffering. In *E. Levinas: Entre Nous: Thinking-of-the-Other*. New York, NY: Columbia University Press, 91–102.

McDonald, M. C. (2019) *Merleau-Ponty and a Phenomenology of PTSD: Hidden Ghosts of Traumatic Memory*. New York, NY: Lexington Books.

Murphy-Erby, Y., Hunt, V., Zajicek, A., Norris, A. and Hamilton, L. (2009) *Incorporating Intersectionality in Social Work Practice, Research, Policy, and Education*. Washington, DC: NASW Press.

Payne, M. (1991) *Modern Social Work Theory: A Critical Introduction*. London: Macmillan.

Ratcliffe, M. (2012) The Phenomenology of Existential Feeling. In Marienberg, S. and Fingerhut, J. (Eds.), *Feelings of Being Alive*. Berlin: de Gruyter, 23–54.

Ratcliffe, M. (2015) *Experiences of Depression*. Oxford: Oxford University Press.

Svenaeus, F. (2014) The Phenomenology of Suffering in Medicine and Bioethics. *Theoretical Medicine and Bioethics*, 35(6): 407–420.

Rogers, C. R. (1959) The Essence of Psychotherapy: A Client-Centered View. *Annals of Psychotherapy*, 1: 51–57.

Rose, N. (1999) *Governing the Soul: The Shaping of the Private Self*. London: Free Association Books.

Sharf, R. (2012) *Theories of Psychotherapy and Counseling. Concepts and Cases* (5th edition). Belmont: Brooks/Cole.

Teater, B. (2010) *An Introduction to Applying Social Work Theories and Methods*. Open University Press.

White, H. C. (2008) *Identity and Control: How Social Formations Emerge*. Princeton, NJ: Princeton University Press.

Zakariás, I. (2019) Othering and Recognition: National Ideologies in Donor-Recipient Encounters in Hungarian Co-Ethnic Philanthropy. *Revue Europeenne des Migrations Internationales*, 35(1–2): 215–237.

Index

Printed in Great Britain
by Amazon

40754304R00123